LAIRA FIREMAN

Footplate Recollections of a GWR Fireman

PHILIP E. RUNDLE M.B.E., M.Inst. T.A.

Irwell Press

DEDICATION

To my Wife, Joyce, for her considerable patience, her love, and most valued support.

To my daughter, Sue, for her care, concern and understanding in most that I do, and to my granddaughter Philippa, for teaching me to 'scan' and bailing out when the computer had a mind rather too much its own.

To my Brother, Bill, a former Engineman, and to all of the retired Footplatemen and former colleagues at Laira, who kindly invite me to visit the at their 'Playschool' from time to time, and particularly among them, if I might be permitted, the Late Don Lee B.E.M., for his valued friendship and kind interest.

Above – author at right, brother Bill at left; the occasion is a reunion with Hugo Manuel (middle) a chum from our first school, St. Mewan. We had not seen each other for more than sixty years!

First published in the United Kingdom in 2009
by Irwell Press Limited, 59A, High Street, Clophill,
Bedfordshire MK45 4BE
Printed by Konway Printhouse.

Contents

ACKNOWLEDGEMENT

To the Members of Saltash Branch of Toc H. in Cornwall, who first asked me to speak to them on my footplate experiences, and then asked me back fifteen time afterwards!

To the many Railway Photographers, and for their marvellous work and expertise. I did not need to take photographs of the locomotives. I went to work and saw them! Praise be that they had the foresight to see that those halcyon days could not last forever. I have a fairly comprehensive library and collection of their works which made the selection all the more difficult. I owe an immense debt of gratitude to those amongst them who so readily gave their consent to use their images.

To Colin Squires (President) and David Coles (Curator) of Saltash Heritage Museum for the information and photographs of Saltash.

I would particularly like to thank Ken Coventry for the loan of some of the photographs. Acknowledgement also to the authors and publishers of those works. I shall ever be indebted for the invaluable help and advice which they gave.

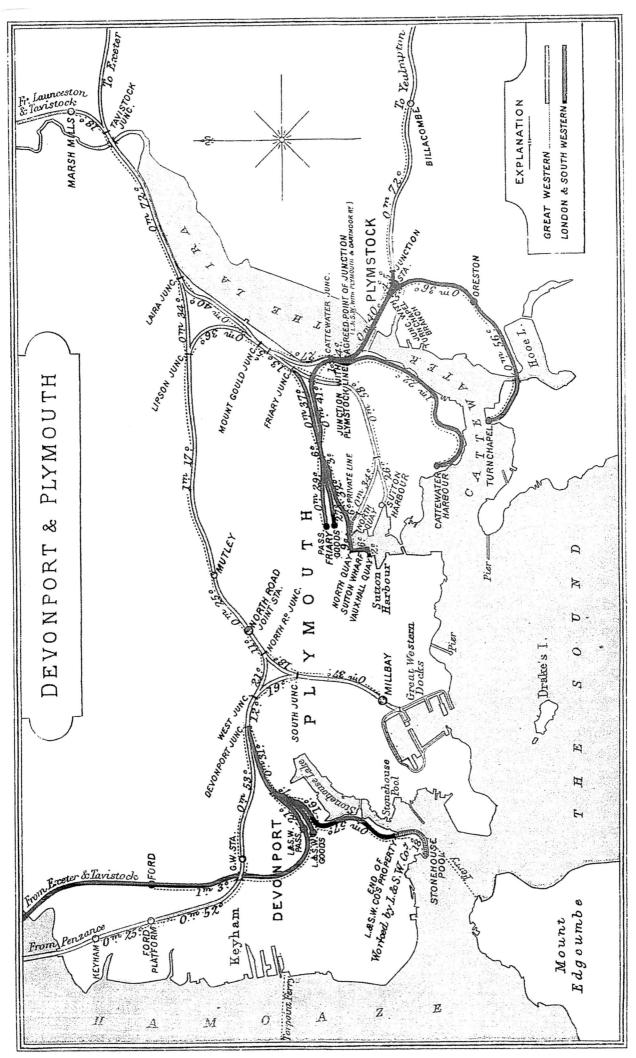

DEVONPORT & PLYMOUTH

iv

Introduction

The sound of a steam locomotive hauling a regular passenger or freight train was once commonplace but alas, is now only a fond memory. We all have, I suspect, some favourite memory from that by-gone age, and mine of course are of the Great Western, when express passenger trains were blessed with names to conjure up the imagination. Millions of holiday-makers made their way to the resorts of South Devon and Cornwall; the Cornish Riviera Express, known to all who worked her as 'The Limited' because at one time her load was *limited* to a specific number of coaches and the Torbay Express along with the Cornishman, the Flying Dutchman and others were almost household names – well, in some households. Memories were interlaced with the railway, woven into our everyday life; going on holiday or even on honeymoon, travelling to school or just train spotting, all linger in the mind as a picture, from those halcyon days. For me, an unforgettable highlight would be a King or Castle thundering up the fearsome 1 in 41 gradient of Hemerdon Bank east of Plympton, with the exhaust echoing through the trees and rolling across the countryside. For the residents of my adopted home town of Saltash it might of course, be something altogether more homely, the 'Saltash Motor', 'the Flier', as it was known, simmering away in the station, four coaches on, filled to overflowing with supporters on an Argyle Saturday as it waited patiently for a path back over the Royal Albert Bridge.

So where did it all start for me? Strange to relate, it was not in the Locomotive Department. To be accepted for work on the footplate normally required knowing someone – preferably

Four car Saltash-Plymouth auto service at the east end of the Royal Albert Bridge in the 1950s. The suburban service ran over thirty 'motors' (as the locals called them) in each direction. *R.E. Vincent/Transport Treasury.*

a relative – already working within that Department. No problem, for my elder brother was already a Fireman of a couple of years standing, at Laira, the Great Western's extensive engine sheds at the east of the city. Another requirement, of course, was that there had to be a vacancy in the first place. Regrettably this was not the case, and I

was advised to apply to join the Traffic Department at Millbay, and then transfer as and when a vacancy at Laira came about. This I did and, on a June morning in 1945, duly arrived at Millbay station,

with my father, for an interview. We were shown into a most imposing office with a huge walnut polished desk and leather upholstered furniture. Much more imposing and impressive though, were the two gentlemen standing behind the desk to greet us. Resplendent in their GWR uniforms with sleeves adorned by gold braid, I met for the first time Chief

6016 KING EDWARD V with the up Royal Duchy at Laira Junction, 15 July 1958. *R.C. Riley/Transport Treasury.*

Inspector Harris and Inspector Selley. I explained why I was applying to join the Traffic Department, not hiding the fact that for me it was to be a temporary arrangement. My mind was full of going to Laira. After answering many questions, and in particular about my standard of education, we were requested to go to a side room where a clerk served us with a cup (monogrammed *GWR)* of coffee and biscuits. As the officers did not join us I presumed that they were deliberating. We were recalled into the office after a while, and Chief Inspector Harris asked my father if he was happy that, with a grammar school education, I had nonetheless chosen to 'waste it' to pursue a career on the footplate. Better opportunities existed in their department, firstly as a clerk, with promotion to station master, and thereafter, who knows, an *Inspector*. Father was most impressed and nudged me to accept. But I went against his judgement and politely refused, stating that it was still my intention to work in the Locomotive Department. My ankle hurt for weeks from the timely kick beneath the walnut desk. I was in the event offered a position as a 'Lad Porter' at Devonport station. This would eventually lead me to my chosen career at Laira engine shed, Plymouth, and a life on the footplate.

So, this is my footplate story, with a bit of Plymouth life in the 1940s through to the 1960s as background. It is not intended to be a work of great technical detail – of shovels of coal/mile, timings, locomotive engineering and the like. We did not do our job with that uppermost in our minds. Like most people, we went to work each day and simply did our best. We worked from A-B with an aim to keep to the timings, to arrive at the destination safely and to have satisfied customers. We did our work as though it were second nature, as we had been trained to do. Probably the only gesture to technical detail was the driver of a passenger train checking his watch at station stops and specific points along the track. We were great talkers and the swapping of tales and experiences in the enginemen's cabin, or the social club, was constant. This is much of the basis of my book, an 'everyday story of footplate folk'. I have attempted, where possible, to include photographs to illustrate various aspects of the text and I trust that you will enjoy it. It is my intention to make a donation from the sale of each book to St Lukes Hospice, Plymouth.

Philip E. Rundle M.B.E.
Saltash, Cornwall, April, 2009

Right. **Old Plymouth 1. The Esplanade, Plymouth Hoe. Steeped in history as Plymouth is, no tale is more famous than that of Sir Francis Drake, whose statue dominates the whole of the Hoe. Standing at the back of the Esplanade, Drake is for ever watchful in case another fleet of unfriendly sails suddenly appears from around the headland at Rame. The Esplanade extends for the whole length of the Hoe and as well as being the grandstand for military parades and displays, is also remembered for the open air dances during the Second World War.**

14XX 0-4-2T 1434 standing in Millbay station, ready to work empty stock to North Road station for a Tavistock branch service in July 1956. Millbay had closed to passengers as a wartime economy measure, in 1941. *R.C. Riley/Transport Treasury.*

Laira's own 7814 FRINGFIELD MANOR and Old Oak King 6028 KING GEORGE VI with the up Cornish Riviera Express on the lower section of Hemerdon Bank. With steam showing at the lower part of the cylinders and the safety valves blowing off, I wonder if the fireman of the Manor has been a bit zealous and overfilled the boiler, causing 'priming' of the cylinders. *R.E. Vincent/Transport Treasury.*

Old Plymouth 2. Looking north of Mutley Plain, to the shops. Mutley tunnel and the Great Western main line ran beneath the Plain in the area just beyond the Baptist Church on the left, about where the horse-drawn carriages are, in the middle of the road.

CHAPTER 1

Devonport, St Budeaux and Laira

The following Monday morning I reported for duty at Devonport station under Station Master Charles Devonshire. In those days, as well as the station master, there was a station foreman on 'day' duty, two clerks on each shift in the booking office, a leading porter and lad porter. There was a shunter who worked on the platform when not required at the goods depot, and three signalmen. The job of a lad porter, as you'd expect, was not particularly glamorous; it included cleaning the toilets, polishing all the brasswork, and sweeping the platforms. In addition, the lad porter would attend the platform for the train arrivals and, when doing nothing else, make the tea! Twice a week the Devonport-based NAAFI food stores arrived, a lorry load of boxes of various pastries and cakes for the various Naval Shore Establishments. Each box required weighing, recording, costing and labelling, and then transferring by station hand trolley to the up platform for despatch on a particular passenger train. If we were lucky, there would be a few free samples to have with our cuppa.

I well recall that our leading porter was not the easiest of persons to work with. I often had the feeling that I was carrying out some of his duties while he was sat down in the parcels office. This always seemed to happen when the station master or foreman was absent, but being a very green and trusting young lad from Cornwall, it took me a little while to work it out! I had been at Devonport for about three or four weeks when I was ordered to report to the station master's office. On arrival he bade me sit down (an unheard of privilege) and I had to wonder what I'd done wrong! His news was the worst. The staffing at the station was to be downgraded (he himself was to be transferred to Keyham station) and *I was to be made redundant, with a fortnight's notice*. This was not the start to a glorious career I'd had in mind. I made contact with Laira the next morning but, still no vacancies there, and the future seemed bleak. On the Monday morning of my final week, I was again summoned by Mr Devonshire, to be informed that the lad porter at St Budeaux Platform had handed in his notice and was joining the Royal Air Force. His job was mine if I

Inside the Round Shed in April 1962. Its title was something of a misnomer because the building was square, with a turntable in the centre, though in truth the great majority of British 'roundhouses' were actually square. Only in the rest of the (sadly misguided) world were 'roundhouses' normally round! Our arrangement in this country was of course superior; it allowed a simpler building with a higher roof and permitted the stabling of all classes of locomotives, for those roads in the 'corners' were of course longer than the rest. In lockers against the walls, we kept all manner of things from a set of dirty overalls for 'prepping', to the tea can! From left to right are 2-6-2T 5572, 4-6-0s 1003 COUNTY OF WILTS and 6988 SWITHLAND HALL, pannier 4658, 2-6-2T 4555 and another Hall, 6938 CORNDEAN HALL. The roundhouse roof suffered over the years and working conditions were greatly improved about 1946 when these renewed smoke chutes, in asbestos concrete, were put in. The ancient GWR originals had been made of tarred wood, which at some sheds occasionally caught fire! *Terry Nicholls.*

Old Plymouth 3. The forecourt of Plymouth North Road in 1939, the redevelopment of the station was delayed by the outbreak of war and was not finally completed until the 1960s. The area alongside the advertising boards is now a two-storey car park.

wished to accept it. Saved at the last minute, by the RAF!

At St Budeaux I teamed up with Leading Porter Graham Hammill. He was an ex-signalman from Hayle but because of an accident was unable to continue his duties in a signal box. Graham instructed me in the intricacies of issuing tickets and other station work, including maintaining the oil lamps of the signals between the two signal boxes, St Budeaux East and Royal Albert Bridge. Each morning a couple of boxes of fish arrived from Plymouth for the shop in the Square; for delivering these every day, at the end of the week I'd get either a half crown or a choice cut of fish to take home; Friday really was 'fish day'. I had been at St Budeaux for the best part of six months when the news came that I had been waiting to hear. *A vacancy existed at Laira shed, and was mine if I still wanted it!* I certainly did, though when it came to it leaving St Budeaux brought mixed feelings, including a faint regret for that half crown every Friday. I had certainly enjoyed the work and the place.

It was a clear sunny morning in August 1946 when I reported, with anticipation and some trepidation, I confess, to the timekeeper's window at Laira. My firm resolve was to be not only the finest engine cleaner in history but also, in time, a driver of the 'Limited', the Cornish Riviera Express. After a fairly peremptory interview with the Laira head foreman, Mr Harold Luscombe and

with spotlessly clean hands and shining face (the only time that I was to look like that while a cleaner boy) I was taken to the chargehand cleaner's cabin, and there met for the first time Tom Day. Tom was an elderly man (or so he seemed to a youngster) and an ex-engineman who for medical reasons had been unable to continue his career on the footplate. Over the years he had become something of a 'father figure' to the cleaners. I was to find out in later days that he was a kindly man, but as will become clear, he had discipline to instil, and this would not be my early impression of him. As a new lad I was given, on this first day, a special task. The up 'Limited' was to be hauled by a renowned Great Western locomotive, 6000 KING GEORGE V. Mounted on the front of this engine was a brass bell. It had been presented, together with two cabside emblems, by the Baltimore and Ohio Railway of America, at the Fair of the Iron Horse, to mark their Centenary in 1927, and in recognition of the sterling performance put up by 6000 running in the USA during these celebrations. My task was to clean this mighty bell. Armed with a pad made of hessian sack with sea sand soaked in a mix of engine oil and paraffin in one hand and a wad of clean cotton waste in the other, I dutifully followed Tom to the outside of the four road 'New Shed' where 6000 was standing. She was already starting to gleam from the attention of my new-found workmates who had begun much earlier (it was the last time I was permitted to

start a cleaning shift as early as 9am!). With much solemnity and ensuring that I realised the weight of history and tradition borne on my shoulders, I was left to my task. Scouring with the pad, and wondering how I could keep the oil from running up under my sleeve, polishing and rubbing dry with the clean waste, I soon settled down to the work. As you can imagine, every so often I'd glance excitedly around trying to take in everything that was going on.

My fellow cleaners were very helpful, giving me encouragement and advice, though soon I'd find that being the junior cleaner qualified me for all of the usual crop of practical jokes. Favourites at Laira included being sent to the stores for some *Red Oil* with which to fill the rear lamps, or with a bucket to get some *Copper Dust* to clean the band which was the hallmark of the Great Western chimney.

My big brother, who happened to be on the shed at the time, further impressed upon me that the task was not to be taken lightly, and to ensure that before reporting back to Tom, I had, in the best of Cornish tradition, 'made her gleam, and done A Proper Job'. This I did, or thought so anyway and, within the allotted time of an hour, I gave a final polish to the bell, and started to walk back to the chargehand cleaner's cabin, glancing back every so often for as long as I could see, to admire the bell absolutely radiating as the mid-morning sun shone upon it. Arriving, almost breathless, at the cabin, I informed Tom

'My' bell! PRESENTED TO LOCOMOTIVE KING GEORGE V BY THE BALTIMORE AND OHIO RAILROAD COMPANY IN COMMEMORATION OF ITS CENTENARY CELEBRATION SEPTEMBER 24TH – OCTOBER 15TH 1927.

that 'I'd finished'. *Finished?* he asked in a tone of disbelief, 'Finished? Are you sure?' (I was later to learn, of course, that this was his tried and tested technique). On my assurance that it was so, he placed his bowler hat (a sign of authority on the Great Western) on his spotlessly bald head and, giving a polish to his spectacles, led me back to New Shed. We entered this shed, a long rectangular building and, deep inside, some 200feet away, KING GEORGE V was standing majestically in the morning sunlight glancing through the rooflights. It was gleaming now from the attention of the cleaners, but shining out most of all was *my bell*. Shafts of sunlight bounced off it, almost obscuring its outline.

Tom stopped where we were, looked at 6000, at me, at the locomotive again, and I awaited his praise, bursting with pride. Turning back to me, and with a quiet voice, but one laden with incredulity (something cleaners at Laira came to know so well) questioned: 'Cleaned it, you say you've *cleaned* that bell?' Hardly understanding, and with tremulous voice, I assured him that it was so. Surely, my mind told me, he was able to see that for himself? Tom took off his bowler and, saddened by the infinite inadequacies of cleaners, rubbed his hand over the baldness of his head, and turned to utter some words which have remained clear to me even to this day. 'Well, son,' he said, 'this is your first day, and that was your first task for the GREAT WESTERN RAILWAY. If you don't intend carrying out

your work in a better manner than this, it will be to your advantage, and most certainly to the advantage of the company, if you were to go out of that gate now!'

This was all, of course, in the finest service tradition of 'moulding' new recruits but was unfortunately new to me. I was stunned. Tears sprang from my eyes, and how my heart sank to the very depth of my boots. It wasn't until some time later that I realised that this was his way of ensuring that I was aware, even on that very first day, that the company that I had elected to serve was indeed God's Wonderful Railway, and that I was ever to be conscious of that fact, and was never to forget it. After that it was necessary that I just went through the motions of cleaning the bell again, and it was passed without comment, as were all of my remaining tasks while I was a cleaner boy.

The job of an engine cleaner was, next to chimney sweep, probably the dirtiest, and the most uncomfortable, on earth. We clambered over locomotives that were covered in coal dust, fire ash and smokebox soot, and crawled beneath into a maze of oily eccentric sheaves, connecting rods, piston rods and cylinder housings in order to ensure that everything was near spotless for the crews that were to get the engine 'prepared' for the road. As well as that it was dangerous and countless times a hot steam pipe or smokebox touched by the unwary brought minor burns and scalds, almost as routine. Every loco man still bears the scars from his time at work. It might be expected that every ingredient was present for discontent and conflict but for all this my cleaning days made for a very happy period of my life. There was the novelty, the excitement and the *comradeship* of my fellow cleaners.

Tom set our tasks according to the shifts that we worked. On 'nights', as a gang we would expect to clean (at the least) the early morning Penzance

passenger, postal, and paper train locomotives, plus the engine for the 7.15 Paddington – usually a King. Added to this would be the early morning pannier tanks (64XX class) for the Saltash motors, and a 45XX prairie tank for the Tavistock branch. It seems a lot, but working together in gangs of four on the tender engines and in pairs on the tanks, it could all be comfortably dealt with.

In addition to the elbow work of actual cleaning we were shown how to re-pack and tighten piston glands, and to climb into a smokebox to clean out char from the superheater tubes. We were able to watch such mysteries as a boiler washout being undertaken. We watched the fitters at work, and realised the importance of good maintenance – still a hallmark of the Great Western in those days. It was altogether a rewarding time of learning, learning, learning. It was also a time of fellowship, of happy laughter and off-key singing. If you've never heard *Beautiful Dreamer* sung in the roundhouse at Laira in the early hours you will forever be musically unfulfilled!

For all of that, our cleaning in those days was expected to be of a very high standard. Although some might disagree, cleanliness of the locomotives was bound up in the *heritage* of the Great Western. I spoke earlier of Chargehand Tom, and of his bald head. When inspecting an engine reported as 'cleaned', he would firstly peer underneath, placing his bowler hat on the front running plate before doing so. After carefully fingering all of those places not apparent to the eye; backs of rods, undersides of framings, springs and so on, Tom would then come out and replace his bowler on his head. A cursory look at the outside, which was always perfect anyway, and he would return to his cabin where a large mirror hung on the wall. The bowler would be removed, the head examined, and only the Good Lord himself could help us if there was a black ring present on that otherwise gleaming bald pate!

6800 ARLINGTON GRANGE at Penzance 29 April 1961. The engine is a perfect example of the care taken by the cleaners. Present day Health and Safety inspectors, however, would certainly have been concerned at the manner in which the nethermost parts were reached! *R.C. Riley/Transport Treasury*.

Laira New (or Long) shed, 22 April 1962. Erected in 1931 using Government money under the 'Loans Act', it was linked to the Old Shed by an opening in the back half of the right-hand wall. Locomotives, right to left, are: 3862 in the sidings behind the wagons; 5082 SWORDFISH on No.1 road, 1028 COUNTY OF WARWICK on No.2 road, 6834 DUMMER GRANGE and 1008 COUNTY OF CARDIGAN. On no.4 road stands 6955 LYDCOTT HALL, with 4927 FLANBOROUGH HALL in the sidings used for the short-lived oil burners. The Photographer, Terry Nicholls was a former Clerk at Laira.

An unfeasibly immaculate KING GEORGE V.

9

Old Plymouth 4. The foreshore beneath The Hoe was known as Tinside, and the centrepiece was the **Tinside Bathing Pavilion**. As can be appreciated from this scene in the 1930s, it was very popular. The large building in the centre is the Marine Biological Institute, with The Citadel immediately to the right.

CHAPTER 2

Medical, Firing Turns and Call Boys; An Unfortunate Milkman

This then was the tradition and heritage which I had elected to become part of that day in 1946. But first, a free ride on a 'Company Pass' to Swindon, there to undergo 'a Medical' at Park House, the experience of all Great Western footplatemen it seems since the start of time. I recall being awed by the fact that I was at the *Home of the Great Western,* and impressed by the vastness of the surroundings. I was also grimly aware that if I failed the tests, there would be no future for me on the footplate. There were half a dozen others present, and with a familiarity that seemed normal to footplatemen the world over, we soon became fellows in adversity! We were lodged overnight in a house in Bathampton Street, bed & breakfast for 2/6d and I had been solemnly handed that princely sum by the office clerk at Laira. The place was renowned/infamous for the so-called 'fried breakfast' the following morning. Greater authority than I held that the sausages were taken to the furnaces of the Swindon Blacksmith's Shop for preparation, and then to the Rolling Mills to give them shape and pliability. I can assure anyone reading

this that future fry-ups, done in the shovel on the footplate were a gourmet's delight by comparison. Nevertheless, we survived and, reporting to Park House at 9am, were put through a range of tests and examinations, to determine our levels of general knowledge, arithmetic and writing**.** We had to strip to the skin for the feared 'medical', which involved the famous *Look Through the Ears* to see the wall opposite and the infamous *Cough,* familiar of course to all gentlemen. And inevitably there was *The Glass Jar* to fill, always a trial under such circumstances.

The eyesight tests were of course vital and involved wall charts, coloured skeins, silks of varying colours (rather off-colour, I felt, and not true shades) to test colour blindness and dotted coloured cards with hidden numbers which could be distinguished only if your sight was normal. Eventually, however, all was completed and, with great severity, I was informed that I had passed and was accepted. I was issued with an Identification Card, which permitted me to 'trespass' on the company's property and a Rule Book (known as 'The Bible'). I had to hand over yet another half crown,

which was later refunded, as my initial payment to the GWR Medical and Superannuation Scheme, and given a further free pass back to Plymouth, with instructions to report to Laira for duty the following morning.

I was now *officially* an Employee of the Great Western Railway; an Engine Cleaner, on the first rung of the ladder. I reported back to the shed foreman at Laira the next morning. Still a cleaner boy, but now with an altogether enhanced status. Soon enough, rising through the seniority ranks as a cleaner it was possible to get firing turns on the footplate. This was especially so in the larger sheds such as Laira, and chances came mostly in the summer season when extra demands were made by all the additional trains scheduled for the summer service. At Laira at the beginning of the summer timetable the six most senior firemen, who had passed their examinations to become drivers, were promoted as temporary drivers, and this progression through the links allowed for the six most senior cleaner boys in turn to act as firemen. At the end of the summer everyone reverted back to type!

St Blazey engine shed on 20 July 1960. The building was remarkable for being built in the form of a 'semi-roundhouse' around a turntable, in the long-distant days of the Cornwall Railway. Common on the continent and in North America, there were nonetheless only a handful of such buildings in this country. It is now 'listed'. The water tower has been a convenient point from which to observe 'suicides'... *R.C. Riley/Transport Treasury.*

These first firing turns were usually in the shunting yard at Tavistock Junction (Marsh Mills) or at Laira Yard; the thinking, at least in part, was that this was where the least harm could befall if things did not go quite to plan. For a cleaner boy, however, the first turn, and indeed all of these early firing stints were beyond description; they were in truth the realisation of dreams. A small 0-6-0 pannier tank engine became, albeit for only a shift, a King. The added bonus of these turns was that they counted for seniority and when the cleaner had attained a certain number (I forget now how many) he was paid at a junior fireman's rate of pay, even if still cleaning engines.

There was another most important duty undertaken by the senior cleaners, that of a *call boy*. It was a requirement of the Great Western that all footplatemen should live within a mile radius of the shed, and that the responsibility for getting to work on time, even during what

would now be called unsocial hours, rested with the individual. The GWR instituted a system whereby all men booking on in the small hours of the morning, 1am-6am, could, when booking off, 'order' an early morning call for the beginning of the following shift. The necessary calls were made by a senior cleaner, hurrying round the streets on a bicycle. He would wake each man in strict rotation, and there was no allowance for error – each 'wakee' was required to sign the register as proof that the task had been carried out. Woe betide anyone who was late for duty after signing the register. Even worse perhaps, was the wrath of the hierarchy which fell upon those who did not avail themselves of the call boy and were still late for duty.

The register was a sort of social document in its own right, full of instructions as to how to awaken the individual sleeping beauties. Some required a knock on the knocker, but not too loud, in case you woke 'the missus',

and Lord help you if that particular calamity came to pass. Some required a specific number of rings on the bell, and a wait for an upstairs window to open. This was not without hazards, for not all appreciated being woken up, and unpleasant things (this was the age of the pot under the bed remember) could be thrown out to the acute discomfort of the unwary.

There was even, reputedly, one house where a piece of string dangled down from an upstairs window, the other end secured to a big toe. I confess I am unable to prove or disprove this for I was never fortunate enough to 'have a go'. The mind boggles as to what might have happened in the bedroom at the time. It was always bad enough trying to arouse a deep sleeper who would not answer, before going on to the next call but, whatever, they *had* to be got up! The added difficulty was that the area around Laira was full of railwaymen, and the continuing banging or knocking on doors could

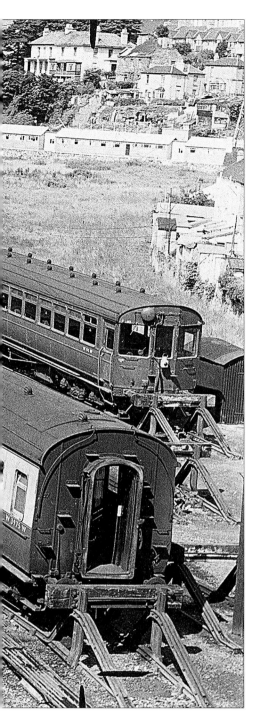

A lovely scene of the railway in its pomp at Laira Junction, 15 July 1957. Little 14XX 0-4-2T 1408 has charge of a local to Tavistock on the up main while everywhere around is as busy as ever; the Lee Moor tramway is still in place, the yards are full of stock, a P.W. Ganger wanders the rails, smoke and steam erupt around the coal stage and the queue of engines, once again, spills out on to the goods loops. The three signal bracket beyond, which it has just passed, govern (from left to right): the river sidings, loop line to Tavistock Junction yards and the up main line. *R.E. Vincent/Transport Treasury.*

having finished the houses in St Blazey, he was leaving the town for Par Moor; trusting in his pony, who probably knew the round and stopping places as well as its master, he settled down to let the swaying motion lull him into a short nap. All of a sudden, he was aware of a violent shaking and the alarming clanking of the milk measures on the churns. Coming wide awake he found that the cart had abruptly stopped. Dismounting, he hastened around to the front to find the pony quite agitated and trembling. They had arrived at the point where the main railway line crossed over the Par Moor road, a place known as 'Five Arches'. Looking further ahead to determine what had frightened the horse, he saw with horror that some 'poor unfortunate' (as they were usually described) had decided to end his life by hanging himself from one of the arches spanning the road.

Calming the animal and tethering him to the fence by the road, our shocked milkman hastened back to St Blazey to rouse the local constable, along with nigh on half the residents of the town. Hurrying back to the arches, the constable lowered the unfortunate to the ground and, upon examination, found that the corpse was none other than a life-size dummy, such as might be used for first aid lessons – in a railway premises perhaps... It was well known, after all, that the railwaymen at St Blazey (the engine shed in particular) and Par were most keen on first aid. It did not therefore take very long at all for the village policeman, in true Holmesian style, to reach the right conclusion and, with the co-operation of the shed foreman, root out the culprits. I am given to understand by my elder brother (who seems to have been suspiciously privy to the plot) that the punishment was suitably draconian!

Of course at Laira we had no such rascals, although I do recall on one occasion two call boys plotting on how best to alter the front gate numbers of a row of houses at Laira known as Western Drive. The idea was that No.1 should go to No.29 on one side, and No.2 to No.30 on the other, and so on. It was decided that the work could be carried out while away from the shed on call up duties. At the appointed hour, the lads left the shed, 'knocked' up a couple of blokes out of bed and doubled back to Western Drive to alter the gates before pedalling off furiously to awaken some more engine crews. Repeated over and over, until the task was completed, and two absurdly proud and happy lads reported back to the shed; all call ups completed and, unknown to the shed, all gate numbers interchanged. As in many doomed conspiracies, the criminals had, somewhat stupidly it has to be said, overlooked a vital fact. Western Drive, like so many round about, was of course a street of railway houses, and they had been spotted by a railwayman coming off duty; worse still, he had phoned the shed! Hauled up in front of Chief Foreman Harold Luscumbe, they were given a very severe dressing down, warned as to future conduct and fined a sum in accordance with the Rule Book. Worse still, they were

awaken the next door neighbour, himself in all probability a member of a train crew, not long arrived home and dropped off to sleep, and he was not going to take kindly to being woken up once more.

Cleaners/call boys were also noted for their high spirits and an uninhibited view of practical pranks and though I truly believe that all we did was meant in fun, the unfortunate victim might not have always agreed. A favourite at Laira was to get hold of a firelighter's paraffin can and swop the contents for water. We would then watch eagerly as he attempted unsuccessfully to light the fire in some locomotive firebox. Of course, they got wise soon enough and then it was a good idea to make yourself scarce! There is a story from St Blazey, where my elder brother did his engine cleaning, concerning the unfortunate experiences of a local milkman. He had a traditional round, a horse and cart full of churns of milk and measures, very early in the morning often before first light. On this particular day,

sent back to Western Drive in *their own time* to rectify the damage, but now of course, under the full gaze and scorn of those who lived in the houses. In hindsight perhaps it was not worth all of the effort and aftermath. But at the time my mate and I thought it was.

Perhaps the gods were looking down on me before I could get into any more hot water for, on arriving at the shed a couple of mornings afterwards I looked at the notice board to see that I had been 'made' a FIREMAN, and was to report to Slough engine shed for work the following week. It was March 1947 and one of the worst winters ever, though I hardly noticed. Although it seemed much longer, I had been a cleaner boy for just eight months!

Slough shed and surrounds, circa 1948.

CHAPTER 3
Slough Engine Shed

Promotion, whether for fireman or driver, came according to seniority and/or vacancies and it was with some relief that I heard of my promotion, and placement to Slough. It was normal practice on the Western for a man, on promotion, to be assigned to the first vacancy on the system. If you were lucky this, by coincidence, might occur at your home shed (especially a big one like Laira) but as often as not it meant transferring far away, to somewhere you'd never been, or even heard of. Once sent away from his first shed it was most men's intention to transfer back 'home' as soon as possible, though many of course put down roots and stayed, or moved on somewhere different altogether. The system ensured that men tended to concentrate at big sheds from smaller establishments – one reason why so many West Country and Welsh men could be found in London at Old Oak Common for instance. Transfer back again was dependent on vacancies arising and there would be a queue in front of you before your turn came up. On appointment to Slough I was informed of how may of men around the railway of comparable grade

were waiting to return to Laira before me. The system also ensured that men from any shed were scattered about the system, most of them waiting the chance to get back; it was a 'first away, first home' system, all scrupulously recorded and I recall that there were some fourteen exiled firemen wanting to return home to Plymouth before me. It was a case of keeping an eye on the appointments list on the Slough shed notice board.

Slough shed was altogether different from Laira, much smaller, a bit ramshackle in parts and sited by the station, within the London suburban area. Upon reporting to the shed foreman, I was first of all taken to the hostel where my accommodation had been arranged. This was a large old country house set in a rural wooded area just off the Windsor Road, adjacent to the District Hospital, and about ten minutes walk from the shed. Back at the shed, I examined the notice board and duties roster to find that I was 'paired' with a Driver Jones, and scheduled for 'shed duties' at 6am, the next morning. 'Dai' as he wanted to be known, was perfectly pleasant and made me welcome. He was, unsurprisingly, a

Welshman, from Abercynon in the Valleys, but had set up home at Slough. Straight away, he sympathised with a young man away from home for the first time, having had the same experience himself. He was cheerful, considerate and took me under his wing, explaining and showing me everything that I needed to know about the shed and our workings. One lasting memory is of him teaching me to play cribbage, which came in handy later on.

The workings at Slough shed covered suburban passenger services to Paddington, Reading, Oxford, and down the branch to Windsor & Eton, though to us it was just 'Windsor'. For this work we had locomotives of the 61XX class of large prairie 2-6-2Ts. We also had what were called 'zonal' duties, which mostly required relieving crews of goods trains and taking them on to various destinations. Usually they were bound for Acton yard, the main marshalling yard for the London area, but at times to places much further off. A feature of London in those days was the infamous 'smog', the 'pea-souper' as it was locally known and a somewhat alarming

54XX pannier tank 5409 at Slough shed on 20 May 1951. I can recall this loco, but never worked on her, and was not at Slough long enough to get the seniority required to work auto trains. Slough had three types of tank engine fitted with the gear. Two 14XX 0-4-2Ts worked the Windsor and Marlow branches and two 74XXs and this one 54XX were on the Watlington Branch. I always wondered about the latter, for it commenced at Princes Risborough, quite a distance to travel from Slough. Oxford was the next nearest shed, but was also quite a way off. *R.C. Riley/Transport Treasury*.

Windsor & Eton Central. The town was served by two stations, the Great Western (ours) by a branch line from Slough, and the Southern Railway with a line from Staines. We were the best of course, because we had a Royal waiting room (I do not know if the Southern had one!) and Queen Victoria travelled by GW to London. I still think back to my 'special' trip. Little did I think then that one day I would meet Royalty in the flesh! *A.E. Bennett/Transport Treasury.*

phenomenon that was new to me. It was a fog so thick that it was virtually impossible to see the proverbial hand in front of one's face, and of course it severely affected the train timetables. Working practice gave preference to passenger and perishable traffic, and all other services were directed into the seemingly endless 'loop' lines at Iver and Hayes & Harlington (the latter the home of 'His Masters Voice'). It was possible to stable six or seven goods trains at a time, nose to tail and, as the one at the front was got safely off on the next stage of its progress the next train would be made ready to go; engine crews would return from the comfort of the preceding guards van, and all would move up one place. And wait.

This, of course, would then allow another goods train to join the queue at the rear. In extreme conditions movement from the loops was virtually non-existent for hours on end, and relief for the train crews was effected by 'zonal' crews from the various sheds, travelling the line to the nearest station by ordinary passenger train, light engine or engine and guards van – by hook or by crook in effect. Yet so severe was the dislocation to working during a pea souper that it was not entirely unknown for a relieved crew, upon booking on again, to be relieving the same train, only two or three places further forward in the queue! As can be imagined this type of duty involved long hours of inactive duty, and it was here that the cribbage board and card schools came into their own.

The crew on the engine of the leading train did not have the comfort of a guards van, of course, and had to stick it out on the footplate. It was here that I found out the true reason why the Great Western adopted lower quadrant signals, in which

'the board' (the signal arm) dropped down instead of being hauled upwards. In order that a continuous watch did not have to be kept on to the loop exit signal, the fireman would climb the ladder of the signal post carrying a bucket from the footplate, place the said bucket on the arm of the signal, and return to the footplate. When the signal eventually came 'off', the arm would drop and the bucket would fall to the ground with an immense clatter, enough to awaken the dead. A quick recovery of the bucket, and on went the train. As a young fireman I felt that it was very considerate of the powers-that-be!

The locomotives at Slough were all tank engines, 61XX prairies for the main passenger duties to Paddington, Reading, and occasionally Oxford and Princes Risborough. These engines were capable of very fast acceleration, and even the stopping trains were booked and ran with 'A' class (express) headlamp codes and timings. With coupled driving wheels of 5ft 8ins, they fairly 'ate up' the track once in full cry. The boiler pressure was 225lb. Free steaming, they were an absolute delight to work on. We also used 57XX 0-6-0 panniers for passenger, 'trip freights' and shunting, and 14XX class 0-4-2Ts for the couple of the branches on which we covered the local service, Marlow and Windsor.

Dai was very helpful with advice and encouragement, and I seemed to cope pretty well under his guidance, and he had great patience. As a young lad, away from home for the first time, I found him to be most understanding. He regularly made enquiries as to my lodgings and general well-being, and he would ensure that, when weekends permitted, I travelled home to Saltash. When we had

to work on a weekend I was always invited to his home to share the Sunday roast with himself and his wife. I have never forgotten their kindness.

Odd though it might seem, while I worked with him I never knew the English translation of the Welsh Dai – my only excuse that I was lad brought up in the innermost depths of Cornwall, and had led a sheltered life! I did not like to show my lack of knowledge by asking him or his wife, but always wondered. It was not until I returned to Laira and mentioned this in the enginemen's cabin that I was enlightened by another 'immigrant' Welshman, and informed that it was indeed David. I had much leg pulling from then on, and to this day cannot comprehend how I could have been so thick!

'The branch' (though it was more like an extension of the main line really) to Windsor was something of an exception. It was not an 'ordinary' branch of course, for in addition to the Royal parties who travelled to and from Windsor by train in those days, there were the 'young Gentlemen' of Eton. When their holidays (the 'half' they called it) came about, special trains would be laid on to take them to Paddington and again to bring them back to the college when term resumed. I have to admit that they were a splendid sight dressed in black coats and striped trousers, with toppers to match! Most gave the impression of being 'decent chaps' and would come to the footplate and make a comment or two, but a few of course had to let us know that they were socially the elite and, really, speaking to the likes of us was just not the done thing, old chap!

The working of specials from Eton for the Henley Regatta was particularly memorable. Everything went well on the outward journey, but champagne-fuelled high spirits took over on the return trains. Dai warned me to make sure that I stayed in the comparative safety of the locomotive. I can only say that on the one and only occasion I worked one of these trains a good time had most certainly been had by all, and the singing was a delight to hear though my mum would not have been pleased for me to have heard the words of some of the refrains.

The Windsor line was only a short one, three miles or so on the level and not a daunting prospect, though it was as well not to get it wrong. 'Standing orders' were 'a couple of shovelfuls on the fire, and don't make too much smoke, THEY might be home'. I booked on one morning for what I thought was a spare turn, to find that we were booked *Special Coaches, Windsor*. On asking I was told that some Royal coaches were being detached from a through express, and we were to take them down to Windsor. From what Dai knew, I was able to work out that it would not be Their Majesties, King George V1 and Queen Elizabeth, for they would have been brought from Paddington behind a gleaming Castle, and gone through Slough as though it never existed. No, it had to be Royalty of a little lesser rank. Upon getting on to the footplate I found a gentleman there in a grey serge suit, bowler hat and shining black shoes. A Footplate Inspector, no less. This did not help my confidence at all, I must say. The footplate on a 61XX was a little congested at the best of times, and to have a third person present, especially one of some elevated status, made it all

the more daunting. What if my dirty shovel was to brush against the trouser leg of the serge suit, or, the Lord forbid, the dust from the coal mar the shine of the gleaming black shoes? Eventually the express arrived and departed, and the signalman let us off shed to couple up to the beautiful, gleaming Royal coaches, watched closely all the time by the inspector. The 'right away' came, with much blowing of whistles, flag waving and the rest and I thought about putting some coal on to the fire. In the confined cab I wondered as I swung the shovel whether an errant stroke might well bring the curtain down on my career. However, all went well and we ran down to Windsor, and into the Royal platform

I recall two things vividly from that day. Firstly, I was aware of the inspector congratulating Dai for stopping the train in just the right spot for the proverbial red carpet. It was not that difficult really, for the edge of the platform was marked out for 'two coaches, three coaches' and so on. Secondly, I had no idea, and still do not, as to who we took to Windsor that day. The Royal platform at Windsor was on the driver's side, and where I wanted to stand to look to see what was going on, this inspector stood, and left no more room for me! I did not think that he would have taken it lightly, a very junior fireman asking him to move over. I like to think that, taking into account the circumstances, that it was the two Princesses, Elizabeth and Margaret, one of whom is now our most beloved Queen. This however, created a large doubt in my mind in after years. I felt that on that day, I did a magnificent job as a young

Fireman on the Great Western. Little did I realise that it might not have been so.

In 1994 Her Majesty was gracious enough to bestow an honour upon me by awarding The Most Excellent Order of the British Empire. On the day of the Investiture, I travelled from Cornwall to London, only to find that Her Majesty had travelled from London to Truro in Cornwall to present the Maundy Thursday money! I cannot believe that she found something not to her liking all those years before on the train to Windsor, and remembered it for so long and held a grudge, so that she did not want to present my Honour personally! However, I was not too disappointed, for the Investiture was carried out by H.R.H. Prince Charles, the Duke of Cornwall. To a true Cornishman, next to Her Majesty, that would do! While looking up events for this book, I found that the western fork at Slough station which led on to the Windsor line, was also known as 'The Queen's Curve', so-called because it was more or less only used by Royal trains.

Although we worked trains to and from Paddington, surprisingly enough we did not go 'on shed' at Old Oak Common all that often. The locomotives for all the passenger train work at Slough were the redoubtable 61XX prairie tanks with no need to turn them for the return journey for they ran just as well bunker- first as chimney first. Normally on arrival at Paddington we would set back with the coaches into a siding, run round, and eventually reverse them back into our departure platform. On certain rosters without a quick turn-round, we would then go in to the engine yard at Ranelagh

Prairie tank 6160 at her home shed Slough on 20 May 1961. Used extensively on the London suburban passenger services, they were first class engines, very free steaming with quick acceleration. *R.C. Riley/Transport Treasury.*

Bridge, which also gave us an opportunity to 'service' the locomotive.

My first visit to Old Oak was from a 'zonal' working (ordered from central control as required) when Dai and myself relieved, I believe, a Didcot crew on an up goods destined for Acton. I recall that it was in the early hours of the morning and it was still dark when we arrived at Acton and released to take the engine to shed. Even so, as a west country lad, visiting the 'smoke' for the first time I could not help but be impressed. I thought Laira was a big place, but this was *massive*. Naturally, coming in on the ash road, my first sight was of the coal stage. Two roads and, I afterwards found out, ten 'tips' for replenishing the tenders, and at the west end the brick and stone arches supporting the bank. The water tank atop the coal shed appeared big enough to be a swimming pool and Dai informed me that it held somewhere around 300,000 gallons. *Ye Gods! What if you fell in!*

If that were not enough, Dai led me to the Engine Shed and it deserved the capital letters, I can tell you. Not just a building, more a *Cathedral*. Although the interior seemed a little dim and hazy with smoke and so on I could see enough to stand amazed. Four, yes FOUR, 65ft. turntables, each with something like 25 bays radiating from them. I noticed that two tables were serviced with an outgoing road in the side walls. By this time, almost speechless and yes somewhat awestruck, it was time to report to the office for our return job. I still had to try to take more in, though, such as the repair shop (so big they called it 'the factory' with who knows how many roads leading in and an overhead transverser crane. The sidings sprawled for ever and held innumerable carriages – far off was the equally vast carriage shed. My mind boggled and then of course I realised that this was London where everything seemed larger than life. It was impossible not to be impressed.

Afterwards back at Laira I listened to the Old Oak Common crews on double-home workings, and the age old inter-shed rivalry to 'prove' that they were superior to us. I played my part, defending the west country, but it was difficult not to think that they might just have good reason to think that way! Slough, of course seemed tiny in comparison but, it was MY shed, my first as a full fireman, and I was proud of it.

I had reason to visit Southall shed on only one occasion. Again we were on zonal workings, and landed up there after receiving instructions to travel as passengers from Slough and then report again for orders. It was later thoroughly modernised but in my time the shed was an elderly straight six road open one end building. The whole seemed to be 'squeezed' in by the trackside and as such appeared elongated with a turntable a long way off one way and a water tower similarly in the opposite direction. Now strange to tell, after reporting in, it turned out that we were to return back to Slough, again 'on the cushions'.

And what of Paddington, for an impressionable young man? It was

London, that place we viewed from afar, and would never see. What did impress me was that it was so very busy! Even on the more remote platforms, the ones that we ran in to, people just hurried and scurried. Whistles, engine and guards, sounded constantly, in a never-ending to and fro of trains arriving, departing, never getting in each other's way. It was never still, never silent, and of course, they spoke funny, *mate!*

One other memory of the workings at Slough remains to this day; this was the 'trip goods'. Slough was an industrial area, and the many factories along the main line all had their own sidings, and were visited each day by a small goods train, usually hauled by a 57XX pannier and brake van. Each factory would be visited in turn working towards Acton, dropping off a couple of wagons and picking some loaded ones up, and so on our merry way. At times in a factory, the train crew would be given a sample of the wares produced, which was most welcome. Slough of course, was renowned for the *Mars* factory and further up the line, at Hayes & Harlington, was the celebrated His Masters Voice factory with the distinctive chimney with the name inscribed upon it. I don't recall ever coming away with a gramophone from HMV, but always got bars of chocolate from Mars. I confess to still having a taste for the bar that helped you work rest and play.

Looking back my stay at Slough was regretfully all too short, for my time with Dai and other workmates there was interesting and very worthwhile. But as was understandable, I was ever eager to return home to Laira and was always scanning the notice board for staff movements. When Laira was shown I'd alter my own 'list' accordingly. And so, in September of 1947, and after only some six months away from home, I saw the long awaited order: *Slough to Laira. P.E.Rundle, Fireman.*

Left. **Prairie tanks 6133 and 6165 on shed at Southall on 30 July 1961. 6133 was from Slough and had been there most of her working life. Times are changing and both 61XXs, once immaculate, are looking rather neglected, and certainly not as I recall them.** *Alec Swain/Transport Treasury.*

Below. **Slough's 0-4-2T 1448 standing in Marlow station on 21 June 1952. In my time at Slough we shared the workings of this branch with Southall shed.** *R.C. Riley/Transport Treasury.*

Laira shed about 1950.

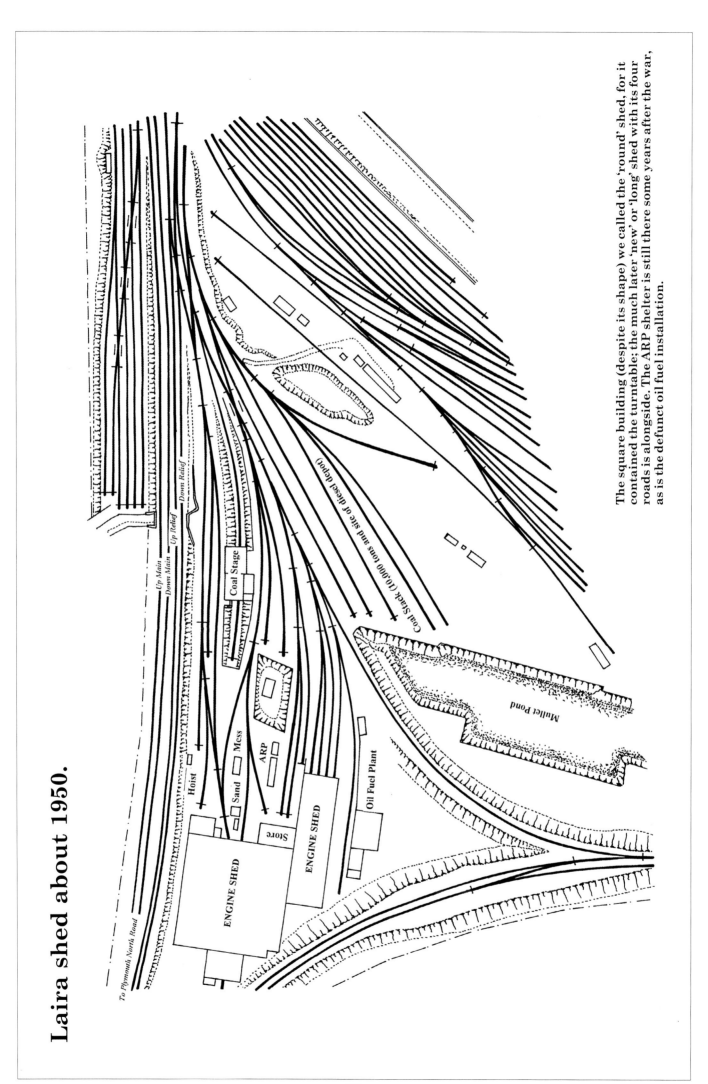

The square building (despite its shape) we called the 'round' shed, for it contained the turntable; the much later 'new' or 'long' shed with its four roads is alongside. The ARP shelter is still there some years after the war, as is the defunct oil fuel installation.

To Plymouth North Road

Up Main
Down Main
Up Relief
Down Relief

Coal Stage

Coal Stack (10,000 tons and site of diesel depot)

Hoist

Sand
Mess

ARP

Store

ENGINE SHED

ENGINE SHED

Oil Fuel Plant

Mullet Pond

CHAPTER 4
Laira; Pilot Link

It was natural that I should be glad to return to Laira, for this was a shed of Kings, Castles, 'Double Homes' (in which crews lodged away from home overnight), Ocean Mails and all the rest. I was placed in the Pilot Link, the most junior link, whose workings were as follows:

Shed turning (including working wagons on and off the coal stage)

'Prepping' (preparation of engines for their next job)

Marshalling yard shunting

Banking engines on Hemerdon.

My driver, at the start, was Don Jenkins, a fairly senior driver in the link, who was soon to be promoted out, and replaced by Les Plummer. The opposite to Don, he had newly 'passed' and this was his first link as driver. Although both men were very willing to teach me the trade and the art of good footplate practice I confess to being a little unsettled to start with. After the heady days of passenger work at Slough it seemed a bit of a come down; I was soon to realise that I had a lot to learn.

'Shed turning' was virtually an administrative duty. Locomotives that had taken coal from the stage, tenders/bunkers replenished and their fires cleaned, would then be stabled in the desired position, so that they could leave without (or with minimum) rearrangement on their next turn of duty. We also shunted full wagons of coal on to the stage and removed the empties afterwards. Laira was in essence divided into three areas for this. The roundhouse (we called it the 'Round Shed' with its 28 turntable roads, was generally the domain of the tank engines, although tender engines would be stabled in the longer roads at the corners. The 'New Shed' (sometimes called the 'Long Shed') was normally reserved for tender engines – Kings, Castles, Halls, Granges, Manors which were rostered for passenger duties. Between the sheds were the 'Intermediate Sidings' on which goods engines were stabled.

Coal was loaded manually from the stage on to the tenders and bunkers of locomotives beneath, the men shovelling it from open wagons to half ton wheeled tubs which were then manhandled out and up-ended so that the contents fell down to the locomotive; I describe these stalwarts and others in Chapter 15.

Prepping' was getting locomotives ready ('prepared') to go off shed and to work. For my driver it would mean replenishing the oil cups, inspecting to see that there were no obvious defects and, if there were, getting them corrected. My task would be to ensure that a full set of tools was present, examine the smokebox, ensure that the door was secured air tight, and check the sand boxes. In between I would gradually build the fire up, trim the coal in the tender or bunker, trim the lamps and generally have a good clean up of the footplate. When both of us were ready the tender tank would be replenished from a water column. 'Prepping' was a dirty job at the best of times, but worse was raising steam after a locomotive had undergone a boiler wash. There would be no steam at all in the boiler to work the 'blower' (the forced draught to get the fire going) and until there was, the footplate would be filled with dense, yellow, sulphurous smoke.

We were given an allocation of engines for a shift; it would be something like two tender locos, a couple of tanks and perhaps a boiler washout. There would also be a couple of engines, perhaps, that

Old Plymouth 5. The Hoe, showing the west end of The Esplanade, the Shelter below, and again, the magnificent buildings forming the backdrop.

Old Plymouth 6. An early Cremyll ferry on the Cornish side of the Hamoaze, shortly to cross to the Plymouth side at Mutton Cove. Mount Wise, opposite, is the residence of the Port Admiral. Paddle Steamers also sailed to Stonehouse and the River Yealm.

would just require a check that all the tools, lamps and oil cans were ready for the crews who would book on to 'prep' their own locomotive.

The work of local shunting, that I had already experienced as a senior cleaner, was centred (as mentioned earlier) on the yards at Tavistock Junction (Marsh Mills) and Laira. In those days 'the Junction' boasted three shunting engines on 24 hour duty for six days a week, and two on Sundays. The up yard consisted of some twenty or so long sidings which received the freight traffic from Cornwall as well as from the local area. The wagons were then marshalled into trains for forwarding, although some would be labelled for local destinations. Twice a day the shunter would take the latter across the main line to the 'new yard' which lay adjacent to the down main line, and was made up of some 12 sidings and two reception roads. It received the freight trains from various and far-flung places north of Plymouth. These were then re-marshalled for their various destinations; Cornwall, Plymouth and its environs and branch lines. The local freight stayed in this yard to be distributed by transfer goods workings (more of these in due course) while the Cornish traffic was shunted into the adjacent 'down yard'. This consisted of approximately 15 sidings and a 'head shunt' and handled all of the Cornish goods traffic. Shunting taught me how to control the amount of steam and water in the boiler of a tank engine. One moment it had to be sufficient to maintain a heavy session of shunting, the next to try to stop excess steam blowing

from the safety valves while waiting for the next train to arrive. In both Don and Les, I could not have had better tuition.

Banker duty was carried out in the Pilot Link in those days, though later it was transferred into the No.2 Goods Link. We had large 31XX class 2-6-2Ts for this work and spent our working day assisting freight trains up the fearsome I in 41 Hemerdon Bank, by pushing from the rear. Upon reaching the top, we would return back to Tavistock Junction, take on water and wait for the next 'customer'. In the busiest period, at night when the freights were making their way east, two bankers would be on duty, and during peaks such as the brief Cornish broccoli season, the whole shift would be non-stop. Respite only came from the need to top up the tanks with water, and occasionally a trip back to Laira shed to re-fill the bunker with coal. Four trips for each night 'banker' would be the norm, increased to perhaps six in the new potato or broccoli season. I know of one Laira crew booked on 'spare duty' who were sent to Tavistock Junction to 'help out' during a busy spell who landed up doing *twelve* trips up and down the bank. They found out afterwards, to their chagrin, that the 'booked' banking engines and crews had done nowhere near that number! The locomotive would not be coupled up for the journey, leaving the main train to continue non-stop at the top. The work was hard on both the engine and crews, for once leaving the bottom of the bank in 'Plympton Sidings' (the two long up Tavistock departure roads) the regulator would be opened 'right across' with the lever fairly forward (that is, 'flat out').

The bonus for a fireman was that a boiler of water would almost take us to the top, necessitating putting the injector on to place water into the boiler when the ATC sounded for Hemerdon signal box. The injector would then remain on all the way back down the bank; on arrival there the boiler would be full, and the steam gauge would recover while taking on water in the tanks.

The GWR Rule Book (*Bible* by nickname) but properly entitled *Rules and Regulations for the guidance of Officers and Men - Rule 149(c)* states that: *When the Driver of the Engine in front has received the Guards signal to start, and he is satisfied that the necessary fixed Signal has been lowered, he must call the attention of the Driver in the rear of the train by giving two "crow" whistles, which must then be acknowledged by repetition from the rear engine, and, until these "crows" have been given and acknowledged, neither the train engine nor the assisting engine must move forward.*

A two crow series of whistles was made up of one long blast, two short ones, a long, two short and two more short. It doesn't require much effort to imagine what the good ratepayers of nearby Plympton felt about this chorus on a clear summer night, repeated and then followed by the blast of two locomotives working flat out to move a train out of the goods loop, through Plympton station and up the Hemerdon bank. And this, in the season, all night long!

4920 DUMBLETON HALL of Newton Abbot shed, 15 September 1963, standing on the siding adjacent to the ash road at Laira shed. With the onset of the diesels the loss of space in the New Shed saw this siding in regular use for the stabling of locomotives. She looks in excellent condition, with a tender full of decent size coal for her trip back to her home shed. *Terry Nicholls*.

Outside Laira New Shed in the mid-1950s, a typical scene in a typical locomotive shed; steam and smoke, locomotives in varying degrees of readiness. As the picture shows, this building was mainly used for tender locomotives, on passenger duty. Facing the camera in road No.2 is 7815 FRITWELL MANOR, a long way from its Gloucester home. *R.E. Vincent/Transport Treasury*.

1006 COUNTY OF CORNWALL of Penzance shed, in the siding by the coal stage. The absence of headlamps and lack of any steam would indicate that she still has to be readied for her journey back down through Cornwall. Small prairie tank 5536 on the coal stage job. *Terry Nicholls.*

The view from the water tank, 17 July 1960, eastwards along the main line. It is a Sunday, and the locomotives are queuing for coal, all the way out on to the goods loop. In the distance, on the far side of the main line, are the up sidings, where the auto carriages were stabled. At middle right, just past the signal, is where I almost derailed MALLARD. *R.C. Riley/Transport Treasury.*

The Saltash ferry approaching the Cornish shore in April 1950. The buildings on the skyline at the eastern end of the bridge mark the former camp for US soldiers, stationed there in readiness for D-Day. The ground occupied ran all the way across to the Nissen huts, visible to the left of the bridge. That area is now occupied by the eastern end of the Tamar road bridge and its dual carriageway. *R.E. Vincent/Transport Treasury.*

Laira shed on 27 June 1955 and 6869 RESOLVEN GRANGE stands on the siding next to the outgoing road; pannier tank 9770 is on the coal stage above, either retrieving empties or dropping off 'full 'uns'. The Grange, a Penzance engine at the time, has passed through the coal stage and had her fire cleaned and so on. She has obviously been freshly prepared for her next turn of duty; fire made up (wisp of smoke from chimney) and tender trimmed with tools in place, 'pep' pipe attached and hanging over the side and the headlamps trimmed and hanging on the hooks in the cab *R.E. Vincent/Transport Treasury.*

Large prairie tank 5175 with the early morning 'down snaily' entering the east end of Wearde loop, 13 July 1957. This was the original line of the Cornwall Railway before the deviation in 1908. Part of Defiance Platform can be seen on the left. This is the train to which I refer in this chapter; it will take advantage of being 'put in' to allow the early morning passengers to pass, filling up its tanks from the column at the west end at Wearde. *R.E. Vincent/Transport Treasury.*

Millbay, an elevated view of East Dock in 1927. Coaches stand in the siding for a mail train, with the 'dockie' saddle tank and its shunting wagon alongside. A Castle is on a train at the departure sidings, extreme left; in the misty background Drake's Island can just be made out. Jewsons Timber Yard is in the foreground.

CHAPTER 5
The Transfer Link

Promotion and progression for footplatemen was by seniority, and in February 1948 I duly came out of the Pilot Link and was placed in the Transfer Link. Its workings entailed moving freight around the various yards in the Plymouth area; Tavistock (always called 'Tavvy') Junction, Laira, Millbay, the docks, Devonport, Keyham and into HM Dockyard, to St Budeaux and down into the Royal Armaments Ordnance Sidings. We also worked local goods into Cornwall, to Yealmpton and to Sutton Harbour. The locomotives on this sort of work were mainly those maids of all work, the 57XX pannier tanks, and my driver, an ex-main line man, was Tren Gill. Tren, for medical reasons, was unable to continue his normal duties, and therefore was accommodated in this link. He loved to recount his days on the main line and I learnt a great deal from him that would stand me in good stead in future years.

Transfer goods work was exactly as the name suggests; it was the transfer of wagons from one yard to another. We would start in Laira yard, collect a brake van and proceed to Tavistock Junction to pick up a train of wagons. From there we might go back to Laira yard again to set

down and pick up more wagons, and on to Millbay to do the same. Then it was on to the goods yards at Devonport and Keyham, both of which enjoyed extensive traffic in those days. While at Keyham we would drop down into the Royal Naval Dockyard, and link up with the Navy's own railway system, before progressing to St Budeaux and the Armaments Depot. It was the rule in this place (which, unsurprisingly, no one thought to break) never to place coal on the fire, in case an errant spark escaped the chimney and blew us, and maybe half of Plymouth, to kingdom come. Across the track was a very different railway, they painted everything the wrong shade of green, and drove on the wrong side; GW locos were right-hand drive, other companies drove from the left. They called themselves *The Southern!*

In Millbay Docks we worked the little 1361 class of 0-6-0 saddle tanks, and marshalled wagons for the considerable perishable and grain traffic which came in by sea in those days. To this would be added traffic for the various trades which went on in there. These included timber and coal yards, marine engineering and metal works; all relied on the railway. When the Atlantic liners came in to

Plymouth, with our little tankie we marshalled the Pullman coaches for the Ocean Mail Trains that sped the well-heeled passengers up to London. A feature of shunting the docks was that one seldom saw a shunter. The track was full of twists and curves around the various basins and wharves and the work was largely carried out using a system of whistle signals, as follows:

1 whistle = go ahead, 2 whistles = go backwards, 3 whistles = stop.

Tren, unfortunately, was a little rotund. The footplate on a 'dockie' was rather cramped and the reversing lever was only about 15 inches or so from the side of the cab. At times I'd hear a plaintive 'help' from his side of the cab, and find that he had got himself jammed between the cab and the lever. I'd have to go over and press his stomach in so that he could move the lever or vice-versa! At times I would pretend not to hear, and then his entreaties quickly turned to threats!

The railways' freight working, all across the country, rested on an ancient institution, the pick-up goods, which served every wayside station or siding, delivering full wagons and taking away empties. We had a 5.15am pick-up goods,

The little one road Millbay Docks engine shed with its water tank outside. Engines ceased being stabled at the docks when the main Plymouth shed at Belmont sidings was closed and the locomotives moved to the new shed at Laira.

Large prairie 5148 at Liskeard on 10 July 1955 with the 9.25 Tavistock Junction-St Austell pick-up goods. This train slowly worked its way westward, shunting at Menheniot, Liskeard and Doublebois where there would be an exchange with St Blazey crew working their way east from St Austell with a similar train. *R.C. Riley/Transport Treasury.*

from Tavistock Junction into Cornwall. Such trains often took forever and the nickname of this particular one, 'the snaily' tells you everything about it. First stop going west was St Germans and from there we'd work our way to Menheniot, Liskeard, and possibly Doublebois, shunting the goods yard in each case, setting down and collecting wagons. Our locomotive was the inevitable 51XX prairie tank. To cover the main line in sufficient time to get the crews back home we 'swopped' engines at Liskeard. A St Blazey crew had been inching their way towards us with a similar train, again starting out early in the morning, eastwards from St Austell. The usual changeover was effected at Liskeard (we'd take their engine – often a 53XX mogul but sometimes a 57XX pannier – back to Laira and they'd have ours, and the next day they were swopped over again) but occasionally we would have to work on to Doublebois before meeting with the up 'snaily'. Tren was never very happy about this and would exchange some old fashioned looks with the St Blazey driver, thinking, possibly rightly, that he had been hanging around deliberately. Should it happen twice in one week, then he became livid. He would ensure that it did not happen a third time, for Tren would then waste as much time as he reasonably could while shunting Menheniot and Liskeard. If, as happened on one occasion, the up pick-up made

good progress and met us early, at Menheniot, he was all smiles.

By the time I arrived in the Transfer Link passenger services on the Yealmpton branch had ceased, leaving only a single goods train, once a day. We had a regular pannier tank, 4656 on this turn, booking on at 10.15am, to get the engine ready, and going off shed at 11am for Laira yard. Departure from the yard was at 11.30am, usually with 12-18 wagons, mostly loaded for the needs of farmers and agricultural merchants; fertiliser, livestock and fodder as well as domestic coal for the village. The working was a leisurely affair; arriving at Plymstock, where the branch proper started, the 'staff' (the electric train token for the single line running) was collected, and away we would go, knowing that we were to be the only train on the line that day.

Firing was kept to a minimum, for there were no great demands in working the branch; it was a matter of just keeping the steam gauge up, there or thereabouts, and the boiler three parts full with water, and all would be well. Most of my time was spent cleaning and polishing up the footplate. Being a regular engine it was possible to take personal pride in its appearance. On the outward journey we shunted at Billacombe, Elburton Cross, Brixton Road and Steer Point, where a brickworks furnished traffic for the railway and at one time the *Kitley Belle* and her sister

river steamers would offload day trippers, who returned to Plymouth on the railway. Arrival at Yealmpton was booked for 12.58, and we had travelled less than seven miles in about two hours! Yard duties at Yealmpton involved shunting the goods shed and sidings and, occasionally, the cattle pens and after that it was time to tend to the needs of the engine, taking on water and oiling. We were scheduled to depart at 2.18pm and the only scheduled stop on the return was at Billacombe, to collect wagons from Moore's Quarry, to arrive back at Laira yard at 3.12pm. Released to go to shed we booked off duty at 4pm, unless the foreman had found a job of work for us to make up our eight hours.

Sutton Harbour boasted just one goods train, running on three days a week, out of Laira yard. The locomotives had traditionally been drawn from a rapidly diminishing collection of veteran pannier tanks, 1930, 1990, 2038, 2090 and 2148, dating back to the 1890s and kept at Laira for two reasons, I believe. One was because the wheelbase was especially suited to the sharp curvature of the track on the quayside and wharves and, secondly, they could be equipped with one of the 'V' or 'plate' snowploughs on the front buffer and sent to the Princetown branch, to run up and down it in severe weather. The native small prairies of the 44XX series were, it would seem, not suited to this. In addition to the sidings in Sutton Harbour, shunting took place at Northey's Sidings, and in the petroleum depot at Cattedown. The track to Sutton Harbour has long been taken up, and now forms a part of the Embankment Ring Road into Plymouth.

Every weeknight a 57XX pannier would leave shed at 12.10am for Laira Yard and there collect a train for St Germans, shunting at Saltash on the return journey. The wagons contained mainly agricultural feedstuffs, fertilisers and domestic coal, the bread and butter (as it were) of local freight working. The train also regularly included a couple of petroleum tanks for the depot on Quay Road, immediately beneath the goods sidings. The train arrived in the very early hours of the morning, about 1.00am and shunting was scheduled to stop at 2.30am in deference to the people living near the station. It was hardly a generous concession and, with due respect to them, I often thought that if they had not got to sleep by 2.30, there wasn't much hope after that! If required, we would have short shunt at 4am, before leaving with the train to Saltash.

Most of the traffic for Saltash was local goods for delivery in the surrounding area (by a Great Western lorry, driven by Bill Hingston) and household coal. Milk tanks, filled from a road tanker from the local dairy, were brought and collected by the Saltash auto train (the 'Saltash Motor'). Shunting at Saltash was usually completed before the first auto train of the day arrived, and we were due to depart again at 5.45am. It was a matter of some anxiety for me that this train might disturb the residents of Coombe Road, beneath the station and goods yard. In fact it was hard to see how they could possibly stay undisturbed, such was the clanking and banging of loose couplings during the early morning shunting. The problem was my parents lived close to the station and would walk along Coombe Road to reach the town. My mother, especially, was very proud of the fact that both her sons were on the footplate, and delighted to tell the residents that *her son, Philip, was on the morning goods train!* Not so enthralled were her listeners, I'll be bound. When visiting home after the St Germans turn of duty, I would try to 'sneak' along the road before anyone saw me and gave me a piece of their mind about being woken up in the small hours.

I confess to having thoroughly enjoyed the Transfer Link, and especially working with Tren. It was a time of learning, made more interesting by the varied type of work. So it was with very mixed feelings, on a day in late June 1948, that I opened and read a very important letter labelled ON HIS MAJESTY'S SERVICE, informing me that I had been called up for NATIONAL SERVICE, and was to report to 9 Training Regiment, Royal Engineers at Cove, Hampshire, on the 8th July 1948.

Pannier tank 9716 at Billacombe on 12 March 1958. The train is the 10.40am Laira Yard-Yealmpton branch goods, returning at 2.15pm from Yealmpton. Passenger services had ceased in October 1947. Once through Plymstock station the goods was the sole train on the line. Traffic included wagons of household coal, agricultural goods and animal feedstuff, in addition to general merchandise. Steer Point provided heavy brick traffic from time to time and there was stone and sand from the adjacent Billacombe Quarry. With the gradual decline in goods traffic the service was reduced to Mondays, Wednesdays and Fridays until the branch finally closed completely on 26 February 1960. *Hugh Davis.*

Pannier tank 2148 with the Laira yard to Sutton Harbour goods train on 28 March 1951. The 19XX and 21XX class of tank were kept at Laira partly for this duty, their short wheel base suited to the tight curves of the track on the dockside quays. *Alan Lathey/Transport Treasury*.

Plymouth Docks in the 1930s. All of the docksides and wharves had tracks and the little 1361 class shunting engines would work over the whole system. This view shows, bottom left, Eastern Kings Point and West Wharf, where a large grain silo was erected for the animal feedstuff coming in by sea. The track and sidings continued towards the top of the picture with the quays enclosing the Inner Basin connected by a swing bridge. The Graving Dock in the Inner Basin is extreme left and the sidings continued around the northern side of the Basin, with its massive warehouses. The track can just be made out coming from behind the last warehouse on the right. Proceeding now to East Dock, the junction with the outgoing line to Millbay station can be seen. East Quay had timber yards but was mainly concerned with the ocean mail and liner traffic which came to the dock at the extreme bottom right.

1364 on East Dock. The water tank of the little engine shed is visible above the vans and the track to the left is on the quay that encloses the Inner Basin. The headlamp arrangement on the engine is not the 'A' code as borne by express passenger locomotives but is instead the code for shunting work. *R.C. Riley/Transport Treasury.*

Saddle tank 1364 shunting Millbay Docks on 14 July 1955, at the junction where the track from West Wharf meets with East Wharf and the out-going road to the Millbay and Plymouth North Road stations. The shunters truck (the dummy or chariot as it was known) is attached to the engine and the shunters can be seen just behind the box van. Because of the severe curvatures of the track the shunters were seldom seen and the work was guided by whistles. *R.C. Riley/Transport Treasury.*

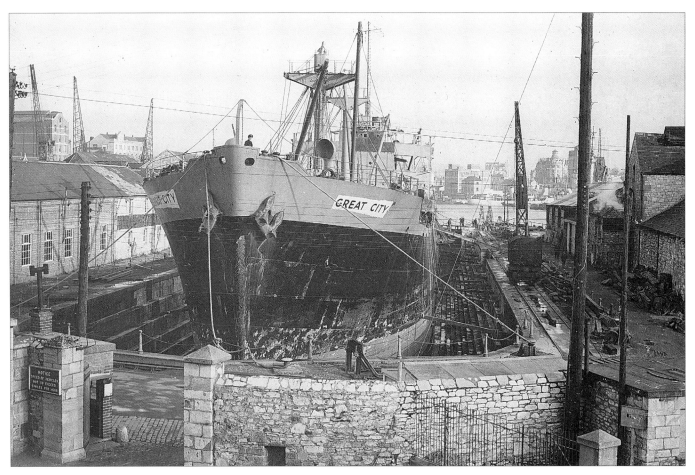

October 1966 and SS GREAT CITY is berthed in the Great Western's Dry Dock in the Inner Basin. The western entrance to the docks can be seen bottom left, along with the quayside track leading to West Wharf.

The Great Western tender CHESHIRE, fastened alongside a four-funnelled liner in Plymouth Sound, probably about 1930 by the look of the tender and the warship going across the bows of the liner. A small amount of mail has been transferred and is on the foredeck of the tender.

Tender CHESHIRE alongside a liner in Plymouth Sound, with the mails stored on the decks.

Tender LIVERPOOL with the mails being offloaded and manhandled to the waiting mail vans.

Millbay Docks tender *Sir Richard Grenville* on 4 July 1955. All traffic, mail and passengers arriving by the liners was transferred to tenders in the middle of Plymouth Sound and then ferried ashore. *R.C. Riley/Transport Treasury*.

Tender *Sir John Hawkins*, 4 July 1955. Both tenders were built by Earles of Hull. *Sir John Hawkins* was launched around 1930 and her sister some two years later. They earned their keep in the summer when not tending the liners by sailing excursions to ports on the Devon and Cornish shores. *R.C. Riley/Transport Treasury*.

Belmont and Harwell Street sidings at Millbay, 1 May 1961. Belmont sidings (left) was once the site of the Plymouth engine shed. In my time, it was used to store wagons and served as a shunting spur. In later times it became a carriage siding. Harwell Street (right), had a large covered shed where carriage cleaning took place. *R.C. Riley/Transport Treasury*.

64XX pannier tank 6414 with a two car auto arriving at St Germans, 16 July 1956. The train is passing the goods shed and yard before entering the station. The siding to the right was used for petrol and fuel tank wagons, supplying the fuel depot by the embankment, glimpsed on the right. On the opposite side of the road to this depot was a row of council houses, the reason for shunting stopping 'early'! *R.C. Riley/Transport Treasury*.

The Doublebois goods returning to Liskeard. The engine would shunt the sidings by the goods shed behind the engine, and also sidings adjacent to the terminus of the Looe branch at Liskeard. It would then travel eastwards to Menheniot to complete the shunting there, collecting hoppers of railway ballast from the quarry sidings. *R.E. Vincent/Transport Treasury*.

Pannier tank 1930 with the Sutton Harbour goods at Friary Junction, on 30 May 1925. It was something of an institution, running three days a week from Laira yard over many years.

Pannier 2032 with the Sutton Harbour goods at Northey's sidings in April 1952. The track bed now forms part of the Eastern Ring Road, from the Embankment to Coxside in Plymouth. *Alan Lathey/Transport Treasury*.

Pannier 2148 on the Sutton Harbour branch, passing under the SR line to Friary in April 1951. The train shows that the load to Sutton Harbour was mainly empty wagons. On the return they would be filled with all manner of seaborne traffic, including scrap metal. *Alan Lathey/Transport Treasury*.

2097 at North Quay Junction in 1953. The scrap metal can be clearly seen. *Michael Daley.*

2148 shunting Sutton Harbour quayside on the afternoon of 10 August 1951. It was a very busy dock complex and shunting was made more awkward by lorries suddenly appearing from nowhere or straddling the rails, with the driver gone for a tea break! *Alan Lathey/Transport Treasury.*

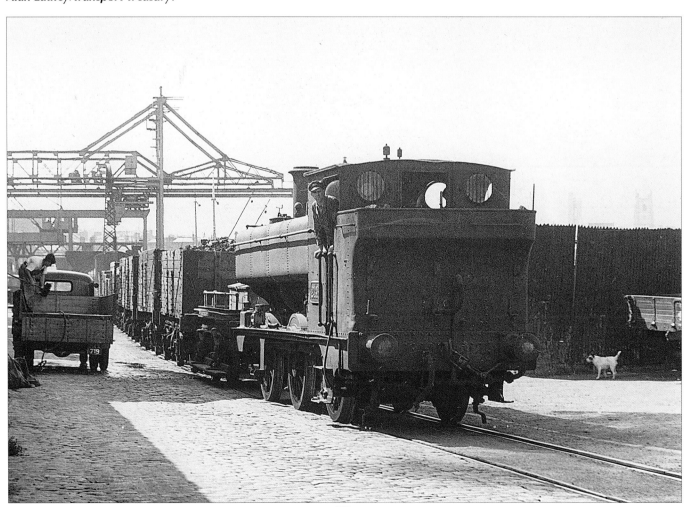

Yealmpton Station, just over six miles from the junction at Plymstock. Prior to the abandonment of passenger services in October 1947 the branch was served by eight trains a day, on weekdays only. The goods ran every day, leaving Laira yard at 11.30am and arriving at Yealmpton a little before 1pm. The return working left Yealmpton at 2.18pm, due Laira yard at 3.15pm. *Maurice J. Dart Collection..*

57XX pannier tank 9716 on the Yealmpton goods at Brixton Road in March 1958. This was a lovely old branch; passenger services had stopped and the line was all ours. Sadly the goods traffic was in decline too.

The Longmoor Military Railway in May 1946 with Austerity 2-10-0 79250 McMULLEN on shed. It had been named after Maj.Gen. McMullen, the Commandant of the Railway Training Centre 1937-1939. *R.C. Riley, Transport Treasury.*

LMR 70179 (ex-GWR 2466) at Longmoor in May 1946. During the Second World War the British railway companies were required to provide locomotives for work with the military. The Great Western supplied this class as well as a number of the 53XX Moguls. *R.C. Riley, Transport Treasury.*

CHAPTER 6
National Service and then Two Weeks 'Z' Training

I suspect that most young men of my age with a good civilian job felt at that time as I did – decidedly not overly keen to leave it for two years in the Services, but, in hindsight, I am glad I went. At 9 Training Regiment, Royal Engineers the first eight weeks consisted of basic training; fitness, drilling, rifle and Bren gun proficiency, in order for us firstly to be soldiers. The following four weeks was more specialised, learning how to be a Royal Engineer – *a Sapper*. We carried out timber bridging, learning how to use wood spars and how to lash them together, 'watermanship', that is Bailey and pontoon bridging, mine clearance (which I did not care for) and demolitions. I must have pleased them for they made me a Lance Corporal and, other than a short spell at Elgin in Scotland, was stationed permanently at 9.T.R.R.E as a Training NCO for the rest of my two years and three months service. I accept that this has no direct bearing on a railway story, other than after demobilisation and a return to civilian life, I was called back to the Army to serve for two weeks for what was known as 'Z' Training. For this I was instructed to report to the Army Transportation Unit of the Corps of Royal Engineers, on Longmoor Downs in Hampshire.

For this fortnight's 'Z' Training, it made no difference to the Army that for my earlier service I had served over two years in a Field Regiment acquiring expertise in training recruits in the art of bridge building, and then blowing the darn things up again. I was now to be a Military Railwayman. Furthermore, because I had attained the exalted rank of Full Corporal RE in my previous Service, I was to be a *Railway Engine Driver (Steam),* notwithstanding that in civilian life I was only a fireman, and a very junior one at that. After a day spent on rules and locomotive practice, for the next couple of weeks I drove all manner of Locomotives on passenger and freight trains on the famous Longmoor Military Railway, situated between Bordon and Liss in Hampshire**.** The railway had about eight miles of 'main line', mostly single track, and there was also a branch circuit called the Hollywater Line, used mainly for training; relaying, block circuit for training 'blockmen' (signalmen) and the like. Longmoor had an unofficial motto: *You can tell a Longmoor Sapper anywhere, but you can't tell him much!*

The 'coal' used on the LMR consisted of briquettes, about 9in x 6in x 3in, made of compressed coal dust, similar to the 'ovoids' sold as domestic fuel at that time. To a Great Western man, brought up in the tradition of best soft Welsh steam coal this stuff was anathema, and I confess to a secret admiration for my Sapper fireman who regularly produced good steaming results with such inferior stuff. He was, however, an LMS fireman in civilian life, so perhaps that had something to do with it. Never in my wildest imaginings did I expect to encounter fuel of that nature again. Alas I did, and it was on the Great Western of all lines, in Cornwall, at Truro engine shed...

Before the Army had finished with me and my fellow 'Z' Reservists, we were to be 'extended' in order the better to demonstrate our abilities. Someone 'higher-up' had decided that a good idea would be to send all the regular soldiers at Longmoor on a weeks leave, and *leave the Reservists to run the Railway*. That in itself seemed fine to us; we were quite pleased really, although the depot Staff Sergeant was heard protesting to the Camp Commandant; something uncomplimentary about a 'bunch of bl—dy amateurs'. That hurt, because in the main we were all railwaymen in civilian life. The sting in the tail, which we were not told immediately, was that this 'higher-up' had also improved upon his brilliant idea by suggesting to Southern Command that it would be a *ripping good show* to stage a mock battle scheme. We felt like gladiators in Rome, or worse, the unfortunate Christians. Using Regular and National Service units of the army stationed in the Aldershot and Farnborough areas, the eventual target would be the *capture of the Longmoor Military Railway*. We were duly issued with rifles to carry on the footplate.

On the appointed day, I was booked on a late evening shift to work a trip goods on the Hollywater branch. I recall that it was a Friday, and the thoughts of both myself and my fireman were that by the time we finished, booked off, and got to the barrack room, we would not get much sleep before travelling back home the next day. However, Hollywater it was, with a Hunslet 0-6-0 saddle tank. We left the depot and yard with a 'made-up' train, for after all we were really just going through the motions. We called into Woolmer Yard and did a bit of shunting before going on to Whitehill where we used the short cut-off line to go on to the branch. We shunted again at Hopkins Sidings and then travelled all the way past Hollywater and Holm Mills to Griggs Green. All there was here was a long siding running parallel to the track, used extensively for re-laying training. All we did, really, was to shunt wagons of

sleepers and rails from the siding to the branch line, alter their order in the siding a couple of times and reform our train. By now the summer evening was turning to dusk, and it was decided to have our snack. Talking about the week, enjoying a cup of tea and thinking very much of home, we became very relaxed only to hear a voice from the ground on my side of the engine: *Don't move or do anything silly, you're captured!* I looked down and saw a wicked-looking bayonet pointing at me, fixed to a Lee-Enfield .303 rifle, held by a blacked-face chap wearing a tin helmet covered in camouflage.

Well now, what does one do? I thought. My fireman decided he wanted to be a hero, and grabbed for his rifle from the rack, which was fine for him; after all the bloke with the bayonet was on my side! I suggested that, as we were going home in a few hours, discretion was the better part of valour, and that the chap on the ground looked as though he wasn't exactly playing at soldiering. I found out, on clambering down from the engine, that he was from the Green Howards Regiment. Gaining psychological dominance, I asked him what he expected us to do, pointing out that we had a locomotive to look after. I mentioned that if he marched us off to a concentration camp or the like, the boiler would eventually empty and the locomotive would blow to pieces, and with that the powers-that-be would not be happy, at all.

He was giving some thought to this when a Green Howards officer arrived. After discussion the officer informed our captor that he was to stay with us until a certain time, when the exercise was due to end, and then allow us to go on our way back to Longmoor Yard and Camp This he duly did, and eventually we were 'released'. I reported to our officer the events of the night, and it seemed we had done the correct thing for some of the attacking forces had been a trifle overzealous, leaving a few of our chaps a bit battered and bruised. We booked off, and the next morning departed from Longmoor for the journey home.

A very enjoyable week, especially for the opportunity to have been an engine driver even for a short period, but it was a marvellous feeling being the man in charge; it showed what a couple of stripes on the arm could achieve! Yet the thought has ever remained that I ended my career in the Army as a *Prisoner of War!* And as such by the actions of the *British Army!* At least they didn't put it on my service record...

The single coach auto train North Road-Tavistock, approaching Mutley tunnel on 27 June 1955, with pannier tank 6414. *R.E. Vincent/Transport Treasury.*

CHAPTER 7
No.2 Goods Link

So, soldiering days over, I returned to normal life again at Laira shed. It was early in 1952 and I was promoted into the No.2 Goods Link, there to team up with a driver called Claude Bolt. This was my first true main line link, and here I was to learn what firing a locomotive was all about. In Claude I could have no finer tutor, for, as well as being a gentleman, he was also a first class engineman. This driver, perhaps more than any other, was to have a great and lasting influence upon me. He taught me the essentials of my trade. How to produce steam and water in great quantities when necessary, and how to conserve the same when it was not required. He also gave me fatherly advice when I found the problems of everyday life a burden, and gave me counsel when I needed guidance, which seemed to be often.

One of the many rostered duties we had in the No.2 Goods Link was the 1.40 am early morning train from Tavistock Junction to Truro. The train was destined for Drump Lane, Redruth, and was a semi-fast freight with a number of vacuum brake fitted wagons. Apart for an occasional stop at St Austell to set down, it was normally a straight run to Truro, where we were relieved by a Truro crew who took the train forward. For Claude and myself, it was a walk across the track to Truro shed, have our breakfast, and then prepare a locomotive ready to work the 7.30am 'stopper', back to Plymouth. The regular Truro engine rostered for this duty was at that time the pride of the place, 4906 BRADFIELD HALL; later on, with their introduction to Cornwall, one of the 1000 County class 4-6-0s took over. This particular morning Claude and myself left the enginemen's cabin and walked across the sidings to where 4906 was stabled. Climbing up on to the footplate, you can imagine my surprise and disgust to find the tender full of the despised briquettes. It did not help any to see good Welsh steam coal in the wagons in the sidings adjacent!

Claude, who unlike me was a very placid man when things were not right, was prepared to go to the foreman and take him to task for not, at the very least, mixing this poor stuff with some decent steam coal. But to his surprise (expecting me to 'blow my top') I calmly informed him that I was perfectly happy thank you, and that the rubbish held no fears for me. I proved it to him by making up a fire of some excellence and, on the journey to Plymouth, provided sufficient steam and water for perfectly good time-keeping. It was not easy, I confess, but BRADFIELD HALL was an elderly lady at that time, and rode a little rough on her springs, which was helpful in shaking the fire up and keeping it bright.

Stopping at every station also helped, and gave me time not only to recover the water level in the boiler but to get the steam gauge back 'on the mark'. Most importantly, we made Plymouth North Road *on time*. In later weeks, in the enginemens cabin at Laira, Claude and I took delight listening to our fellow crews who had worked the 'stopper' and could not keep time, cursing the poor steaming quality of the coal. They could not understand how we had escaped such problems. But then, their firemen had not had the advantage that I had in watching a young Sapper plying his trade on the Longmoor Military Railway. The secret he had revealed to me back then was: *break the darn things up, to expose a rough 'face' that the flames can 'bite' on*. We never did not tell them though!

My first turn of duty in the No.2 Goods Link with Claude had been the early morning Tavistock goods. I was of course eager to prove myself so turned up early on the Monday morning to ensure that when we went 'off shed' everything would be in order. I made up a good body of fire in the box, or so I thought, cleaned the footplate up, and even made a 'can' of tea. I was going to show him how proficient I

As the two coach Saltash auto leaves the bridge on the way to Plymouth on 15 May 1954, the driver in the leading vestibule exchanges a nod with the fireman on 6953 LEIGHTON HALL (a Reading loco at the time). The Hall has a Grange or Manor attached, no doubt to assist to Newton Abbot over the South Devon banks. They are on the way to Wearde sidings, a mile beyond Saltash, to collect empty coaching stock for a special weekday summer excursion Saltash-Goodrington. *R.E. Vincent/Transport Treasury.*

Small prairie 5541 at Tavistock station on 2 May 1961, at the head of a Launceston-Plymouth train. These engines were generally used on the Launceston trains, with pannier tanks on the Plymouth-Tavistock section. *R.C. Riley/Transport Treasury.*

was in the art of providing steam in a pannier tank, and finished up doing exactly the opposite... The goods was due off Laira yard at 5.25am and was to run to Tavistock in front of the early morning passenger which left North Road at 5.50am. Normally the goods was fully laden with the usual rural commodities; fertiliser, animal fodder, household coal and so on. It was very tightly scheduled so we would, if all went well, stay ahead of the passenger all the way to Tavistock up a gruelling gradient of 1:41 in some places. This was important, for getting to Tavistock on time meant that we would be able to have our breakfast at leisure before shunting began. Running late, and our train would be held at Horrabridge for the passenger to overtake us, with the effect that when we arrived at Tavistock the station shunter would be waiting, as would all the traders, and we would have to grab at our food while carrying out the shunting.

We received the signal to let us out of Laira yard and ran alongside the River Plym towards Tavistock Junction. At the turn on to the branch, Claude remarked that if we had a clear road through Marsh Mills, and I collected the 'staff' for the single line without having to stop, we could keep the train swinging along. A relaxed breakfast beckoned. Luck was on our side and as we came around the bend and under the bridge into Marsh Mills station I could see the signalman there with the 'staff', and duly informed Claude. My cry of 'right' as I caught it was met with the regulator going right across on to the second valve. It was from this moment that the trip, for me, threatened disaster. Despite all best efforts, I

struggled for steam all the way up the branch. It was nightmarish, not helped by the autumn leaves on the track making us lose adhesion, and requiring the sanding to go on constantly. I certainly was not idle, far from it, and that was where the fault lay. In my eagerness to please and show-off, I had been guilty of the fireman's greatest sin, that of *overfiring*, and had done so from the very first moment that I'd stepped on the footplate. Even while making the fire up, I had not waited for the layers of coal in the box to burn through before adding more. A complete waste of energy and time.

The fireman's *golden rule* is that *coal should be placed upon fire; coal must not be placed upon unburnt coal*. This I had forgotten on that first showing. No word of reproach came from Claude, though I am now sure that he realised how I felt, and that I was not very proud of myself. He was however aware that, in my inept way, I had worked hard to correct things, despite making things worse instead. Needless to say we were held back at Horrabridge for the passenger to go past and when eventually we reached Tavistock the shunter was there with his pole, ready to start work right away. We shunted Tavistock yard for the rest of the morning, at one time going off to Pitts Cleave Quarry sidings (towards Launceston) to collect wagons of stone. We eventually came back down the branch with a fully laden train once again. From this I learnt a little of how to assist a driver with the braking of a goods train, using the locomotive handbrake. After taking the train into Laira yard we were released to shed; we placed the

engine on the coal stage road and went to the office to book off.

Before departing Claude quietly told me to do nothing with the fire the next morning until he arrived. Back on our pannier tank next day he undertook the making up of the fire, and I had to watch. Eventually we left the shed, with possibly only half of the fire that I had put in the previous day, but *what a quality of fire it was*. Going up the branch that morning I only fired when Claude told me to, and placed coal only where he directed I should. Not only did we have all of the steam and water we could want but at times I was able to leave the firehole flap down, and even have a sit down myself. What a difference; I had learnt how to prepare a fire and how to make steam in an engine. I do not believe that I ever made the same mistake again. The Second Golden Rule was *little and often*, and this was well and truly brought home to me on the Tavvy Goods!

The workings of the No.2 Goods Link included trains to Truro in the west and Newton Abbot to the east, and these places marked the limits to which the drivers in this Link 'learnt the road'. The crews worked branch passenger and goods to Tavistock, double headed passenger trains over the South Devon banks to Newton Abbot and banked freights up Hemerdon (which I had first done in the Pilot Link). There were also spare turn rosters, in which we covered any duty (within reason) sometimes with a different driver. In order that a fireman could eventually become a driver it was necessary, amongst other things, for him to pass an examination on the workings of a steam locomotive, as well as being tested for a thorough knowledge of the GW rule book (the 'bible') at Swindon. To this end it was accepted practice for instruction to be given at Mutual Improvement Classes which were held, in the men's own time, on Sunday mornings. The instructors were volunteer enginemen who, with the aid of 'cut-away' models provided by the company, would explain the intricacies of steam, the meaning of weird things such as 'lap and lead' and, from the Rule Book 'Wrong Line Orders'.

The idea was that this would be followed up, whenever possible, with practical tuition on the footplate. Claude was an instructor and I recall many a teaching session with him. Sitting in a loop with a freight train waiting for a clear road, waiting on a banking engine between trains, or out on the road hard at it shovelling coal, he would suddenly shout a question at me, and expect an immediate answer. I would have to respond to a specific engine breakdown, what action could be taken, if any, and which procedure would apply to protect the train.

Railwaymen of whatever calling seemed to have a quality about them that made them 'men apart', and this was not only in the job they did, the manner of their work, but also and perhaps more importantly in their outlook on life. They had a certain type of character, were memorable (though in hindsight there are a couple best forgotten) and amongst these were the gangers, the men who oversaw 'their' stretch of track and kept

it, and the surrounds, in such excellent condition. They knew every inch that they were responsible for, and its particular needs. Such a man was the ganger at Liskeard.

Claude and I were rostered to work a train of cattle wagon empties from Tavistock Junction, destined for Marazion, for use in the broccoli specials. We were to be relieved at Truro. Our locomotive was 4-6-0 6873 CARADOC GRANGE, one of Laira's best, and this class were superb over the Cornish road. I confess a disappointment, that in this modern day not one of the class has been restored and preserved. It was a miserable day, raining cats and dogs and blowing a gale. As we pulled out of the yard Claude remarked that if not already washed and cleaned, the cattle wagons would be by the time they were needed. We had nearly a full load for a Grange over the Cornish main line but all bode well, for as we made the pull from Laira Junction to Mutley tunnel the steam gauge hardly moved off the 'mark'.

Going through North Road station, Claude looked at his watch and commented that we were most likely to be diverted into a running loop somewhere, as a passenger was due off North Road for Cornwall soon. I took this as a warning to let the level of the water in the boiler drop a bit, so that when we stopped there would be less chance for blowing off excess steam. The first possibility was Royal Albert Bridge, before crossing the Tamar, so I let the boiler drop on the climb to Devonport, and

dropped the flap from the firehole door to cool things down a little. As we approached St Budeaux East Signal Box, however, the anticipated diversion into the loop did not happen. Instead the bell rang in the cab to signify that the distant signal was 'off'; we were clear to stay on the main line, at least to Saltash. I collected the 'staff' for the bridge and suggested to Claude that we might be put in at Wearde, after the station at Saltash. But it was not to be; distants still in the off position, bells ringing merrily in the cab, we were to continue on the main line. I now had some hard work to do for I had let the water level drop, and with the Cornish road always demanding, I preferred everything to be in first class order at this stage of the trip.

The next possibility was Menheniot but as we rounded into the station we noticed the up 'snaily' (of earlier fame) occupying that loop as she collected ballast wagons from the adjacent quarry. We were perplexed now. Claude knew that the passenger must have been chasing us, and the only passing place left was Doublebois. However, all was soon revealed. Coming around the corner at Cartuther, we at last had a siren in the cab to tell us the distant signal for Liskeard was at caution, and we should anticipate adverse signals on the way in. Sure enough, running to the outer home we could see that it was 'on', but a toot on the whistle and it 'dropped'. We crawled now all of the way to the station and as we came on the viaduct I informed Claude

The return Tavistock goods at Marsh Mills, on 29 August 1961. It was booked to stop here on the return journey, to collect wagons from the Lee Moor China Clay works, and from the Ordnance Sidings beyond the white gates (left). This section of line now forms part of the preserved Plym Valley Railway. *R.C. Riley/Transport Treasury.*

Old Plymouth No.7. The Bandstand, Plymouth Hoe, in 1922. Taken from the top of Smeaton's Tower, showing the Esplanade, the road from West Hoe to the Barbican, and Tinside. The popularity of the concerts is demonstrated by the number of seats surrounding the bandstand; typically, some of the strollers are naval ratings.

that a *red flag* was showing from the signal box window. This meant the signalman had instructions for us. Stopping at the box and: *panic stations;* the passenger was at Menheniot, and the down main had to be cleared. We were instructed to pull ahead to clear the cross-over points, and then to shunt back on to the up main, eventually coming to a halt standing on Liskeard Viaduct.

While we were reversing the train, and negotiating the cross-over to go on to the up road, Claude instructed me to keep a good look out for an adverse signal from the guard. All went well but, as we came to a stop I noticed the local ganger walking along the down main, hammer on shoulder, sack over his back and with that 'rolling gait', so peculiar to lengthmen as they judged their pace to suit the sleepers. At that same moment we heard the protesting whistle of the passenger as she reached the distant and found it at caution. It was still raining hard and the cross wind on the viaduct, some 150 feet or so above the ground, was even making the engine and train rock. I warned Claude of the approaching ganger and he suggested that I invite him up to shelter and have a warm until the line was clear. This I did and it was accepted gratefully. He clambered up and, loosening his oilskin, lifted it as he turned his back to the fire to give warmth to his nether parts. While he was passing the time of the day with Claude, the down passenger went by, the crew shouting a few ribald expressions of displeasure for daring to have checked their progress. As if we could have done anything about it – we had been prepared to 'go in' as far back

as the Royal Albert Bridge, after all. Enjoying the quick burst of banter, the ganger, making a remark concerning the fraternity of footplate crews, turned to me and enquired after my health. I assured him I was fine except that I had a concern...

'What would that be?' he asked.

'Well', I replied , 'I'm a bit worried about the way your viaduct is swaying around.'

Thinking on it for a moment before answering, as was the way with country railwaymen, he turned back to me and said that I might well be right but 'it was when it didn't sway, would be the time to worry!' Of course, in his untold experience, he knew that the structure was designed to move a certain amount with the elements. With that, he thanked us both for our hospitality, climbed down from the footplate and continued on his way.

Most express passenger trains required an assisting engine over the tortuous banks of South Devon. Eastward from Plymouth we had two; Plympton to Hemerdon and Totnes to Dainton. West from Newton Abbot there were two more; Aller Junction (where the Torbay line left the main line) to Dainton and Totnes to Rattery and I touch on these again in Chapter 14. This work usually involved either Hall or Grange and later Manor 4-6-0s, coupled in front of the train engine as a pilot. Even Kings and Castles could be rostered for this duty, especially on a summer Saturday when two Kings would work the second part of 'The Limited' from Newton Abbot to Plymouth.

This piloting was rostered to the No.2 Goods Link, and very enlightening it was too. The Rule Book stated that the driver

of the leading engine (the junior man after all) was responsible for the handling of the train, observing signals, braking and so on. The driver of the main train would for sure be a top link engineman from Laira, or Old Oak Common. Again, it was a matter of learning as we went along, building experience for the future. At times, as with banking, we'd suspect the train engine might be easing off a little, leaving the assisting engine to work hard for both of them.

A rostered turn in this link which I particularly enjoyed – probably because I did not have to get out of bed at an un-earthly hour – was the 11.10 am semi-fast Penzance goods. We booked on at 10.00am and 'prepped' an engine, usually a Laira Hall, and worked the train from Tavistock Junction to Truro. I booked on one morning in the summer of 1954, to find that our engine was to be 6913 LEVENS HALL, one of Laira's best. I was fortunate to find that the footplate had not been 'robbed' of too many tools (a common abuse in those days) and with a little bit of searching (and *robbing* in turn) was able to get everything ready. A quick look in the firebox revealed that the firelighter had done me proud. Opening the dampers to get the air flowing up through the firebox, I was able to spread his fire over at least two-thirds of the grate area. A few selected lumps, about 6-9 inches, were put on to burn through while I did the 'outside jobs'. This meant trimming the lamps and pulling the sand levers; taking the handbrush down from the footplate I walked to the front of the engine, checking that there was a deposit of sand on the rail showing that all was in order. Placing the lamps on the front buffer beam and putting one on the nearside bracket, I climbed up to check the smokebox. Opening the door, a quick glance confirmed that the tubes had been cleared and were not blocked; the baffle plate was secure and the jumper ring on the top of the blast pipe was free to move up and down and not stuck solid.

All well, I shut the door and 'reamed' it tight to ensure a secure fit, and brushed off the loose char from the running plate.

Back on the footplate the coal which I'd put on was burnt through and with the long pricker fire iron I could now spread the fire all over the box. A touch on the blower (forcing the draught) and I started to make the fire up with some decent lumps from the front of the tender. Claude had arrived by this time and after a few topical remarks, I passed the oil cans and feeders down to him and he carried on with his part, the inspections and oiling. Into the tender now to trim the large lumps of coal into a manageable size for shovelling, selecting out a few big prize ones to complete the making up of the fire. Ensuring that no coal can fall off over the side and bringing a fair bit forward from the back of the tender, I check the fire and place on the remaining 'prize' lumps selected earlier. Start to clean up now, brushing the footplate back towards the tender, trying not to let much go over the side in case it hits my driver. The steam gauge is coming around and I can put on the injector to place water into the boiler and after shouting a warning to Claude, I wash down the footplate to get rid of the dust. Sprinkle the 'pep pipe'

over the tender to damp down the coal – most important for we shall go tender first to 'Tavvy Junction' to collect our train. Ease the blower now for I want to control the steam now that the fire is burning through and getting hot. A few shovelfuls on the back end to 'deaden the fire down a little' will help.

Now it is about the final preparations for leaving shed. Claude has finished oiling the motion and calls if I am ready to fill the tender with water from the adjacent column. Scrambling back over the coal I catch the chain as he swings it towards me; pulling the arm of the column around I place the leather 'bag' attached to the end of the arm, into the tender. Again a shout to Claude and he turns on the water. Back to the footplate to top up the boiler ensuring that we will leave shed with a full complement of water in both boiler and tender.

The task now is to clean up the footplate. Using a wad of dirty cotton waste I place some oil on it and wipe down the back of the firebox which protrudes into the footplate and leave a small film of oil there to catch any dust floating in the air. The tender must be getting full so back over the tender in time to warn Claude, and as he shuts off the valve, I lift the bag out of the filling hole and give the arm a push to swing the column back to its original position. After that it's a quick visit to the enginemens cabin with the can to make the tea. Back in the cab we proceed to the telephone to inform the signalman at Laira Junction box who we are, where we wish to go to, and that we are ready to proceed. The 'board' comes

off, Claude opens the regulator and we go 'off shed'. While this has gone on we've poured ourselves a cup of tea from the can. We edge quietly over the points and around behind the signal box and on to the loop alongside the River Plym. There was a dead end siding here, known as 'Ocean Siding' which was always a bit of a joke, for the river here was very wide and tidal and at low water amounted to little more than acres of mud. Very 'un-ocean' like! Enjoying our tea and having a quiet talk we come to 'Lord Morley's Bridge' and are signalled into the down side of the yard at Tavistock Junction. The shunter would already have set the points for us to run back on to our train, and he couples us on.

The leading wagons were usually vans I recall, forming the vacuum brake fitted part of the train. The guard came up to give Claude the loading which I do not remember, but this train was always somewhere around a full load for a Hall over the Cornish line. Now was the time to sort out the fire and get ready for the off. The fire was bright and I felt that there was no need to put a fire iron in to stir it up. I always tried to keep that action to a minimum for the introduction of an iron generally disturbed the fire on the firebars, causing cold air to come in and hasten the formation of clinker. I've described the Cornish road in some detail elsewhere in this book so will only mention some specific parts of the journey. We were not booked to set down at any location, but knew that we would be 'put in' at times to allow more prestige trains to pass.

2-8-0 3816 pounding up the 1 in 41 of Hemerdon Bank, with a banker on, 14 April 1952. The train engine is a long way from its home shed, Severn Tunnel Junction. Impressive (there was a cold snap that day) is the effect of the exhaust steam and smoke in the sky. The clouds escaping at the front end of 3816 and the outpourings at the rear from the banker indicate that both locomotives are working flat out, though they still have the steepest section to come. *R.E. Vincent/Transport Treasury.*

And now the banker comes past. Large prairie 3186 is indeed working 'flat-out' as revealed by the steam escaping under extreme pressure from the cylinders, and the exhaust being blasted high into the sky. It would seem to be a fine day; witness the guard standing on the platform at the rear of his van. *R.E. Vincent/Transport Treasury.*

The right away came and the signal was off for us to make the down main line. As Claude picked the train up carefully (so as not to snatch the couplings on the wagons at the rear which had loose couplings) and as we moved forward I kept a watch to the rear to exchange a wave from the guard in his van. This was to signify that the train was complete; at night we would exchange signals with lamps swung slowly from side to side. That taken care of and reported to Claude I was able to start to make up the fire. Already LEVENS HALL promised good steaming for the hand on the steam gauge had hardly moved. I placed a few shovelfuls to the corners of the front end and tended to the back corners. A slight blackening of the exhaust showed it to be having the right effect, as we picked up speed towards Laira Junction, ready for the climb to Mutley tunnel, a couple of miles ahead. No problems at all as we steamed past the shed and I noticed Forman Fred Manley standing watching, ever present cigarette in hand. Lipson Junction, where the line ran off to the Southern station at Friary came and went and it was on up to the tunnel. I had purposely let the water level in the boiler drop down to half glass, for with a hot fire it would be a problem stopping her from blowing her head off through North Road station. Into the tunnel and I put the injector on with an approving nod from Claude who had realised my intention. Down through Platform 4, I believe, and on to North

Road West signal box where we were signalled with distants off for the Cornish Road.

Claude reminded me that it was normal practice for us to be put into the loop at Wearde, just west of Saltash, to allow the Paddington parcels, 11.30 ex-North Road, and the Menheniot auto which followed behind to get past us. This was a hint to manage the boiler level accordingly and with LEVENS HALL steaming well I was able to keep the firehole flap down. A clean pick-up of the staff at Royal Albert Bridge signal box and for me an opportunity to tidy up the footplate, brush up, wash the front with the pep pipe and spray some water over the exposed coal surface in the tender. As we approached the western end of the bridge I attempted to look to the end of Coombe-by-Saltash viaduct to see if I could determine the signal, but no such luck. We soon found out, however, for after hanging out the staff at Saltash and running under the platform bridge, we could see the starter signal and the advanced with the distant at caution. Sure enough we were signalled into the loop, a section of the original Cornwall Railway which ran to Wearde alongside the banks of the River Lynher, and a glorious setting.

At Wearde I went to the box to inform the signalman that we were there, under the strictures of 'Rule 55' and to sign the register to that effect. This was done at Wearde, in the doorway of the box, definitely not *inside* the box, whatever the

weather, this was forbidden – see Chapter 13. Then it was back to the footplate to wait patiently for the parcels to pass so we could proceed. To pass the time I went on to the tender to throw some coal forward, as a help for later on.

Wearde is a idyllic scene in fine weather. There always seemed to be boats of every description moving, and looking back it was possible to see the Plymouth Shore across the River Tamar and the Naval Ordnance jetty at Bull Point.

As it turned out we were to be lucky, for after the parcels passed we were signalled away to continue our run to Truro where we were to be relieved. We were able to follow the parcels without mishap until approaching Liskeard, where it had stopped for 6 or 7 minutes for station duties, and we had almost caught up. Although the distant signal at Cartuther was at caution for Liskeard, as we came around the corner the 'bobby' (signalman) had all signals pulled off and we had a clear road again. Claude checked his large timetable on the pull up to Doublebois and informed me that the parcels was not due to stop again until Par, so it should not affect us again. Down the bank at Largin we dropped, the vacuum fitted vans proving a godsend. Through Bodmin Road and on down towards Lostwithiel, the Hall now had a full head of steam and the boiler was fairly full with water. I was reluctant to place any more in for after Lostwithiel Claude would be opening the regulator on what we called the second port for the steep climb up to Treverrin Tunnel, and if too full the engine would start to 'prime' as water entered the cylinders – this could cause untold damage. No worry however, for as we neared Lostwithiel the distants were again off and Claude eased the regulator open, gradually picking up speed over the level crossing and the curving line through Lostwithiel before opening wide; dropping the reversing lever down a couple of notches we went full out for Treverrin.

Claude had checked his watch at Lostwithiel and it was just after 1.00pm. Another look at the timetable and he confirmed that, all being well, the parcels would have completed his station work at Par, and we should now have a clear run to Truro. This suited me for our engine was steaming her heart out, and it was a pleasure to work on her. The prediction was right for as we ran down to Par from the tunnel the bell on the Automatic Train Control (ATC) rang away merrily in the cab to inform us that we were now clear, at least to St Austell. This was the news we were looking for and with the regulator opened up towards the second port, and the lever dropped down to perhaps 35% we sailed up the climb to St Austell and Burngullow. Nothing to hurt now between there and Truro, and my thoughts started to turn to being relieved, but not before I got some coal forward for the Penzance fireman, as well as leaving things a little 'ship-shape' for him. I went into the tender

between the two tunnels east of Truro, Polperro and Buckshead to do this and then swept and tidied up the footplate and damped it all down. By now we were approaching Truro. We ran into the goods side of the station at somewhere around 2.30pm and, handing over a locomotive in good condition, we got off well satisfied with our efforts. It had been a 'good' trip.

We were booked to work back the 1.55pm Penzance-Newton Abbot 'stopper', due to leave Truro at 3.10pm, so as there was no need to visit Truro shed we walked on to the platform and sat down quietly to eat our 'dinner'. A quick visit to the station buffet produced hot water for our can of tea. Conversation was a little limited as we ate, but Claude reminded me (as if I could forget) that our train back stopped everywhere, even at Probus & Ladock Platform and Grampound Road station as the first two stops before St Austell, and later on at Menheniot and at St Germans between Liskeard and Saltash. Our train ran in and on the front was 6813 EASTBURY GRANGE, a Newton Abbot locomotive working her way back home. It looked a bit long to me for a stopping train, and the Truro driver confirmed that as he gave Claude the loadings. His mate had given me no cause for concern with a simple 'she's steaming well mate', and so it was.

A 'good' Grange would make light work of the Cornish road. Their slightly smaller driving wheel diameter was an advantage on the climbs, and we were

not short of those in Cornwall. They usually steamed freely, too, even when the fire was getting a bit 'dirty', as this one would be after working from Newton Abbot to Penzance and back. We were right away to time again and with a characteristic 'shuffle' as the driving wheels gripped the rails we were on the move. I got a fire iron out of the rack and levelled the fire over the box. It gave me a chance to see what sort of a fire the Truro man had bequeathed me. Not bad, I thought; there was a good body of fire and I could certainly do something with that. I noticed Claude smile as he saw my satisfied grin, and with a knowing nod to each other we settled down to 'go home'. A fireman had to 'play the boiler' with a stopping train in order that the thing was not blowing her head off every time we stopped. I was aware that this was one of Claude's pet hates, so I tried to keep the water level to about three-quarters of the gauge glass.

The journey back was so good that there was little out of the ordinary to make a story. Our hardest work was from the dead stop at Probus & Ladock Platform to Grampound and Burngullow, and later from Par to Lostwithiel and up to Doublebois but this was almost effortless for me as EASTBURY GRANGE responded to our every need. She was an engine and a half! The only thing that could go wrong was to miss the staff at Saltash for the run across the Royal Albert Bridge, but I was determined not to spoil the day with a

Old Plymouth No.8. Plymouth Hoe in 1922, showing Smeaton's Tower and the Bandstand. Smeaton's Tower was originally built as a lighthouse on Eddystone Rock; completed in 1759, it took three years to build. It was removed in 1882 piece by piece and presented to the City of Plymouth to be erected as a memorial to John Smeaton. It was erected on its present site on Plymouth Hoe in 1884.

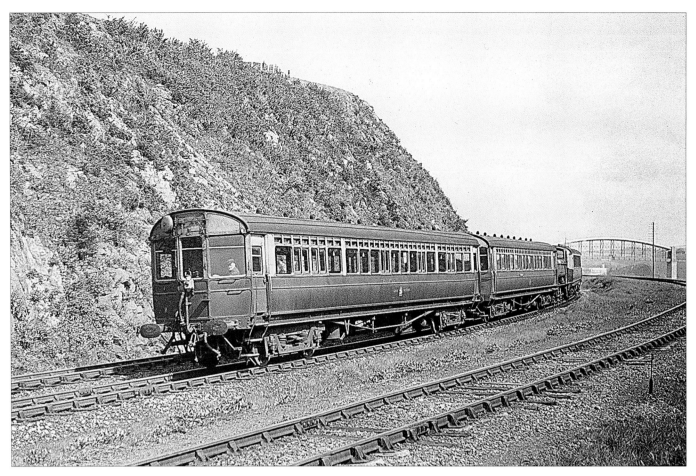

Four car auto train west of Saltash, probably on a service extended to Liskeard, in April 1949. Note the Coombe Viaduct to Wearde loop line, to the right. The acute change of direction of the line after leaving Saltash is indicated by the position of the Royal Albert Bridge in the background, more or less at a right angle. *R.E. Vincent/Transport Treasury*.

silly mistake like that. The operation was generally done with a careless familiarity, but on this occasion I concentrated and plucked the tablet and carrier from the signalman's hand as clean as a whistle. Of course, all that bravado was not necessary for we were stopping there anyway, and if I had missed it the bobby would have brought it up the platform to me anyway! It was pride though, stopper or not, to do it in the best of Western tradition. Which I did. Plymouth North Road was reached to time at 5.10pm and we were relieved by a Newton Abbot Crew. We caught a bus to Laira and booked off duty. A first class days work.

Before I leave this chapter I have two further recollections from the footplate while I was with Claude. The first confirms the nature of the man, and bears out my earlier description of him. The second concerns my early nature, which at times could be rightly described as impetuous. I recall that on a cold wintry day in late November, 1958 or 1959, we worked the 2.00pm afternoon passenger from North Road to Tavistock. Taking on water on arrival, and before crossing over to the up platform for the return journey which did not depart until 4.40pm, another hour or so, I noticed a passenger standing on that platform presumably waiting to catch our train to Plymouth. He was of African descent, or similar and back then, this made him something out of the ordinary. We were aware that at times when prisoners were released from Dartmoor prison they were taken by road

to Tavistock to catch the train and, discussing this with Claude, we felt that this was the possibly what had happened. In the event we placed the coaches in the up platform and 'ran around' the train with the engine, coupled up, and then I went to the signal box to make the inevitable can of tea. On my return the chap was still on the platform and in the meantime the guard had told Claude that he was 'popping' down to the town for some reason, and had locked the coaches up for safety. Sitting on the engine Claude was quite concerned as the man on the platform must have been shivering with the cold. He told me to invite him on to the footplate where he could have a warm up from the fire and, if he wished, a cup of tea from the can. This I did and the offer was readily accepted. I confess to looking a little askance at him, for he certainly was a 'big' chap! On the footplate he thanked us profusely, and sipped his tea. Claude made some conversation with him, but suddenly with no prompting from us he mentioned that he had indeed just been released from Dartmoor. He said that if that worried us he would get off the footplate again. Claude told him that he was still welcome to stay up with us whereupon he recounted his story. It seemed that he had just finished three years in the prison for 'GBH'. He came from the Birmingham area and had been out of work for some time and ran out of money, borrowed from the moneylenders and was unable to repay. In desperation he turned to robbery and house-breaking. The last occasion was a shop, and the

shop-keeper resisted and he had hit him over the head and fled. Eventually caught, he was brought before the courts and sentenced.

Claude asked if this had now taught him a lesson and that he would go back to lead a normal life. To which came the reply that he doubted it; with a reputation for violence and a prison term, he would find work difficult to come by, and might well do the same again. He said that it was not his wish to re-offend, but circumstances might mean that he would have to. I asked him that if he was caught would mean returning to Dartmoor, and he agreed that it would more than likely be the result. 'But', he said, 'at least I'll be warm, fed well and have a bed!' Prisoners no longer feared the punishment of prisons, he opined, even the most hardened. We were open mouthed – you don't (or didn't) meet giants freshly released from Dartmoor (then Britain's best known and possibly most notorious prison) all that often after all. It was a bit like the beginning of *Great Expectations*. According to his account the Government had ended the use of the 'Cat of Nine Tails' while he was in Dartmoor and he said the cheer that echoed through the place could probably have been heard in Plymouth! With that the guard arrived back from his shopping and unlocked the coaches, and our 'guest' left after expressing his gratitude. He came up to the engine again at Plymouth North Road to say thank you once more, and to receive from us our best wishes and hopes that things might turn out better for him in the future. He did say that he had decided not to return to Birmingham but to try a fresh start elsewhere. He's hardly likely to read this book, but I do still wonder what happened to him.

The second recollection concerns the annual Country Fair held at Tavistock, a grand occasion known as the 'Goosey Fair'. In the 1950s it seemed that everyone and anyone came to Tavistock for Goosey Fair, and in those days plenty of geese were to be seen. The town would be packed with people, many arriving by train which was pleasing even though it made more work for the fireman. Stalls selling all sorts of anything flourished, and none more so that the 'cheapjacks' selling 'high class' dinner sets and so on at knockdown prices. At the Launceston end of Tavistock station was a small overbridge, and from that vantage point it was possible to look over the east end of the town and see all that was happening. On the day of my story we were again working the 2.0pm from Plymouth so with plenty of time to spare I informed Claude that I was going up to the bridge to have a look round.

As I looked out from the bridge I could see beneath me one of these crockery stalls, with the 'gentleman' in control doing his utmost to sell his crockery. I have always admired their juggling-style tricks and the patter: *how much am I askin'? Not – Not even – Give me just –!* And so to a knockdown price that no one could resist. A fraction of the original! Very well done I thought and watched the people buying set after set, and the spiel still went on. And I realised why! - to keep

their attention from what his assistant was doing. From where I was watching I could see all that was happening on that stall and behind it. The trick was that the offered articles were not those that were sold. *A switch was made behind and beneath the stall.* Although the pattern and chinaware to all intents and purposes, looked the same, it was not. And I could see that and the persons buying could not. I felt that it was my moral duty to bring the matter to their attention, and unwisely perhaps, started to call out and jeer. Well, I thought, I was safe, on private railway property and up and away from the stallholder. How wrong could I be; I was permitted to continue for a short while, and with him shouting back very uncomplimentary remarks, particularly with regard to my parentage, I could see the people below in the road really quite enjoying the exchange.

Suddenly I was aware that his assistant was missing from the stall, and to my horror noticed that he was walking up the approach road to the goods yard and station. My moral outrage cooling somewhat, it was time to move, I thought, and I sprinted back to the engine as fast as my legs would carry me. Noticing that I was out of breath, Claude asked as to what I had been up to, and I quickly gave him the gist of the proceedings. He saw the funny side and had a laugh, but I was watching out for my approaching nemesis. Sure enough he eventually arrived at the engine and had the temerity to accuse me of insulting them and ruining their sale. Upon my denial and declaration (who me?) that I had no

idea of what he was talking about, he announced that it had to be me, because it was someone in dirty railway overalls and shiny cap! With that Claude came to the rescue, and informed him that he had not seen me leave the footplate; furthermore a train had just left the down side for Launceston. Perhaps it was the fireman on that train he was talking about. It worked, and leaving behind some undisguised threats, he eventually went away, much to my relief. My putative career in trading standards enforcement over, I expressed my thanks to Claude for saving my skin, and he replied that I did not really deserve it, but made the point that he had not told any lies. He indeed did not actually *see* me leave the engine, and that a train *had* left Tavistock for Launceston sometime earlier that day! As I said at the beginning of the chapter, he was a gentleman, as well as a good mate. I courted and married my wife, Joyce, while I fired to him, and he and his wife, Kathleen, gave us a wonderful wedding present. He later gained promotion to a more senior link, and I missed him.

Loading broccoli at Angarrack, 9 April 1960. Cattle empties were pressed in to service for this extensive and lucrative trade. In the height of the season almost every spare opportunity in the timetable would be used for broccoli and, later, Cornish potato specials. *R.C. Riley/ Transport Treasury.*

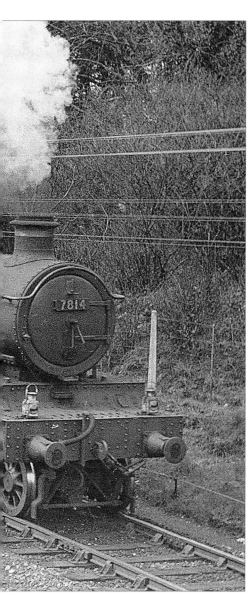

Left. Laira's 7814 FRINGFORD MANOR assists 6019 KING HENRY V of Old Oak Common, on Hemerdon, 8 April 1953. With eleven carriages on, the Manor will work through to Newton Abbot and then perform the same task for a down train. The King appears to have a packing gland leaking on an inside cylinder and the Cockney fireman might regret that loss of hard-earned steam before he gets home. *R.E. Vincent/Transport Treasury.*

Bottom left. Truro's 6855 SAIGHTON GRANGE and 6981 MARBURY HALL of Penzance at the head of the first part of the down Cornish Riviera Express, at Stoneycombe, on 19 July 1958. This was a summer Saturday working whereby the train destined for either Newquay or Falmouth took over the working of the train from Newton Abbot. The King which had brought it from London detached at Newton Abbot and coupled up to the following train to assist over the banks. *R.C. Riley/Transport Treasury.*

Below. Truro engine shed, from the east, on 8 April 1960. Only these three roads and the workshop next door formed the engine accommodation; the remainder of the building belonged to the Carriage & Wagon Dept. Coal stage and turntable to the left. The building occupied an area cut into the high ground to the west, by the mouth of Highertown Tunnel. *R.C. Riley/Transport Treasury.*

6004 KING GEORGE III, of Laira shed, near Westbury on 22 July 1956, with the down 11am Paddington-Plymouth. This was the first King that I had fired, on the 'midnight' from Plymouth to Exeter and had (appropriately?) a nightmare of a trip! *R.C. Riley/ Transport Treasury.*

Small prairie 4410 entering Princetown station, 5 July 1955. The working regulations stated that the train had to stop at the home signal (seen by the rear of the train) which would be at 'danger', blow the whistle and proceed into the station when the signal had been pulled to the 'off' position. The train is a 'mixed' one and was required to include a brake van at the rear. This picture certainly reminds us of the bleakness of the Moor. *R.C. Riley/Transport Treasury.*

CHAPTER 8
Spare Turns Roster

Although the rosters for the No.2 Goods Link were for work only between Newton Abbot and Truro and up the branch to Tavistock, a fireman would occasionally be paired with a driver from a more senior link on a 'spare turn' duty. In this manner we'd find ourselves on jobs to Penzance, Exeter, Taunton and Launceston. It was never quite the same firing to a strange driver though in most cases, of course, their expertise was unquestionable, and their comradeship and understanding could not be faulted. Finding myself 'spare' one warm sunny summer afternoon, I had just booked on and was instructed to report to the shift foreman. All my past sins swam before me as I knocked on his door, but all was well, He informed me that the fireman for the 5.20pm stopping train to Truro had called in sick, and I was to replace him. The return working was the up 'Kensington Milk', a *Top Link* turn and a very superior duty for me. I was told to get to North Road station turntable as quick as I could and to team up with Driver Fred ..., whose surname I will omit in deference to a first class engineman.

You were on your own when it came to getting to the turntable and its stabling roads, tucked away in a triangle, on raised ground west of the station. A 'light' engine going off shed was always a good

bet or, in this case, up to Old Road, Laira, catch a bus to Mutley Plain and, literally, run the rest of the way. I confess to being excited, and hoped that a more senior fireman did not book on in time, so that I lost the turn. I arrived at the turntable, very short of breath, and started to climb up on to the footplate. Fred looked up, and enquired as to 'who I thought I was, and what was I doing on his footplate'. I tried to explain the situation to him but he cut me short; so far as he was concerned I fired to Claude Bolt, and he was not having such a novice fireman for *this* turn. To make matters worse for me, he added: *If you were your brother it would be alright.* I tried again, telling him of the foreman's instructions; adding, for good measure, that in any case I was the only spare turn man available. Not quite true, but I wanted this turn! This he reluctantly accepted, and then laid down the law, by stating that he would be recording his protest on the 'train sheet' and, ominously, that *any loss of time-keeping due to a shortage of steam would be recorded against me!* Not the best way to instil confidence, by any means.

With that, the ground signal came off and we were directed back the short distance east to the station and on to the coaches standing in Platform 2, as I recall. I coupled up, made a can of tea,

hoping that would put him in a better frame of mind, and then started making preparations for the trip, as I had been taught by Claude, but aware of his baleful gaze all the time. He did condescend to enquire my name, and to how I liked to be called. A start at least I thought. The ice melted a little more when he remarked that if Claude had trained me, then we might just get there. Well I had no doubts as to my ability; given half a chance, I could cope.

From the 'right away' I was aware of Fred's scrutiny in all that I did. Trying to do everything by the book, I allowed the water level in the boiler to drop a little on the climb to Devonport in order that when the regulator was shut for stopping at stations I could put the injector on to get water into the boiler and stop the safety valves blowing off excessive steam. We stopped at Devonport and Keyham, and all seemed to be going well. At Royal Albert Bridge box I was full of nerves as I caught the staff for the single line, and gave a silent prayer of gratitude that I had not missed it. After the station stop at Saltash I tried to settle down, only too aware of Fred watching my every move. It was not a good feeling and it had the effect of forcing silly mistakes which I would not otherwise have made. Fred kept informing me as to when he would

4410 approaching Ingra Tor Halt with a Yelverton to Princetown 'mixed train' including a 'perishable' van in July 1955. The halt was six miles from Yelverton, approximately half way along the branch. It was known for an official GWR notice, warning that: IN THE INTERESTS OF GAME PRESERVATION AND FOR THEIR PROTECTION AGAINST SNAKES ETC., DOGS SHOULD BE KEPT ON A LEAD. *R.C. Riley/Transport Treasury*.

4410 shunting at Princetown, June 1955. Note the brake van, the luxurious overnight accommodation used by the author on the occasion when he worked as a relief fireman on the branch. *R.C. Riley/Transport Treasury.*

be working the engine 'hard or light', which helped, but I was also conscious that too much smoke or excess steam blowing off could invite criticism.

On into Cornwall we travelled and I gave of my best, with no word of reproach from the driver's side but, come to that, no praise either. We were relieved at Truro, and it was with a sigh of relief that I was able to hand over a locomotive in 'good nick'; reasonable fire in the firebox, a full head of steam and a boiler full with water. After the tunnels at Buckshead and Polperro I had been able to get a good amount of coal brought forward in the tender to give a start for my relief. Good show, I thought, and the Truro Fireman seemed happy. As I stepped down to the platform I heard Fred say to the Truro Driver that he hoped that everything was alright, but that he *had only had a novice for a fireman.*

The return working was the evening train of milk tanks for the depot at Kensington in West London; a revenue earning train and timekeeping was all. When she ran in I saw that we had a Newton Abbot Castle on the front and I thought, *here we go, I'll show you who's who.* I did, and we had a cracking journey. She responded to my every action and, unbelievably, I might even have caught Fred nodding in appreciation at times. At Saltash I again collected the staff without mishap, and hung it up again at Royal Albert Bridge box without any trouble. Tidy up now, for Fred had reminded me that a Newton Abbot crew would relieve us at North Road station. I

proudly handed over a locomotive in good order, but yet again heard Fred inform the Newton Abbot driver that *he only had a novice for a fireman* and added: *but he wasn't that bad!* Praise indeed.

I suppose no recollection of Laira would be complete without some talk of the Princetown branch. Fearsome in its remoteness, it was endlessly fascinating to all who experienced the Line. Although the distance from the junction at Yelverton to the terminus, as the crow flies, was just six miles, the entire length of the track as it wound its way upwards and skirted the Tors was almost *seventeen* miles. It was notorious for its ferocious winters and as I mentioned in Chapter 5, Laira held on to one or two of the older pannier tanks, fitted with snow plough, ready in steam in the Round Shed at periods of expected snow on the moor. As an 'outstation' of Laira, the little single road engine shed at Princetown had two sets of men permanently based there, and Laira men only became involved as holiday relief or as cover for sickness; even then normally only the fireman was involved. Ron Hext, the senior fireman at Princetown was a 'passed' driver and he it was who would usually take over the driving duties. I was booked 'Princetown holiday relief', and on the following Monday was to travel passenger to Yelverton on the 12.10pm train, to catch the 1.20pm to Princetown and work with Ron on the afternoon shift, servicing the engine afterwards to get it ready for the next morning. I had to lodge overnight at Princetown, travel back to

Laira on the first passenger the following day (Tuesday) and then work the branch again on Wednesday and Friday. Ron would be responsible for my supper and breakfast.

Monday morning duly came and I took the train from Plymouth, eventually meeting up with Ron Hext at Princetown. We had three trips to do, starting with the 2.12pm to Yelverton and finishing with the 7pm from Yelverton, arriving back at Princetown at 7.40 in the evening. Then we had to stable the locomotive, one of the elegant 44XX prairie tanks; clean the fire, replenish the bunker with coal and fill the tanks with water. I could then have a wash and clean up, and go home with Ron for supper. My grand 'lodge' was the branch brake van and on Ron's advice I saved a few hot coals on a shovel to light the stove in the van! A little luxury never went amiss.

On the first trip from Princetown, I started to fire as though I was on the main line but this was a different world altogether. Ron told me to sit down and 'admire the scenery'. This I did, and was impressed; it was magnificent. At Yelverton we had a novel way of running around the two carriages so as to be engine leading on the way back. We pushed the carriages up the gradient leading towards Dousland (the first station on the branch) and then dropped into a siding. The carriages then ran back past us into Yelverton by gravity, the guard bringing them to a halt using the handbrake. We then came out of the siding, dropped back on to the carriages, and coupled up for the next trip. Days on the Princetown branch were happy-go-lucky, or so it seemed, running in such a leisurely manner. The same strict railway rules and regulations applied of course as on the main line but it just did not feel like it. On the second run back from Yelverton, the 2.50pm, we got to Burrator Halt and the guard came up to Ron, to announce 'She isn't here'. So we waited. A local lady always caught this train on a Monday after visiting a neighbour, so we waited and sure enough after a few moments she arrived, got into the carriage, and on we went as though nothing untoward had occurred!

After the last trip of the day, with the engine looked after and the fire lit in my 'lodgings', I'd go home with Ron for an enormous pasty. Then I'd go 'home' and Ron would turn up in the morning with my breakfast, a flask of tea and bacon sandwiches with plenty of time left to wash up in hot water from the engine and work the first train to Yelverton. Well that old van was at least warm; I am not too sure about comfortable but no one ever thought to complain. I suppose it was not too bad under the circumstances, but I barely slept a wink through the incessant bleating of the local sheep. Upon hearing of my difficulty, Ron declared that perhaps we could do something about that on Wednesday! This he most certainly did. On Wednesday, after completing labours and supper, he took me across to the local pub, The Plume of Feathers and there introduced me to the locals as a Top Link fireman from Laira. Double home man, Cornish Riviera to London, non-stop, no less. The locals were most impressed, for they were not to know the truth! For the rest of the evening they

were kind enough to keep my glass filled, as Ron told them story after story, and I pitched in with a feeble 'yes' now and then. Nothing kept me awake that night, but my head told a tale the next morning.

The problem I found with spare turns was the fact that you were paired with a driver whose habits you were not attuned to. I confess to often feeling a little apprehensive. I knew that I could do my job with the best of them, given half a chance but I seldom felt comfortable even though, in the end, it usually turned out alright. Fear and trepidation for nothing. In the early summer of 1953 I was booked with Driver Frank Bunce on the 'up midnight' from Plymouth to Exeter. I knew of Frank inasmuch as any young fireman in the No.2 Goods Link would be aware of a No.2 Passenger Link driver, and he always seemed approachable. The trouble was that the train engine was always a King, and I had never fired one at that time. I spoke with Claude before booking off the previous day, and he gave me a few words of advice, but mainly urged, *do what you have learnt to do*. Booking on deliberately early, I found that we had 6004 KING GEORGE III. I settled down to carry out all the preliminaries; sand boxes, tools, lamps, smokebox and so on and even got Frank's oil cans and 'feeders' ready for him. I suppose nowadays an action such as that would be classed as 'creeping' but for me it was trying to give *a good impression*. Starting now on the fire, I levelled it over the grate adding a few suitable lumps from the tender as I started to build it up making sure, of course, that each layer burned through before adding more. Shades of the Tavistock goods! Frank arrived and we exchanged pleasantries. I informed

him of my trepidation at the prospect of firing a King but he gave me every re-assurance, and said that with the training which Claude had no doubt given me, he was sure I would cope. Well, I have to say that all seemed perfect by the time we left the shed and I even made a can of tea. Going tender first to North Road station, I recall feeling just a little bit important.

At North Road we coupled on to the additional sleepers standing at Platform 8; these would be attached to the front of the main train arriving from Cornwall. I connected the steam heating to keep the sleeping beauties comfortable and snug on their journey. The assisting pilot to help to Newton Abbot coupled on to our front, and the usual banter ensued concerning who was going to do the major work on the banks. Everything looked good; full head of steam, full boiler of water, fire looking perfect, and then the 'right away'. As the regulator opened my steam gauge gave a flip backward. Not to worry, that was normal. Out with the fire iron and give the fire a stir up going towards Mutley tunnel. Down through Laira and along the banks of the Plym, steam now blowing off as we ran towards Hemerdon bank. Frank gradually starts to ease the regulator open fraction by fraction and at the same time dropping the lever a snick at a time lengthening the cut-off through Plympton. We're now flat out, regulator wide across on second port, cut off 30%, and then my steam gauge goes backwards. *Trouble.*

Fire iron out, rake the fire, look for holes, all that I had been taught. I work, I sweat; I swear, royalty or not! But no good, it was useless, or I was. Frank came over and had a look, gave a bit of advice but I

Old Plymouth 9. The magnificent Plymouth Pier from the Hoe, July 1922. A paddle steamer is moored to the end of the Pier, possibly chartered on pleasure trips along the coast to either Looe, Fowey, Dartmouth, or maybe for an 'all aboard the Skylark' trip along the Tamar.

struggled, and to tell the truth I did all the way. Thank the Lord for the assisting engine, and for the reverse slopes which gave me a chance to get a little bit of recovery. My concern was that after Newton Abbot, we would be on our own; no second engine to Exeter, and there I would be handing over to a Taunton or Bristol fireman. At Newton I got down from the footplate and went to the front end where the other fireman was uncoupling. I placed my headlamps on their brackets and had a chat. He of course, had realised that I was in trouble and made sympathetic noises. I tried the smokebox door to check it was tight, for it could allow air into the partial vacuum that drew the hot gases through the tubes to heat the water in the boiler, and that would not do. But no; everything was fine. Thought was given to the possible culprits; the baffle plate and the jumper ring in the smokebox could cause bad steaming if not secure and working properly, but I knew I had checked them at Laira.

Frank had looked at the fire for me while I was away, and he could see nothing wrong there, which was some small comfort. But we had to go on, and now on our own for some 20 miles to Exeter. I have never put so much effort in as I did over that stretch. The sea wall meant nothing. I saw none of that beautiful Devon scenery. All I saw was a red hot fire, a dropping boiler level, and a steam gauge that struggled to keep somewhere near the mark. Thankfully, Frank was an engineman and a half, nursing her and me all the way. I picked up water at the troughs at Exminster and made some

attempt to get things right for my relief fireman, poor chap. What was I going to say to him? We ran into Exeter and I was loth to hand her over in this condition. I heard Frank, bless him, explain to his relief driver that I was only from a junior link, and hadn't experienced a King before. I confessed to some relief at handing over 6004, and he gave me a pat on the back and told me to go and have a cup of tea. We went to shed to await our return working and all of the time I was expecting to hear of an SOS for a train stuck at Burlescombe or somewhere on the way to Whiteball. But no such call came, so I must assume that he'd coped better than me. The train must have eventually reached Paddington safe and sound and the King would have got to Old Oak Common shed without 'failing'; if it had there would have been an inquest, and for a certainty my original preparation of the engine would have come under scrutiny. Questions would need answers!

I was subdued while we waited for the return journey, relieving our train on the down platform. On the way across the tracks, Frank quietly made encouraging noises. The up train had gone, he explained. That journey was over. Yes, I had had it rough, but had done my best. Forget it. Think only now of working back to Plymouth. 'One bad trip' he said, 'did not make you a bad fireman'. It helped. I climbed aboard the next locomotive, a Plymouth Castle, 5058 EARL OF CLANCARTY, and I was relieved to hear 'she's great mate!'. And so she was, and she steamed. Along the sea wall I could look and see the lights twinkling on the

water as daybreak was coming in. At Newton Abbot, we collected a pilot on the front. I spent time in the tender getting coal; forward, and remember thinking that *this was firing*. We climbed up the bank from Aller Junction where the Torquay line left the main, through the curving line at Stoneycombe and, though the fire by this time was getting a little dull – signifying clinker on the firebars – 5058 gave little trouble. Down the other side to Totnes, through the middle road, and both locomotives opened up full power to haul our train up to Rattery, Marley tunnel, Wrangaton and all the way home to Plymouth. I did myself proud, and our Castle did us all proud. A good engine crew needs a good locomotive. We were a team. Eventually we arrived at Laira shed to book off and Frank's last words to me were *Well done youngster!* Praise indeed. But I have always thought of that fireman relieving me on 6004. I fired a King on many occasions afterwards, and never experienced any difficulties. The thought remains – what did I miss during the preparation?

Old Plymouth 10. The Hoe, Tinside and foreshore, from the Citadel, July 1922. To the east the first headland past the Pier was Eastern Kings, marking the entrance to Millbay Docks. Beyond that was Western Kings where the mouth of the Hamoaze and the River Tamar can just made out. On the land beyond, on the Cornish side, are Mount Edgecumbe and Cremyll.

6801 AYLBURTON GRANGE, a Penzance engine, heads the up 'Kensington Milk' through Menheniot on 16 July 1956. Two milk trains were scheduled, this one in the afternoon and a second in the early evening. The tankers would have been picked up at St Erth and Lostwithiel. *R.C. Riley/Transport Treasury*.

The fireman of 6911 HOLKER HALL, on the down Cornishman, hands the staff to the Saltash signalman on 25 June 1955. Although it was not particularly encouraged, this method permitted the signalman to have the token a few moments earlier than he would otherwise have hold of it; he was then able to exchange it for an up movement almost before the down train had cleared the platform. This was especially helpful on a summer Saturday. *R.E. Vincent/Transport Treasury*.

The great bridge, looking towards Cornwall in April 1949. The lower part of Saltash, to the left of the bridge, was cleared of houses and redeveloped as part of a regeneration scheme in the late 1960s. Of note is the tower of SS.Nicholas & Faith Parish Church. As a bell ringer I have been able to visit the top of the tower and from there it is possible to look directly through the centre spans of the bridge. As this was the only high structure present when the bridge was built it is suggested that Brunel used the tower as a 'sighting mark'! *R.E. Vincent/Transport Treasury.*

CHAPTER 9
The Cornish Road

Workings at Laira shed were varied and extensive, ranging from the 'double home' passenger jobs (London and return next day) at the top, to shunting in the marshalling yards and everything in between. Regrettably I never experienced the former, but I had a great admiration for and looked up to those who had; there was an elite air to such men. However, I always felt that no part of the system made more demands on engines and their crews than the Cornish road. Picturesque in its varying scenery, severe in the geographical setting, to observe the gradient profile was to remind yourself of nothing so much as the very misused blade of a saw.

Locomotive power varied according to the range of duties covered, though many classes were 'mixed' and able to cover all demands. The Castles all but lorded it over the prestige passenger and perishable trains, although many would say a good Grange with its smaller wheels would serve just as well. The Halls were maids of all work and the Counties, once the draughting had been improved, gave sterling results on the gradients. Add the 2-6-0s used on both passenger and goods traffic and it can be seen we had a class for every occasion and let us not, of course, forget the branch lines with their 0-4-2Ts, 0-6-0PTs and 2-6-2Ts for any eventuality, including the clay traffic around St Blazey.

Engine preparation needed to be thorough for the line could be unforgiving if things were not going right, but to get it spot on was a pleasure. So join me as we ride on the footplate of a Castle over the rails from Plymouth to Penzance. Leaving Plymouth North Road the falling gradient lasted to Cornwall Junction, affording just enough time to level the fire (if needed) and place a few selected shovels of coal in the firebox before the regulator was opened even wider, and the reversing lever drops a 'click' or two to perhaps 30 or 40% for the pull up to Devonport. Through the station and the speed increases for the run down through Keyham and Western Mill viaduct, with a chance to replenish the boiler before the pull up to the Royal Albert Bridge commenced. I've mentioned it two or three times, so readers might appreciate the haunting fear whenever collecting the single line token staff that permitted the crossing of the Bridge. Don't dare miss it at this busy bottle-neck, for that would mean stopping and walking back to collect it, with passengers and, worse, colleagues in the know, looking out of windows and doors to see why the train had stopped... With all going well though, and the passage of the great bridge safely negotiated, there were wonderful views to be had of the River Tamar and mouth of the Lynher, views that changed with every nuance of the weather and season. The staff hangs secure on the hook at the

end of Saltash platform, and with bells ringing in the cab to show a 'Clear Road Ahead', the regulator is again opened up, and the reversing lever gradually notched back to 20% or so to shorten the length of the piston travel. Speed increases as we run along the banks of the River Lynher and head for St Germans. Tending to the fire now, shovel to tender, left hand grabs the chain to drop the firehole flap, then back to the shovel to place the coal in the firebox. Not just anywhere but a spot carefully calculated to be of the most value. A few up the front, over the mound in front of the firehole door to tend to the middle of the fire, and then fill up the back corners. A glance out of the front window will show a small black colouration in the exhaust from the chimney to confirm that each shovelful has landed in the right place. Then, most importantly, sweep the footplate of any coal which had dropped off the shovel – easy to turn an ankle on an errant lump, given a swaying footplate. Turn on the hose (the 'pep-pipe' as we knew it) and damp down the front of the footplate to lay the dust. Finally, spray the exposed face of the disturbed coal in the tender; such 'house-keeping' was routine and a constant, and I've mentioned it elsewhere. No let up now, through Shillingham tunnel we speed, and now comes the start of a long pull up through St Germans and on towards Menheniot.

The boiler level has dropped with the

6869 RESOLVEN GRANGE on a down passenger train on Trenance viaduct, St Austell, 8 July 1955. With ten coaches on, the fireman still has a bit of work to do with a further couple of miles of 'up' gradient to go before the top at Burngallow. A fair number of crews felt that a 'good 68XX was equal to a Castle on the Cornish Road. The smaller diameter wheel of the Grange probably gave them the 'edge' on the banks. *R.C. Riley/Transport Treasury.*

Very Old Plymouth! This was the extraordinary scene from the Devon shore in 1858. The Cornwall span is raised in position with the end roadway sections still in a temporary alignment to ease movement of the complete truss during the lifting and positioning of the Devon span. This span is in place ready for lifting and the foreshore has all the usual clutter of a construction site. It is likely that the baulk timbers were off-loaded from the two vessels moored alongside the wooden jetty.

On 13 April 1952 a Western National double-decker waits patiently at Saltash passage for her next scheduled run. The eastern end of the Royal Albert Bridge dominates the skyline, and the outskirts of Saltash on the Cornish shore form a backdrop. Ships of the Reserve Fleet show from behind the bridge pillar; the large vessel immediately visible behind the bus is the 'monitor' (a gun platform) RODNEY. Her mast was higher, but she knocked off a portion when negotiating her way upstream under the bridge. *R.E. Vincent/Transport Treasury.*

climb to Trerule Foot, and as the regulator is eased a little the injector can be placed on to refill it. No need to be unduly worried for the first stop at Liskeard is getting near. It will be a chance then to not only keep the safety valves from blowing off excess steam, but to top up the boiler to 'full'. As the bell in the cab rings to signify the Liskeard distant signal is off, I drop the flap from the front of the firehole and take the chance to sit down and admire the scenery. As we cross the Liskeard viaduct I can look down and there, some 150 feet or so below us, the Looe branch passes underneath.

The Liskeard station work completed, whistles blow and the 'right away' comes. The train starts again for the sudden drop down to the Moorswater viaduct. One author once wrote that going on to this structure was like 'launching into space' and it certainly seemed so at times. It was afterwards a matter of climbing from the viaduct up the 1:61 gradient to Doublebois before the eight mile run down to Bodmin Road and Lostwithiel. Aware of the need to contain the steam pressure, I'd allow the water level in the boiler to fall, putting the water injector on at Doublebois as my driver eased the regulator. Most of them kept the regulator open just a fraction on what was known as *drift*, even when coasting, in order to maintain a slight supply of oil to the cylinders. Running down the bank my driver was busy controlling the speed of the train with careful use of the vacuum brakes, while I had a chance to sit down

once again and to enjoy the Glynn Valley, before we came eventually to a stop at Bodmin Road.

Once the junction for the Wadebridge and Padstow branches, the main line station now serves the preserved railway to Bodmin and Boscarne Junction. Station work over, whistles blow and we are given the 'right away' once more. My driver opens the regulator and we set off, still on a falling gradient, for the three miles or so to Lostwithiel. I start to place a few shovels of coal on the back end of the firebox to help repair any damage which the long downhill run might have brought about. You were aware that after Lostwithiel came another long climb with gradients of 1:57 and 1:64 to the tunnel at Treverrin. All was well enough though, running over the level crossing to stop in Lostwithiel station. Noticeable on my side of the footplate would be the coal wagons destined for Carne Point on the Fowey branch, which ran alongside the main line for a short distance. There the clay would be loaded into coastal vessels for distribution to far and wide.

Although the train would be lightened a fraction by the passengers getting off at Par, it probably would have little effect upon our next section, 7½ miles of pulling ground to Burngullow with ruling gradients of 1:60 and 1:64, with a short respite for the stop at St Austell. As we left the station we were faced with a short section of 1:43, and my driver left me in no doubt what was to happen. Regulator across on the second port as soon as he had the train moving the reversing lever

only brought back a fraction, our locomotive fairly leapt to the task. It reminded me of my boyhood days on a farm just outside St Austell, and of the two shire horses we had there. Whatever the task, ploughing, harvesting, chained to the 'binder' machine cutting corn or hay or just between the shafts of a cart of wagon; no matter what, on the command to move, they would lean forward into the harness and pull their hearts out. While I hesitate to compare a GW 4-6-0 to a farm horse in any way our Castle did seem to emulate that sheer power and determination moving out of Par Station. My fire needed a great deal of attention after all the down gradient since Doublebois but I risked a glance over the cab on the drivers side to see St Blazey yard and engine shed in the near distance. Back to the job in hand, and out with the long 'pricker' (fire iron) from the rack to give the fire a good stir up, levelling it over the whole of the firebox and grate. Shut the doors for a second to give it a chance to brighten up, and then down to some serious firing. *Shovel to tender, fill with coal, left hand to the chain of the firehole flap, a sharp tug to make it fall open, left hand to shovel, shovel to firebox, coal placed in position required.* This was *not* a random matter or guesswork; each shovel of coal was placed precisely where it was needed, and this was repeated over and over again as up towards St Austell we went. And she responded; the steam pressure gauge came around the 'the mark', indicating a full head of steam, and the injector was placed on to replenish the boiler. All was well with the world.

At the station I liked to have a look at the people either on the platform or getting off the train. It was my birthplace and as a former St Austell lad, I always hoped to see someone from schooldays – but never did. 'Right away' meant no more time for reminiscing, it was back to work for the last climb to Burngullow. With the next stop at Truro some fifteen miles or so ahead, we had rising and falling gradients to cope with but none as severe as we had already tackled. Past the clay complex at Burngullow – still a Platform there for stopping trains for a couple more years before closure – and the mineral branch runs away on the up side to serve the clay mining areas of Foxhole, Nanpean and St Dennis. It was a falling gradient for three miles now before a short climb up to Grampound Road station, a run down to Probus & Ladock Platform (to survive for a couple more years yet) and the final approaches for the run in to Truro. I take the opportunity to go into the tender to get forward some fresh coal for the final stage from Truro to Penzance, coming back on to the footplate after a warning from my driver of the two tunnels approaching, Polperro and Buckshead. Top up the boiler and I am ready for Truro. We glance at the water gauge on the tender and decide to have a 'top up' from the column on the platform when we stop.

We run into Truro something like one and a half hours after leaving Plymouth and *dead on time*. I climb over the coal to the back of the tender to place the water bag in the filling hole, and my driver turns

the water on. While we're filling up he has a quick look around to check all is well. This done, the tender replenished and we await the 'right away' once again, to restart the train for the final stage to Penzance. A steep pull up to Penwithers Junction, and as we approach Highertown Tunnel we see Truro engine shed nestled comfortably against the high cliffs which heralded the start of the tunnel. Leaving the tunnel the main line takes a sharp deviation to the right, at the point where the Falmouth branch line leaves the main. From here a further climb of five miles or so at 1:62/65 faces us to Chacewater before levelling out to Scorrier and Redruth. Again I undertake some serious work on the fire, to keep the boiler level reasonably high as well as a full head of steam. The countryside has started to alter now as our train runs deeper into the mining area of Cornwall. Altered too was the nature of the track. Instead of the sharp climbs followed by a fall on the reverse slope, the line now seemed to be on one never-ending hill. For me, the hard work would be over by Scorrier and excepting a couple of 'hiccups' the gradient would fall for most of the way. No reason for complacency however. We'll have the same locomotive on our return booking back to Plymouth but we won't need too much of a fire for the stop-over at Penzance shed so I start to allow the front end to thin-out a bit, just keeping a full fire at the back of the box, to give me something to build on for the return.

Leaving Redruth we are on the highest section of track, and have just two more intermediate station stops, Camborne

and St Erth. The latter was (is) the junction for the St Ives branch and normally a very busy station in the summer season. I am able to sit down now, and to admire the scenery once more, this time Mounts Bay and St Michaels Mount as we sweep around the coast at Marazion. We pass Penzance engine shed at 'Long Rock' on my driver's side, and right on time and some two and a half hours after leaving Plymouth we run into the terminus at Penzance; the end of the line and some 304 miles from Paddington.

Simmering quietly in the platform, watching our passengers depart, we wait for the signal to push the empty stock back to the coaching sidings at Marazion, there to be released for the shed. There we turn our Castle to face east, oil and water her and get some coal forward to the front of the tender for the journey back to Plymouth. The locomotive taken care of, it is time for us to think of ourselves. A wash off in the bucket and cross to the enginemens cabin to make a can of tea, and partake of whatever has been packed in our dinner boxes.

All too soon our watches tell us it's time to get back to the engine. Full head of steam now, but a little room in the boiler to put some water in to stop her blowing off at the safety valves A final check around to confirm that everything is ready and I go to the internal 'phone to inform the signalman that we are ready to go off shed for Penzance station and our return train – a Paddington express. At the station we couple up and the guard arrives to give my mate the loading. As we have a Paddington train I am aware

Laira's 5090 NEATH ABBEY on 14 April 1952, crossing Coombe by Saltash viaduct with a return passenger working from Penzance. Note the footbridge attached to the side of the viaduct which I used to get to my parents' home at the top of the market garden, immediately to the right of the last carriage. The signalpost at the rear left of the train has a small arm which directs trains into the Wearde loop, which in effect is the line of the former Cornwall Railway. *R.E. Vincent/Transport Treasury.*

4089 DONNINGTON CASTLE, a Laira engine, with the Up Cornish Riviera Express at Royal Albert Bridge signal box, 13 April 1952. The signalman has brought a tank engine and guards van to a stand by the box, ready to accept the staff as soon as the up train has cleared, when a new tablet can be drawn. The pannier tank and brake waiting to cross westward might be going to Saltash to marshal vans for seasonal traffic – flowers, fruit etc., or Menheniot to collect a train of ballast wagons. The possibilities are endless! *R.E. Vincent/Transport Treasury.*

that we shall have a full load (or thereabouts) for a Castle. Time now to pay attention once again to the fire so it's out with the fire iron once more, and level the fire over the whole of the box. Earlier, at Long Rock, when getting some coal forward I'd cunningly selected some fair-sized lumps and put them at the front of the tender. I now place these inside the firehole to build up the back end. No need to panic, we still have some time left for the coal to burn steadily through. A little forced draught on the blower to disperse any black smoke, and time to polish off the contents of the tea can.

During my short career on the footplate I'd noticed that the period spent waiting before a journey was often given over to some contemplation on the part of a crew. All sorts of things seem to make their way into your mind; the family, the weather, the scenery, passengers joining the train and of course the job ahead to get the train safely and on time to wherever we were going. I recall that once at Penzance, for some unknown reason my thoughts came from a book that I had been reading by S.P.B. Mais, *The Cornish Riviera*, now a much sought after work. In the opening paragraph he writes: *Brunel's Royal Albert Bridge is the means, and an almost majestical means, of transporting travellers from a county which, if richer than others, is yet unmistakably an English county, to a Duchy which is in every respect un-English. You shut your eyes going over the Saltash*

Bridge only to open them again on a foreign scene. The Cornish cream is not Devonshire cream and the Cornish people are not English people. They have something to show the visitor that is peculiar to themselves. Penzance struck me as epitomising something of this. The climate matches any. The sun shines but does not burn, the water is warm enough to bathe in winter (well sometimes) and there are palm trees growing on the Prom.

Soon though, whistles start to blow, doors are slammed shut, shouts ring out, signals drop and the reverie comes to an end. It's 'right away' yet again. Flap up over the firehole, and as the regulator opens, our Castle does a little sideways wiggle on the rails, and sure-footedly starts to move the load on her drawbar. The blast from her exhaust starts to brighten the fire up, just what I had hoped for. We have reasonably level going for 2-3 miles before the pull up to St Erth will give me a chance to get the fire 'right'. A look in the firebox using the blade of the shovel to direct the fumes away will soon reveal any problems in the making but the steam pressure gauge has held up reasonably well, and all would appear to be in order. Just a need for normal and steady firing – *little and often*.

Over the top of the 'nip' (local argot for a short but sharp rising gradient) and we fall down into St Erth. As always plenty of paying customers on the platform. They have come from St Ives, on the branch passenger train now standing in

the bay. Right away, and after Hayle and Gwinear Road we climb the 1:61 Angarrack incline to Camborne; the station work there complete, we pull away, skirting Carn Brae. The castle ruins are a landmark visible for many miles around. Stopping at Redruth I get a chance to replenish the boiler. So far all is going well. Our Castle is steaming freely and all bodes well for a good journey. There is no room for complacency but I am well aware that after Redruth the track will be fairly level going until Scorrier, when it will be down grade all the way to Truro. The regulator will still be open making demands upon my side of the footplate, but at the same time I want to let the level of the water in the boiler drop a little. Just after Scorrier my mate closes the regulator and winds the reversing lever to allow the piston stroke to lengthen as we head down hill. A couple of short sections either side of Chacewater see the regulator open again, but only for about half a mile or so. We check our speed for Penwithers Junction, just to the west of Highertown Tunnel. The junction is quite complex with the Falmouth and Newham Wharves lines leaving the main line on the southern side. We coast around the long curve and enter the tunnel and drop down the 1:80 gradient into Truro station. We stop opposite to the water column and top up the water level in the tender. I take the opportunity to get as much coal forward as I can, to save fetching it later on. My driver checks the motion, feeling to see if any bearings feel warm, and topping up a couple of oil wells to make sure. I get a chance to make a can of tea and pour a cup for both of us. Back on the footplate we get a chance to have a talk about things in general while we wait for the 'right-away'.

The section Truro-St Austell is something of a switchback with the highest point at Burngullow. As we pull away and pound over the viaducts the cathedral with its three spires takes centre stage. Back through two tunnels it is a twisting drop down to the valley before Probus & Ladock. No stop for us though – we have express headcodes up. A climb of two and a half miles follows at 1:67 and we reach Grampound Road; through the station and the regulator is eased but not shut, for the slight fall before the final climb of some three miles at 1:70 to Burngullow. I have kept tending the fire to ensure there is a good body of fire in the box before the long run down hill to St Austell and Par. I shall need all of my best efforts from then on. On the climb our Castle is loving it, almost purring. Her exhaust is loud and clear and the four cylinders hammer out a rhythmic melody. No problems with steaming; she responds to every shovelful, and I am now working the boiler level to let it fall; half a boiler would be just right at Burngullow. Over the top and I have a glimpse of the clay drying pens where my brother and I played as boys. Covered in white clay dust and earning a telling-off when we arrived home! A clay train behind a pannier tank is waiting to come off the Drinnick Mill

mineral line, and a touch on the whistle acknowledges the wave from the footplate crew. A quick brush up of the footplate and damp it down and then it's time to sit down again and enjoy the scenery of my boyhood. Over the road bridge at Trewoon, the nearest village to where I lived and with a rush we arrive at St Austell. Again a look round to see a familiar face and again no luck. Perhaps everyone else left that area when we did!

The run down to Par is approximately five miles, and encompasses some of the best in Cornish scenery. On the driver's side the expanse of the coastline and St Austell Bay comes into view, with the golf course separating the railway line from the cliffs. Approaching Par the large china clay dock complex dominates the shoreline and extends almost to the station. At Par, the platform is again crowded, this time with holiday makers off the Newquay branch – returning home. It is a fact that the more passengers board a train, the heavier it will get; the heavier it gets, the harder we have to work the locomotive, the harder the locomotive is worked the harder the demands on steam and water, the harder the demands on steam and water, the harder for …who else but the fireman, yours truly. It is what we do though, what we get paid for. And I have to admit that most times I love it. No respite from Par for now it is a 1: 62 incline for the two miles to Treverrin tunnel before dropping down to Lostwithiel. That means no worries for water, I can recover the boiler on that reverse slope. Through the tunnel and down the gradient we fly. Brush up the footplate, and while the feed is on to the

boiler use the pep pipe to damp down the footplate and coal. No dust on our footplate. Sit down, it's time to enjoy the view once more. A touch on the brakes on the lower bends and we stop at Lostwithiel blocking the level crossing as always. I often wonder if the car drivers really appreciated us. Serious stuff now for, other than stopping at Bodmin Road, we have a pulling gradient all of the way to Doublebois – Largin bank – 1 in 58 at its steepest.

Up and through Brunel's old Brown Queen Tunnel, the exhaust of the Castle echoing down from the roof, and with a roar as we burst out from its confines. Ease the regulator now for the stop at Bodmin Road. A quick visit to the tender and drag a few good lumps of coal from the sides. I will have need of them shortly, for the firebox on a Castle can be hungry when worked hard as she will be over the next stage. Away we go, full regulator, and the reversing lever only back a little. She likes it though; no slip of the wheels, barking her head off out of her chimney. The best part of six miles of 1:65/70 ahead of us, and on and up we go, over those lovely viaducts, and the fir tree-lined slopes of that beautiful valley, not that I had a lot of time to see it. This will be my last big test, for after Liskeard I shall be letting the fire work down to get the engine to shed and the waiting fire-droppers. But no time to worry about them; my driver and my engine need all my attention. The shovelling has become second nature. No time to think about it – just to do it, and to the best of my ability. And – and – she responded. She steamed her heart out, bless her! My

Laira's 5098 CLIFFORD CASTLE approaching Treverrin tunnel on 24 September 1960. She seems in excellent condition and even with all of the exertion of the 1 in 64 climb up from Lostwithiel there is no sign of a gland or cylinder leaking steam. The cleaners have done a first class job; the splashers are spotless, the paintwork and brasswork gleaming. *R.C. Riley/Transport Treasury* .

driver checked his watch at Doublebois and with a nod of his head, acknowledged all our efforts. Plain sailing now with Liskeard the last stop before Plymouth.

Sometimes, as strange as it might seem, when all was going well you could feel reluctant for it to end. A silly thought perhaps but I am sure that certain of my former colleagues will know what I mean. After Liskeard we wound our way through East Cornwall, Menheniot, St Germans and along by the banks of the Lyhner to the Tamar at Saltash. Must catch the staff, can't spoil the trip at this late stage. No problem, took it from the signalman's outstretched hand clean as a whistle. A shout to my driver and over the Royal Albert Bridge we trundle. I level the fire for the last time, hang the staff perfectly on the hook at Royal Albert box and then sit down to enjoy the last of it to Plymouth North Road. Come to rest. Uncouple from the train, and run light engine to our shed at Laira. Book off, tired but happy.

Above. Truro shed, the country end, on 22 July 1960; a view from Station Road, showing the coal stage, turntable and the two vans of the breakdown train. The old stone shed building has been extended at the front by now to house the new DMU sets. Small Prairie 5562 in lower foreground. *R.C. Riley/Transport Treasury*.

Below. Down passenger train on Forder viaduct, west of Saltash, on 18 April 1949. With a full brake/parcels van on the front and a vanfit on the rear this could be the 3.40pm Plymouth-Penzance, due to arrive at 6.55pm. Hauled on this occasion by a County, 1006 COUNTY OF CORNWALL, this train was the 'stopper service' to cover both the down Cornish Riviera and The Cornishman. I sometimes wondered about the contents of the vanfit. It carried fish from Grimsby, which had left much earlier that day. *R.E. Vincent/Transport Treasury*.

Above. Forder Viaduct on Easter Sunday, 13 April 1952 and 6855 SAIGHTON GRANGE with a section of the down 'Limited'. With no destination boards on the stock, and the varied selection, this could possibly be the Saturdays Only Falmouth portion, 10.35am ex-Paddington. *R.E. Vincent/Transport Treasury*.

Below. Forder Viaduct in September 1954, as a 49XX Hall crosses with what might be a summer Saturday passenger train. With '10+ on' and the make up of coaching stock (only two with destination boards) this could be a holiday train for Newquay, Falmouth or Penzance. *R.E. Vincent/Transport Treasury*.

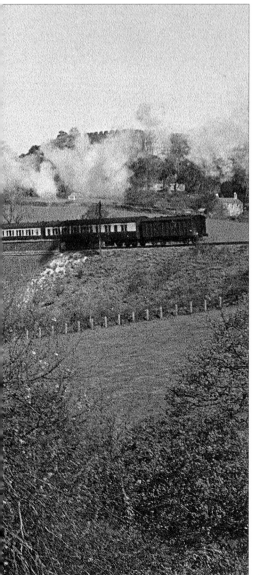

Left. 4946 MOSELEY HALL crossing Liskeard viaduct, 13 April 1950. The engine is working home to Penzance with (probably) the 11.10am Tavistock Junction- Penzance semi-fast freight. This was booked to make only four stops; Truro, Drump Lane, St Erth and Penzance, arriving at 4.35pm. *R.E. Vincent/ Transport Treasury.*

Below. 4970 SKETTY HALL of Taunton shed coming into Liskeard with an up passenger train on 13 April 1950. This was probably the 16.45pm ex-Penzance, a return working of a North of England express. The driver must be having sighting problems with that boiler washout plug blowing directly in front of his cab window. *R.E. Vincent/ Transport Treasury.*

Moorswater viaduct and a down mixed freight, with what looks like a Grange, on 2 October 1954. The view is from the Looe branch, looking north from Coombe Junction. *R.E. Vincent/Transport Treasury*.

A County 4-6-0 on Moorswater viaduct (318 yards long and 147 feet high) with the up Cornish Riviera Express, on 24 June 1955. The structure was rebuilt in 1881 and some of the abandoned stone columns of the old wooden structure remained in place. *R.E. Vincent/Transport Treasury*.

Two Halls double head an up express across Moorswater viaduct, 24 June 1955. This was a Cornish working, as far as Newton Abbot for the crews, who returned with the Falmouth and Newquay portion of the down Cornish Riviera. *R.E. Vincent/Transport Treasury.*

A Grange with an up milk train on Moorswater viaduct, 24 June 1955. The three vehicles behind the van are gas wagons; the gas was used in certain stations, such as Penzance and Plymouth, to replenish the cylinders on the dining cars. That's my old driver Jack Chaston (see Chapter 15) on the path, cycling home after a shift at Moorswater shed. *R.E. Vincent/Transport Treasury.*

A Penzance Hall, 5969 HONINGTON HALL with an up express west of Bodmin Road on 25 June 1955. This was something of a climb for the crews, and it was 'collar work' all the way from Lostwithiel to Doublebois, with a probable stop for station duties at Bodmin Road. The driver appears to be making some sort of gesture to the photographer... *R.E. Vincent/Transport Treasury*.

10XX Class 1023 COUNTY OF OXFORD with the 4.0pm stopper Truro-Penzance, 13 July 1957. The train is climbing up towards Highertown tunnel (below us at right); Truro engine shed can just be seen on the left, before the commencement of the cutting. *R.E. Vincent/Transport Treasury*.

A Hall with the down Cornish Riviera Express on 13 July 1957, about to enter Highertown tunnel. With a stiff climb of 1 in 80 for about three miles, the locomotive seems to be steaming freely. *R.E. Vincent/Transport Treasury.*

Royal Albert Bridge from Saltash Passage on the Plymouth shore, 13 April 1952. It is a view full of interest, with a 2-8-0T working towards Plymouth with empty coaching stock. As the 42XXs were based at St Blazey, this could be spare coaches from a Newquay special being taken back to Plymouth for re-scheduling. The slipway and remains of a pier mark the spot where the American servicemen, based in a camp above the east end of the bridge, embarked for the Normandy landings. The warships are 'reserves' and no longer required, 'mothballed' to protect then from the salt air. As most eventually went to the breakers yard, one wonders if the mothballing was worth it! *R.E. Vincent/Transport Treasury.*

Old Plymouth 11. The eastern end of Plymouth Hoe in July 1922, showing the impressive frontage of the Marine Biological Institute, with the Citadel to the right. Extreme right is the entrance to the waters of the Barbican, Sutton Harbour and Cattedown.

5011 TREGENNA CASTLE of Newton Abbot in the departure platform at Penzance station with the 1.20pm for Paddington, 15 July 1958. The engine has backed on to the train after a sojourn at Long Rock shed, to turn and prepare for the run back home. The fireman has yet to place the second headlamp on the left-hand bracket above the buffer beam. *Alec Swain/Transport Treasury*.

Left. 5078 BEAUFORT of Bristol Bath Road departing from Platform 8 at Plymouth North Road on 15 July, working home with what could be a North of England express. A Hall comes in by the ground signals, known to the crews as 'dummies'; she is destined for Platform 4. *R.E. Vincent/Transport Treasury.*

Below. 1005 COUNTY OF DEVON in the cutting approaching Mutley tunnel, 27 June 1955. This was the site of Mutley station, closed before the outbreak of the Second World War. The building beyond, partially obscured by the cloud of exhaust steam, is Plymouth Eye Infirmary; very handy when a speck of ash needed removing from the eye of a footplateman, on the way back to Laira shed. *R.E. Vincent/Transport Treasury.*

CHAPTER 10
Coal, Water and Tea

Life on the footplate was not always as glamorous, or as straightforward, as we story tellers would like you to believe. Sometimes there was dark side, when things did not go according to plan, or the relationship between driver and fireman was all it should be. And then again, we all of us have our off-days... One memory remains of a trip back from Exeter, with a train of locomotive coal. We had worked up with a Cornish broccoli special, and enjoyed a spanking journey. The Hall 4-6-0 had steamed her heart out, and gave no inclination of how the remainder of the night would be. We had no scheduled return, and had set our hearts on going back 'on the cushions', as passengers. No such luck. Upon reporting to the Exeter shed foreman, we were baldly informed that we were to go to Riverside yard and there relieve a Taunton crew on a train, mostly loco coal, and work it to Laira yard. My driver, whose name I will omit for reasons which will become clear, I hope, was a rather dour individual. All the way up he had hardly spoken a sentence more than he had to, all in the interests of *good practice* you understand. At Riverside the changeover was made a little more hurriedly than usual, with the exchange of information virtually non-existent. A

look around soon told me why. The 28XX 2-8-0s were normally perfect for this class of work and, with a small wheel diameter, were exceptional at climbing the Devon banks. But on this one, conditions were far from right. The fire looked dull, telling of a layer of clinker on the firebars which would affect the draughting. The tender did not have a piece of coal larger than a marble which meant that, as the train had come all the way from South Wales, every fireman before me had raked the tender through and through. This left me the 'rubbish' and I had the hardest part of the journey to come, the South Devon tops of Dainton and Rattery. Well, I thought, I have to give it a go, so I jabbed a fire iron in the box and gave a good stir around, but nothing much seemed to improve. Out of the yard, I put the blower, the forced draught, on a touch and we trundled on. Coal trains are notoriously heavy, just hanging on the draw bar and the names went slowly past; Starcross, the Warren, Dawlish and Teignmouth.

I struggled to keep water in the boiler and some semblance of fire in the box but the steam gauge was nowhere near where it ought to be! All boded ill for the banks after Newton Abbot. We were to go into the goods yard at Hackney, for the train to be re-marshalled, so I thought it

prudent to mention to my mate the possibility of a quick visit to shed. Try and clean the fire a little, and perhaps a tub or two of decent coal, or even, beyond my wildest dreams, *a replacement engine!* Imagine my shock (though, recalling the fellow, perhaps I should not have been all that startled) to be told that there was plenty of coal (coal, there was a laugh) in the tender and that I was the bloke paid to shovel it. My job was to do the firing, so get on with it. Out of Hackney, along the level stretch of track (almost the last before Plymouth) to Aller Junction, there to pick up a banking engine to help us from the rear up the fearsome gradients of 1 in 41 or so. Worse, around Stoneycombe the track became twisting and curving, making for extra 'drag' on the wheel flanges of a really heavy train. We were directed into the loop line and as we passed the waiting banker engine I shouted to them to 'give it their best' or maybe it was more colourful than that. My driver brought the train to a halt and we waited for a clear road.

After a short, apprehensive wait, the signal came off and, with the recognised system of 'crow' whistle calls exchanged between us and the banker, we started up the bank. My worst fears were soon realised and, by Stoneycombe, with the

6800 ARLINGTON GRANGE leaving the west end of Mutley tunnel to drop down to North Road station, 14 April 1952. A Penzance engine, it is a bit of a mystery that 6800 has found itself at the head of the 10.35am Wolverhampton and Birmingham to Penzance passenger train. *R.E. Vincent/Transport Treasury.*

water level dropping in the boiler and the steam gauge betraying all the symptoms on being 'on strike', I could foresee no hope of putting water back into the boiler until the very last minute, near to the tunnel at the summit at Dainton. My driver would need all the steam, albeit low pressure, to get us to the top. We eventually made it into the tunnel and with a sigh of relief, I put the injector on. Steam could be sacrificed now for the benefit of water, ensuring there was sufficient to cover the fusible (safety) plugs at the back of the boiler, as the front of the locomotive dipped down grade.

Once through the tunnel, we came to a stop for the guard to come forward and pin the brakes down on some of the leading wagons for the drop down to Totnes. The 2-8-0, designed to operate most efficiently at 225lb/sq.in. and at least three parts of a boiler of water, was now showing 160lb, with the water very low, just showing in the bottom of the gauge glass. I spent the time in the tender, shovelling coal forward, for every bit that was within reach at Aller, I had shovelled into that hungry firebox. It was so small, almost dust really, that the greater part of it must have gone straight through the tubes, up, up, and away and out of the chimney. Again, by stirring up the fire with a fire iron and putting on some coal I was able, by the time Totnes was reached, to get things in reasonable condition to face the climb to Rattery and Marley tunnel, which at that moment seemed a long, long way away!

The brakes, which had been pinned down on the leading wagons, were released, steam was 'on the mark' and the boiler was full; the banker came up behind, the 'crows' were duly exchanged again, and off we went. Once more we faced a climb that we would be fortunate to make without 'a blow-up', a forced stop to recover steam and water, a dent to the pride of any self-respecting fireman. This time there would be no let out, no escape, water would have to be put into the boiler at some stage, irrespective of the drain on steam. It was a nightmare; I struggled, I shovelled, I raked and poked at the fire. What I sobbed and said under my breath as I swore at that beast of a locomotive cannot be repeated; into it went all the frustration, tiredness and, yes, pride. I listened thankfully to every beat of the exhaust that took us nearer to safety, and the end of the shift. At Tigley signal box I tried an old dodge, putting the fire iron into the firebox, getting it red-hot, and letting the signalman see it. The hope was that, realising we were in trouble he'd ring ahead to his colleague at Brent to tell him of our circumstances, and we'd be put into the loop there to recover.

No such good fortune. Rattery came, the banker left us and into Marley tunnel we went. Out of the tunnel and soon the bell sounded in the cab to tell us of a clear road ahead. My ploy at Tigley was fruitless; much like everything else I did, it seemed, or so I thought, with steam falling off and water in the boiler steadily dropping. We struggled to Wrangaton and thankfully it was downhill now, although the regulator would still be open.

Ivybridge, Cornwood and Hemerdon came and I offered a silent prayer that at least it was falling gradient and not rising, for I do not think I could have managed another climb. By this stage I was just going through the motions, keeping a vestige of fire in the box and enough water to get us safely to Laira yard, and the sanctuary of the shed. Well, yes we made it, and all that time, little came from the right-hand side of the footplate. No words of advice, reproach or even support. I had *shovelled coal* as I was told. But it made me appreciate Claude, my regular mate, all the more!

Of course my story of the coal train was the 'exception to the rule'. Usually it was always possible to find some decent size lumps of best Welsh somewhere in a tender. Also in hindsight, I wonder if the driver that day unknowingly did me a favour, by teaching me that no matter how difficult raising steam at times might seem, with a little endeavour it can usually be overcome. The other thought, again in hindsight, is that perhaps my impression of him centred too much upon his personality. On reflection he must have been a good engineman to have managed that heavy train under such adverse conditions. Maybe we both deserved a pat on the back and, in truth once again, we were only doing what we were trained, and paid, to do!

Water, it sounds almost silly to say, is of the utmost importance, because without it there could be no steam. Locomotives use thousands of gallons of the stuff and tenders and tanks continually need replenishing either from columns or troughs set strategically in the 'four foot'. Taking on water from columns was usually without difficulty; the most important factor was stopping the locomotive in the right spot. Picking up water at speed from the troughs needed a little more expertise. The emphasis was on ensuring that a full replenishment of the tender was made, and to this end sometimes overfilling occurred which would cause small coal to be washed forwards from the tender on to the footplate. An awful mess to clear up!

The water pick-up scoop was slung under the tender by the rear wheels, operated by a screw shaft/gearbox beneath the front of the tender controlled by a hand wheel on the tender behind the driver's position. A water level indicator, with a floating gauge, allowed the fireman to judge how a 'fill' was going. The scoop was made to swing down until the lip was below the level of the water in the trough. The forward movement of the locomotive then forced the water up the scoop into the tender. With the inrush of water the floating gauge rose to give the operator an idea of the level in the replenished tender. With a careful watch the scoop (ideally) could then be lifted once more before the water overflowed the tender. Hazards included lowering the scoop too far so that water pressure caused a difficulty when the time came to retract it. Again if left too deep, or for too long, the spray from the trough or the-over filled tender could cause the front coaches

to be smothered. Not so good if the windows on the leading carriages have been left open, or a passenger is looking out.

An interesting situation arises when a train is double-headed. It is then essential that when the leading engine is picking up from the troughs, the fireman on the train engine ensures that his ashpan and dampers are closed, to protect the fire from any spray from the leading engine. In the summer of course, the level of water in troughs, such as those at Exminster, could become low, with the additional demand made upon them by the additional holiday traffic. In these cases it was often necessary to make an unscheduled stop at the next station with a water column. Water of course brings us on to, possibly, the truly important liquid on any footplate, *tea*. It was said that the way to a engine driver's good books was through a cup of tea, and most firemen learnt how to make it to suit the tastes of his mate very early on. 'Brewed' in the ever-present can, either enamel or aluminium, it was kept warm on the shelf above the firehole door. The first can of the day would probably be partaken of going off shed if an engine had been prepared, and was generally the last responsibility of the fireman but your mate would do it if pushed. On the road, drinking water could be obtained at stations, signal boxes and even at times from a handy restaurant car. Boiling the water was no problem, we had a fire (it was as well to put a smear of thick oil on the side of the can to stop it burning) to bring water to the boil, tip in a correct pre-determined amount of tea and sugar mixed in a special oval tin from a certain mustard company (it had compartments both ends) followed by a quick over wrist swirl and within moments there was a can of maybe 4 to 5 cups.

I came across an interesting set of statistics while writing this book, concerning the firing of steam locomotives. The report stated that 'Locomotives burn more coal per mile when climbing gradients than when running on level ground' – pretty logical I would say! It continued, 'but since they ascend a gradient at a slower speed, they have more time to burn it. It is a mistake to think that much more coal is required to feed the firebox in a given space of time when on rising gradients than on the level. *There is no need to increase the rate of firing to any great extent.* I am not too sure about the correctness of that statement, but I well remember that my back ached more on Hemerdon, Rattery and Dainton than going along the sea wall at Teignmouth. The report contained a whole series of technical data linking steam used against speed and cut-off, and came to the conclusion that the increase in percentage cut-off (the length of travel of the pistons) employed on a heavy rising gradient is more than compensated for by the drop in speed. Nonetheless most firemen, especially in the West Country, would probably hold that an increased amount of steam is used on heavy rising gradients and, as a consequence, heavy firing must take place.

Great Western fireboxes were designed to burn coal from the South Wales pits (probably because it was a convenient source and, rumour had it, the GWR directors had colliery interests too). Welsh coal, unlike the English stuff, had a greater tendency to *swell* as it burned, and would open out similar to a fir-cone. This was when the heat generated was at its highest because it would be burning all the way through. A problem for the fireman was that if one fired 'too heavy up the front of the box' the expanding coal could press against the brick arch and occasionally cause it to dislodge. There were even times when one was glad of a bit of 'slack' to deaden the fire down a little, especially at a destination while waiting for a 'turn round'. But a fireman's duties in the main were to provide endless amounts of steam and water for the driver to ply his trade and to enable him to get the best out of the locomotive (and to contain those elements when they were not required). This was achieved by ensuring that the firebox contained a fire of sufficient quantity and quality, by shovelling huge amounts of coal into an ever-hungry furnace, and managing the level of water in the boiler. And also, some may say, most important of all, by making the tea!

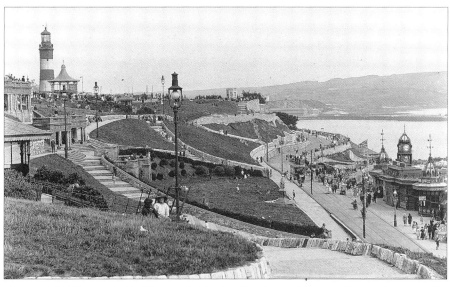

Above. Old Plymouth 12. Plymouth Hoe looking from the west. The pathway to the Esplanade is in the foreground ,with the shelter appearing to sit beneath Smeaton Tower. The road from West Hoe to the Barbican skirts the foreshore, and the entrance to the Pier is right centre.

Below. Laira Junction and on 15 July 1957 the first of the class, 1000 COUNTY OF MIDDLESEX (they were only just considered 'true' Great Western engines by many!) passes with the 7.30am Penzance-Manchester train. 1000 was a Bath Road locomotive, working back home to Bristol. The sidings to the right were home, in the main, to the coaching stock for the auto trains; exceptions included the carriages in the first siding to the right of the three signal bracket, which formed the St Austell-Marsh Mills workmen's train; these were non-corridor coaches, for the workers from Cornwall employed in Devonport Dockyard. For many years, and during my time, the next siding had a sleeping car and dining car for the Old Oak Common men on double home working. The siding on the extreme right at the far end also held a gas tank wagon (and it is in fact there on this occasion) to serve the dining car. *R.E. Vincent/ Transport Treasury*.

Prairie 5569 standing in the platform at Launceston ready to depart for Plymouth with the branch passenger. The photograph brought back a memory of my driver, George Howard, after I had visited the footplate of a Southern railway locomotive. The locomotive simmers away happily enough with just a wisp of steam from the front end, while the train crew pass the time until departure. At the fireman's right knee is the universal metal 'dinner box'; it held the day's food as well as a tin for tea and sugar and an old sauce bottle full of milk. The lid was a hinged flap, deep enough hold the current timetable, special notices, rule book and time sheets! *R.C. Riley/Transport Treasury.*

CHAPTER 11
Pride, Humour, Rivalry

The cab was a special place and has even been called 'the kingdom of the footplate' and, I suppose, so it was. The driver was the man in charge; he had sole control, and his word was law. The fireman worked under his watchful eye and in addition observed signals and, whenever possible, looked out for the road ahead. The conditions were never comfortable. Although Great Western footplates were reputably amongst the most functional and least cluttered, the cab offered little protection from the elements. They were hot in summer and extremely cold in winter. They could be noisy, and often conversation on the road was limited to minimal, grunted bits of information, the position of signals, right away, time-keeping and the rest.

The footplate at times could be dirty, but a proud fireman kept it otherwise. Brush up after every bout of firing, damp down the exposed face of the coal in the tender, to prevent dust flying around, and a light sprinkling of water over the very front of the footplate under the fire hole door (and mind the driver's shoes). The 'front' (which in fact was the *back* of the firebox, and where all of the 'gubbins' were) would be lightly oiled, so as to catch any small particles that were flying around, as I've mentioned. I have known of footplates with the wooden floorboards almost scoured white from the actions of a fireman. Even at the end of a long run, Plymouth-Paddington, say, the whole area would be as clean as when the journey started, 4 to 5 hours and 4 to 5 tons of coal earlier!

It was team work in its purest form and, as described earlier, trust and dependability were all. The fireman was ever aware of the needs and demands from his side of the operation, and would not knowingly let his driver down. A driver in turn would simply just accept that, but would ever keep a watchful eye as to the fireman's side of the footplate, registering (subconsciously, almost) the steam gauge, the level of the water in the gauge glass and so on. He would also be ready with helpful words of advice if he felt that it was needed, though of course, with due deference to the pride which his fireman had in doing his job. Above all else, each (normally) had the greatest confidence in one another. This pride stemmed from the tradition and sense of heritage that had been instilled in us. From the very first day as a *Company Servant* we were convinced that the Great Western was *the best*. Had not Tom Day drummed that belief into me even on that very first day?

The footplate could be a place, paradoxically, of great rivalry, between sheds, between crews at the same shed; even between brothers. At Laira, of course, we considered ourselves to be the finest in the West of England, for did we not work upon the best expresses to London and back, the 'Limited' (the Cornish Riviera) and the Ocean Mails from Millbay Docks? We manned the mighty Kings, and no shed west of Plymouth could match that, nor many to the east of us, for that.

Most plainly, rivalry existed between us and the men of the other railway companies which in our neck of the woods effectively meant the Southern and a suitably superior air was adopted. Laira driver George Howard summed it up for me, on my very first trip to Launceston. Arriving there with an afternoon passenger train, he'd helped me turn the little 55XX 2-6-2T for the trip back to Plymouth and then left me to take on water and tidy up, while he went to the box to check on how the horse with his bet on its nose had fared in the meantime.

The crew of Castle 4056 PRINCESS MARGARET look relaxed as they sit and wait to leave Old Oak Common shed, presumably for Paddington station. The fireman has been busy cleaning 'the front' and has made it shine (a matter of pride). The tea cups are in the tray ready for a 'brew' along the way. *R.C. Riley/Transport Treasury*.

4077 CHEPSTOW CASTLE passes West Largin as it climbs the long drag from Bodmin Road the Doublebois. The train could well be the up Cornish Riviera Express. This is a pleasant wooded valley with the Fowey River meandering through. *R.C. Riley/ Transport Treasury*.

Everything in order on our footplate, I strolled to up to the platform of the 'other' railway which was allowed to run alongside ours, and where one of Southern's locomotives *in the wrong green* was standing. Never having been on a 'foreign' footplate, I politely asked the driver for permission to get on. It was unusual, I have to say, they worked from the wrong sides of the footplate, but strangely though, *the crew did look like us, and even spoke the same language as us!*

Eventually returning to my footplate, I found George already there. He enquired as to where I had been, and listened to an enthusiastic account of my experiences with the other locomotive and crew. At the end of my tale he nodded, and stated quietly but firmly *that while I fired to him, I would not do that again.* 'You see, Phil', he said, 'there's us, and there's them. They don't bother us, and we don't bother them'. I was mildly shocked but to be frank, came to share something of this view of our neighbours; it was almost expected! I was invited some years ago to relate my footplate experiences to the members of Plymouth Railway Circle. During the interval I was approached by the late Roy Wilkes, a former driver from the Southern Railway's Plymouth shed, at Friary. After some polite conversation, he asked if I would clarify a matter which was puzzling him from my talk. Assuring him that I would if I possibly could, he asked, *Phil, what have you got against the Southern Railway and men?* In reply I could only recall a very wet and cold winter evening when I was waiting on Platform 7 in Plymouth North Road station, hoping

for a lift on a light engine returning to shed. Along came a Southern engine, returning from working the branch line at Calstock; it ran in and stopped at the signals. Coming from my sheltered spot I braved the downpour and ran up to the engine to enquire if they were going to Friary – they'd pass Laira shed on the way. Receiving a reply in the affirmative, I then requested a lift to Laira. 'You a Western man?' he asked as the signal dropped for him to go. 'Yes' says I, getting ready to board. 'Not so-and-so likely', said he, and opened the regulator and left me standing there in the rain!

In the days of steam we had a kindly, inoffensive, driver at Laira called Edgar Stephens, but for all his mild disposition away from the footplate, put a regulator in his hand and he became transformed! He was never happier than when he could hear the bark of the exhaust coming out of the chimney, and more than ever if the locomotive happened to be one of the Kings. Not so happy though, were his firemen, for a King worked hard needed constant firing, especially up the front of the firebox and this, if continued for too long a spell, would tax the stamina of any fireman, no matter how willing.

It was reckoned that 'Our Edgar' could do a 'fair speed' through Taunton given a clear road with the 'Limited' or an 'Ocean Mail', without any trouble, or it seemed like it. Down the bank from Whiteball, through Norton Fitzwarren, hear the ATC bell ring in the cab for the distant signal at Taunton informing of a clear through road, and he would be on his feet. Easing the regulator open a little more, notching the lever up a degree or two to perhaps

20-15%, he would cuddle up against the side of the cab, looking intently ahead. Come Taunton it would be *there and gone*. A King or Castle thundering through and what a sight and sound it was. I bet that it lifted all but the heaviest reading material on the counters of the station bookstall. No porter needed to sweep the platform after Edgar had 'passed through'.

I always felt it a bit unfair that the men who drove their locomotives in this manner earned the name of 'hard-hitters', because in most cases their enginemanship was beyond question. Someone once remarked that they had shares in the mines of South Wales, or at least shared the bonus of the miners who worked down them. In most cases if the regulator was opened wide, the control of how hard the engine was driven derived from the position of the reversing lever. A full regulator with the reversing lever at 40-50% cut off at a high speed will make great demands, but the same situation with a cut off at 20-25% would be entirely different. I never felt concerned about the '2nd.port', but I would worry if the reversing lever was continuously being wound forward at the same time.

At St Blazey shed there was a gentleman to rival Edgar Stephens in his method of enginemanship, called Kimber. I am told that he was often known as 'Old Man Kimber', to distinguish him from his son, who was also on the footplate. A story came through to Laira of the exploits of Kimber senior, concerning the timing of a train which he had driven from Par to Doublebois (at the top of the Largin bank) non-stop and it seemed, in a startlingly short time. The exact time taken, I confess, has escaped me, but suffice it to say that whatever it was, to the men of Laira it seemed an impossibility. The problem was, knowing the man, and his manner of enginemanship, no one felt inclined to challenge it. The extravagant claim quite offended one or two of the keener types at Laira, none more so that Edgar Stephens. After all, Edgar reckoned that he could travel the Cornish road as fast as anyone, a claim often attested to by his firemen, and their aching backs! He was repeatedly heard going about the shed muttering 'can't be done... impossible', and the like. After all how could a Cornish driver claim to be superior to the men of Laira? Pride and rivalry bubbled away over the weeks and of course the blokes at St Blazey, Truro and Penzance were no help at all, never missing a chance, in the hearing of a Laira crew, to drop a 'chance' remark.

The *dénouement* unfolded on a day some months later, when Edgar came on to the shed at Laira with a face absolutely beaming after a turn to Penzance and back. He burst in the enginemen's cabin and announced triumphantly to all and sundry that 'No. It *couldn't* be done!' It was, he had deemed, absolutely impossible to run from Par to Doublebois in that time. Edgar had patiently waited for his opportunity and for the circumstance to be right; on that morning he had determined whether it was possible to emulate the feat. It wasn't, and a look at his fireman confirmed it.

He was a wreck, poor chap! From the story told, I can only imagine what had occurred. 'Right away' at Par must have seen the regulator thrown hard across and, as sure- footed as Great Western locomotives were, there had to have been a slip or two as the wheels fought for adhesion with all of that power and effort placed upon them, as the train blasted out of the station for the climb up to Treverrin tunnel. With all of that sudden forward movement, I feel that most likely the passengers in the leading coaches landed up in the rear coach, and the fireman's shovel became a blur as he feverishly fed coal from tender to box; a 'human mechanical stoker'.

Through the tunnel, the regulator closed, the run down to Lostwithiel must have been on the wings of the wind. A slight touch on the vacuum brake for the adverse curves, and through the station, then the regulator opened wide for the blast up to Bodmin Road. Brunel's old structure of Brown Queen tunnel must have had its roof tested as never before by the blast of the exhaust, and now came Bodmin Road station, hardly given a second look as Edgar went all out to prove that what a St Blazey crew could do, the men of Laira, or at least one driver, could do better.

What a spectacle it must have been for anyone in the Glynn Valley on that day, as up over the famous Brunel viaducts the train blasted. Pendalake, Clinnick, Derrycombe, West Largin and Largin itself. The 'bobby' there must have wondered what on earth was happening.

St Pinnock and Westwood, all were tested as never before. It was a good job too, I feel, that it was not during the night, for then surely the Cornish would have added another legend to the canon of folklore - a fire-breathing dragon on the slopes of the valley no doubt. The height of summer would maybe have been worse for, with the size of the red-hot embers being blasted out of the chimney, the whole of the fir woodland lining the sides of the valley might have gone up in smoke. Relief for the fireman would have come only at the top, where, as the signal box at Doublebois flashed by, the watch would have been checked, and the regulator closed with a triumphant flourish. A little jig on the footplate, and it was announced, with certainty, that the alleged time was false! It could not be achieved. Honour had been satisfied. Or had it? I have a theory, a suspicion in the back of my mind, that there never was such a trip. It was instead a story put about by St Blazey, knowing that the Laira men would have to respond. Well they did. Or at least Edgar Stephens did but he had knocked down a straw man, or at least a straw locomotive... That someone at Laira – a premier shed – would rise to the challenge was a given; the very thought of not matching the 'achievement' would be too much to contemplate. Engine crews could be great humorists, truly classic 'leg-pullers' and maybe, just maybe this was one of those occasions. I hope so.

There was always humour in the shed and on the footplate, although we were

Laira's 6999 CAPEL DEWI HALL pilots an unidentified King, pulling the front portion of the up Limited out of Platform 8 to drop back onto the main train, which has arrived from Penzance and is standing in Platform 7. *R.E. Vincent/Transport Treasury.*

Old Plymouth 13. Plymouth Hoe and the view westwards from the Shelter, July 1922. Clearly visible in the roadway are the tracks for the trams which served the city at that time. The area to be seen with the tall buildings is West Hoe and includes the Great Western Docks at Millbay.

always aware of the needs of safety. I was rostered with a short and paunchy driver called Ron, a never-ending wellspring of practical jokes (on anyone but himself of course). We were working a perishable back from Exeter to Plymouth (my first trip back in the dark) on a absolutely terrible night of lashing rain and gale force winds, strong enough to rock the locomotive, and everything 'black as your hat', or as 'black as Newgate's knocker' as the cockneys put it. When I was not actually firing, I tucked myself up into the relative shelter of the front of the cab, keeping a watch ahead through the small window. I was having a pretty good trip, comfortable considering the circumstances until, going through Dawlish, Ron asked me to stick my head out over the side to look for the distant signal across the bay for Teignmouth. If I could spot it early, he said, it would help to keep the train running along. Eager to oblige I left my comparative comfort and looked out, unsuspecting. As if on order, at that moment a massive wave broke against the sea wall, rose in the air the height of a mountain, and crashed down completely over me. I was drowned! I can still hear the cackling of Ron to this day, as I stood there gasping and dripping. I never did see that distant signal from there. Nor did anyone else. It *cannot* be seen!

To the duties of actual firing was added the responsibility, shared by both men on the footplate, to ensure the safety of the train and the passengers. The due observance of the line ahead, of signals and speed restrictions, was vital, accepting of course that ultimate responsibility rested with the driver. Life on the footplate could never be called tedious. No two trips were the same, demands differed. No two locomotives responded the same, they all had something individual about them, which after a time you came to know. A good trip was just that, and a bad one, as illustrated earlier on, could be a nightmare. Even in these latter circumstances though, the comradeship in shared adversity would often shine through and in the majority of instances the true spirit of working on the footplate won through. Each 'partner' played his own role in the joint task of getting the best out of the locomotive. We were a team of three; driver, fireman and by no means least, locomotive.

I recall in the summer of 1955/56 relieving a down express on a summer Saturday at Taunton. The loco was a Laira King, 6026 KING JOHN in perfect fettle and reputed to be the 'strongest' King of them all. Something to do with the cylinders having been re-bored or similar. Getting on to the footplate I was

greeted with the remark from the Old Oak Common fireman that 'she's not steaming all that well mate!' Being a Laira man, and showing all the airs of supreme confidence, I treated this a bit casually and thought to myself that whatever it was that was wrong, I could soon put it right. At the same time, however, my eyes were everywhere; on the fire, the coal, anything that would give me a clue as to what was amiss. Common sense overrode personal pride and told me that the cockney fireman was as able as the rest of us, and his warning should be heeded.

'Right away' from Taunton and we were soon to face the climb to Whiteball, nine miles or so with gradients varying to 1:80 at the steepest point. By Norton Fitzwarren I realised that the Old Oak man's information was only too dismally correct. It was very difficult to maintain a full head of steam but a good stir up with the fire iron, levelling the fire over the box to let it brighten and then build it up again should have transformed the situation. That was the theory, but as always the practical stopped it in its tracks. Imagine my frustration upon sorting through the 'bars and prickers' for the long fire iron, only to find that the longest on the engine was just a bare nine feet or so, and this with a firebox some twelve feet in length. As sure as 'eggs was eggs' if there was problem with the fire, for certain it would be that holes had formed right at the front end. We were at the bottom of the bank, and things were getting desperate and I was getting a little apprehensive. Well, an effort had to be made and so the detested oversize domestic poker went in the firebox. At that a quiet voice from the other side of the 'plate enquired as to 'what I was about?' Really frustrated now and a bit sharp, I replied using the best of footplate argot, complete with the regulation 50% expletives. *About Mate, About? I'm going to give the fire a good root up!* And so on. What the **** did he think I was going to do!

A moment passed, and the same quiet voice remarked, *Root it up Phil? Root the b****r up? You won't even tickle it with that!* I looked at him, and saw what he saw. A man on one of the most powerful locomotives in the country, about to attempt to put it right with a 'hatpin'. He smiled and gave a laugh at his own joke, and the tension was over. I sheepishly put the fire iron back into the rack, and settled down to what I did best and had been taught – to fire the engine, my job. With his calm assurance and expertise, we reached the tunnel at Whiteball and made some sort of recovery on the long run down to Exeter. While stopped in the station, I quickly went across to the engine shed and was able to get a fire iron of proper length, to get to Plymouth.

In Chapter 8 I mentioned that I had 'one more story' of the Princetown branch,

and it concerns that very first Monday morning when I worked the branch as a relief fireman. With Ron Hext as my driver I worked the first train to Yelverton, something like 2.10pm and, after coupling up to the coaches for the return trip, was looking forward to tackling the journey back to Princetown *the hard way.* As Ron opened the regulator for the stiff climb out of the station, I started to tend the fire. Suddenly I realised that we were not travelling at any great speed and glancing over the side, noticed that it was only a crawl. Making a comment to Ron, that this was different from what I'd expected, he informed me that we 'had livestock on'. Barely comprehending, I queried his meaning. I had not seen any cattle wagon attached to our train, and again a quick look back over the train confirmed this. Ron then explained that they had their own way of transporting certain beasts, rather than go through all the official paperwork of getting a van sent up from Plymouth. On this occasion we had a pony to take to Princetown, so, with the owners cognisance it had been attached to the coupling on the rear coach and as long as we travelled slowly, it would be content to trot along behind us...

He wanted me to keep a look out to see if the pony was alright and, not to worry, the sharp curvature of the track would soon show the pony in full view! Further, at each platform stop, the guard would have a look behind his coach and, if all was well, give the 'thumbs up'. I stared in some amazement, but before I

could say anything we had arrived at Dousland, and Ron told me to watch for the guard's signal. Sure enough, the guard left his van, went around to the back of the train and, after a moment, looked up and gave me the universal thumb. Now doubts were creeping in, despite the evidence of my own eyes. Could the guard be party to any sort of leg pull? Perhaps there really is a pony, and perhaps also I had better obey Ron's instructions. After all he was my driver.

Along we went, and every time I started shovelling, Ron would ask me to remember the pony. At every stop the guard went through the routine, and I informed Ron that all was well. At last Princetown was reached. The working instructions stipulated that for safety reasons, the train should stop at the home signal, the whistle blown and, if the station was clear, the signalman would pull the signal for the train to proceed. This, naturally enough, duly took place. I had made up my mind that, as soon as I had uncoupled the engine, rather than get on the footplate again for the run-around, I'd dash round to the back of the coaches to see the phantom pony for myself. Lo and behold, no pony! I had been done, good and proper. A young fireman from Plymouth, and a Cornish lad as well; we were, after all, famously a little slow on the uptake!

Ron brought the engine on to the coaches and I coupled up and, getting back on the footplate, congratulated him. 'For what?, he asked.

1006 COUNTY OF CORNWALL at the head of an express, standing in Platform 7 at Plymouth North Road, 16 May 1954. The light smoke from the chimney shows that the fireman has paid some last minute attention to the firebox, ready for 'right away'. *R.E. Vincent/Transport Treasury.*

'For the trick' I said. 'There never was a pony, we would have squashed it flat when the engine came back on to the buffers'.

'Oh, yes there was' he said, all wounded innocence. 'When we stopped at the home signal, the farmer was waiting, untied the pony, jumped on his back and rode him off across the Moor.'

To this day, I am not *certain*. Would you be, I wonder? The Moor is a strange place... I was very conscious of the reputation which my brother had achieved as a fireman and was often referred to as 'Bill Rundle's brother'. I did not mind really, although I felt a little in his shadow at times. Our paths did not cross that often and when they did it was just a case of talking about meeting up at our parents in Saltash, or something similar. In the summer of 1952, I believe, inspecting the 'roster' before booking off, I noticed that the following day Claude and myself were booked to assist a passenger train to Newton Abbot. Imagine my surprise when, upon checking further, the crew of the train engine was scheduled as none other than Driver H. Roach and Fireman W.L. Rundle (brother Bill).

This, I thought, was my big chance to prove myself, and Claude made a similar observation. The next day I booked on a little beforehand to give time to ensure that when we went off shed, everything was as perfect as I could make it. Our engine was a 49XX Hall, perfect for the task, and engines that could be relied upon as good steamers. I did not have much chance to see Bill, before going off

shed, but we met on the Speedway Road at Laira, ready to go to North Road station, and coupled up. Being the junior, of course, it was left to me to do the honours. As we coupled up, Bill turned to me and made a comment that we should 'give of our best'. We always did when assisting as pilots, and with that off we went to North Road and our train. Well, I had a first rate journey. The engine steamed and steamed, and perhaps in my eagerness I let it blow off excess steam more than I should have merely for propriety's sake. I watched Bill's locomotive over our tender, and had an occasional hand signal, thumbs up or so, when he looked out over the side of his cab. I confess to some admiration, for contrary to what people might think about seeing and hearing an engine blowing off spare steam through the safety valves, this was considered wasteful and therefore bad practice. Bill controlled his steam all the way, with no excess even on the down slopes of the banks. His reputation was well earned and deserved, I felt. At Newton Abbot we only had time for a very few words as I uncoupled and went off to shed to turn and prepare for a return working. Bill was booked to Taunton.

It seemed just one more fairly uneventful trip but the true circumstances were very different, though I had to wait many years to

find out; my fiftieth birthday in fact, when my brother gave me a railway book. Inside the front cover was an envelope with a letter inside:

Dear Brother, I almost bought you 'Double Headed in Devon and Cornwall' Then I had a painful memory of being assisted by you on that train to Newton Abbot. Our County wouldn't steam, and I knew that the slightest touch on the blower would invoke the immediate reaction of a cupped hand to the ear, and an enquiring nod of the head.
Oh yes?
We were in dire straits at Cornwood, I had not put any water in the boiler since Hemerdon! and at Wrangaton we did not have enough steam to lift the smoke, or enough water to wet a postage stamp. The strain of putting on an act of supreme confidence through the front eye glass one minute, and sneaking a red-hot pricker out of the rack, the next, I well remember. Only the supreme confidence of Harry Roach prevented me from saying to 'heck' with it, and screwing the blower out! It did not help any to see your gauge over the tender on the mark. So I did not get you 'Double Headed'. Hope you like this one, Bill. Yes I did, but I liked the truth more. It says it all, rivalry – even between brothers!

Above. **6817 GWENDDWR GRANGE pulling away from Platform 7 at North Road, runs past East Signal Box on 11 October 1953. The locomotive is either going to Laira shed to turn and then work back home to Penzance, or it is crossing over to reverse down to the turntable at the west end of the station, before joining her new train to work home.** *R.E. Vincent/Transport Treasury.*

Left. **An unidentified pair of locomotives – a Manor heading a Castle – passing Laira Junction on 15 July 1957 with an up express. The Manor obviously has excess steam on the falling gradient which bodes well for the climb up Hemerdon to come. The coal stage pilot is busy in the coal sidings beyond the signal box. The prominent two signal bracket controlled entry to the shed as well as the down Lipson loop. Running across at an angle is the distinctive track of the Lee Moor Tramway, which ran alongside Laira goods yard. The down and up main lines run past the front of the box. The tracks leading to the left of the signal box are: straight on to Laira goods yard; branching right, Laira shed and loops.** *R.E. Vincent/Transport Treasury.*

Laira's 5964 WOLSELEY HALL on Hemerdon bank, 3 July 1955. The train is carrying 'H' code headlamps which denotes partial or non-vacuum fitted wagons. In this case the first five have braking connected to the locomotive, but the driver has decided that he requires more assistance, and it can be seen that he has had the hand brakes 'pinned down' on at least a further six wagons. *R.C. Riley/Transport Treasury.*

CHAPTER 12
Hazards

When it came to coal trains the fates seem to have pursued me somewhat. Possibly one of the most frightening experiences to befall a footplate crew was to be involved with a 'runaway', a situation in which the train has taken control of the locomotive and the braking system, when the driver is no longer in complete control. I hasten to mention that these instances were few and far between and were very much the exception rather than the rule. It came about usually through mechanical failure; a vacuum pipe could blow out under the pressure perhaps. Very rarely a runaway was brought about through misjudgement but, probably, it was more often just bad luck.

Paired with Don Jenkins, who I had fired to for a short time in my early days, we worked a Cornish broccoli special to Newton Abbot. After relief on the through road, we were required to take an engine off shed and run to Hackney yard, and then work a train of loco coal back to Laira. The locomotive was a 28XX class 2-8-0, a first rate type for this work. She did not seem to be in bad condition, and I paid the usual attention to the fire and the tender, while Don did some oiling, before leaving to pick up our train. At Hackney, we were not surprised when the guard

announced that we had a full load. The majority of coal wagons in those days were non-vacuum fitted and I recall Don discussing with the guard the need for pinning down a number of the brakes on the leading wagons at the tops of Dainton and Hemerdon banks. The journey to Hemerdon was run of the mill. Going up the bank past Stoneycombe, Don observed that 'she was dragging and heavy' and on the first down gradient at Dainton he had several brakes pinned down on the leading wagons. I played my part, with the handbrake on the tender.

The '28' steamed reasonably freely and presented no undue problems, so that by Marley tunnel I had enough fire in the box to see us home, so I was able to have a well earned sit down. We stayed on the main line through Brent, so now it was all set for Hemerdon; down the bank, looking forward to running easily along the river and off to shed to book off. But little did either of us anticipate the events to come...

A short stay in the loop at Hemerdon to let a 'perishable' or suchlike go past, and we were let out to continue on our way. Before the descent of Hemerdon we come to rest at the stop board just over the brow of the downhill gradient. Here we wait for the guard to come forward, to

confer with Don as to the number of brakes to be pinned down. With that decided, we creep slowly forward. The idea was to secure the brakes progressively until steam was required to keep the train moving forward, even on the falling grade. At this stage Don would pronounce himself satisfied and a blow on the whistle would stop the guard pinning more down; as we drew ahead he could jump back on his van.

Down Hemerdon bank with its ruling gradient of 1 in 41, we went, Don skilfully using the vacuum brake of the engine, me on the tender handbrake. Quietly rolling into the woods, she started to increase her speed. I wound up the handbrake to give Don a chance to rebuild the vacuum. Turn after turn (surely, I thought, I can't keep winding this handle up for ever) but still the train kept increasing speed. Suddenly I had a feeling that all was not as it should be. I was conscious of Don applying the brake with much more urgency and was straining harder and harder on the handbrake. The stink of brake shoes, heating up against the wheels, rose up around us and a glance over the side confirmed that they were smoking! Yet the wheels were picking up speed and I could hear the vacuum piston 'slapping' away. The heavy train was

2-8-0 2803 with a down train of loco coal on the sea wall between Dawlish and Teignmouth. The weather is quite benign and very different from the night that Ron Tregenza played his prank on me. It was also with a train such as this that I experienced my first and only 'run-away'! *R.C. Riley/Transport Treasury*.

starting to push! My mind told me that there had to be a limit to all of our efforts. A glance at Don confirmed that he was experiencing some concern, to put it mildly. Full application of the brake now, with no effect, and we were really in trouble. He shouted that we'd done all we could, and to hold on tight.

There were two whistles on a GW loco, a normal shrill one on the right-hand side for everyday purposes and another on the left with a deep tone, for 'special circumstances'. These were 'special circumstances' alright, and we blew the 'brake whistle', with its distinctive deep tone, to catch the attention of the guard and to alert him to the fact that we were in trouble, if he hadn't realised. More than that, there was the fervent hope that the signalman at Plympton would realise our plight!

Looking back over the train I could see the guard hauling on the handbrake of his van, but I felt that it would serve little or no purpose. Something that Claude had told me, to the effect that in a circumstance such as this the driver could, in the interests of the greater good, order his fireman to 'go over the side', came queasily to mind. I'd be expected to obey without hesitation or question. It seems funny now, but wasn't at the time. I looked out and all along the line were old sleepers and rails, and a dense undergrowth of bramble bushes; a soft landing was the least they offered and I was sure that if Don had given me such an instruction, I would have refused and taken the disciplinary consequences afterwards. I preferred to take my chances on the engine. I am eternally grateful that the need never arose but the alternative was not looking any better; out of the frying pan and all that... I was only too horribly aware that the normal practice was for freight trains at Plympton to be diverted into a goods loop immediately beyond the station and road bridge. It was an evil fortune that this was a very severe turn-off even in normal conditions; at our heightened speed it would throw the front end of the locomotive to one side and derail us. That would mean that the engine, with us on it, would come to a dead stop, and all the wagons of coal would still come on, and pile up on top of us. It was a calculation that, in the circumstances, one tends to repeat over and over.

I continued blasting away on the brake whistle, while Don still tried frantically to get the train under some semblance of control. Into Plympton we sped, rocking as we came around the curve. I knelt on the footplate in an attempt to pick up the signal as soon as I could, for it was partly obscured until the last minute by the road bridge. The bobby, aghast, was looking out of his window as we passed, and then I saw the signal. All but sobbing, tears in my eyes, I screamed the news to Don. *The Main, Don, he's kept us on the Main!* The relief was indescribable. It took us a mighty length of track after Plympton to stop the train, but eventually we did. The guard came up, shaken like us. He lifted the brake levers on the wagons, not that there could be a

lot left of the brake shoes, and we made our way into the reception road at Tavistock Junction. Released to go to shed, we found that word of our exploits had already arrived ahead of us. I confess to being on a 'high' by now, though I'm not sure we called it that back then. I had been involved in a runaway and survived. I strutted into the enginemens cabin, expecting all sorts of a welcome but: no reaction. It was as though what I'd gone through was commonplace but in reality I felt that they were relieved to see us unharmed – comradeship again, but an anti-climax. I had been in my first (and only) runaway, *and no one wanted to know!*

There were other dangers on the footplate, that might not involve an errant train. Something as innocuous as a shovel could prove problematic. The uninitiated could be forgiven for assuming that the Great Western provided a shovel for the purposes of shifting coal (approximately 12½ lb of it at a time) from tender or bunker, to the firebox. Yet it was a 'multi-purpose' tool like no other, useful for toilet functions as well as cooking and it's just as well we'll never see this examined on a cookery programme. Designed as it was with a long blade, and with the moulding in the well to accommodate the handle forming two divided 'compartments', the shovel was ideally suited as a wash basin, but perhaps more importantly, a frying pan. For some inexplicable reason, the main meal on the footplate was always known as 'breakfast' be it morning, noon or middle of the night. And plenty of men loved a fry-up. The shovel would be thoroughly cleansed with hot water (we had plenty of that) and dried with clean cotton waste. Introduced to the firebox where coal free embers would have been carefully prepared (no smoke tainted food here) the shovel was heated sufficient for cooking. Withdrawn, a portion of best dripping or lard would be placed into the back corners of each of the sections, and rashers of bacon placed into one, and 'rounder cut' slices of potato in the other. Back into the fire, heated again, and withdrawn. The bacon and potato would then be turned over and moved a little towards the centre of the shovel, and would be replaced by an egg (held one-handed and broken by tapping against the edge of the shovel) to one compartment. Then a slice of bread was introduced to the other corner. By now the footplate would be starting to smell thoroughly appetising and I have seen mouths watering close by, at the wondrous odour. To the fire again for a quick re-heat, out to turn the bread over, and 'flip' the fat over the egg. Another heating and the finest fried breakfast ever had been conjured forth. Sadly, as intimated, 'breakfast' was not without hazards of its own...

Ideally a locomotive would be stationary for a fry-up but hunger could take over and this was not always possible, so the breakfast would be prepared while running. And that was where the problems arose. You might well recall that in an earlier Chapter, I told of my first day with Claude Bolt on the

Tavistock Goods, and how important it was to run to time in order to have our breakfast before starting to shunt the train and the yard. On one particular occasion we got there late and the shunter was waiting. Claude tossed a coin to see who would eat first while the loser tended to the shunting (some drivers trained and trusted their firemen). I do not know how it was, but I never won, and always ate second; Claude did love his fry-up! The problem lay in the way a steam locomotive worked...

Very briefly, when the regulator is opened the hot gasses of the fire are drawn into the tubes which go through the length of the boiler, thus heating the water. It follows that anything else, if suitably positioned and free to move, can also be drawn inward. To overcome this Claude and I had perfected (beware hubris) a system whereby every time the shunter wanted the engine to move, I would shout a warning: 'opening regulator', and he would keep the shovel away from the mouth of the firebox; with the cry 'closing regulator', the culinary miracle could safely continue. It was all in the timing. This particular morning I prepared the 'back end' of the fire, washed and dried the shovel for Claude and then moved to his side to start the shunting. As he went through his preparations, the routine began. 'Opening regulator' I cried and Claude removed his shovel from the firehole. On hearing 'closing regulator' back went the shovel. And so it went on, bacon and potatoes; egg and bread, all nicely cooking to perfection and all the time I am responding to the needs of the Tavistock shunter and the demands of the local merchants. Claude put the last touch on the fire to finish off breakfast and I yelled *regulator opening Claude* but sadly, not loud enough. *He did not hear me!* Preoccupied with the work, leaning out of the cab, I opened the regulator, the shovel still on the fire complete with perfect bacon, fried egg, fried bread and the spuds too. In a moment all that was left was an empty shovel and a brief puff of fry-up smell through the chimney. Claude was not at all pleased.

In deference to this human tragedy, as you will appreciate, I did not dare fry my own breakfast afterwards, so both of us went hungry. Well, not quite. Claude also had a passion for jam doughnuts (any notion of 'healthy' eating was still decades off back then) so during a break from shunting, I went down to the bakers in Tavistock and bought us a bag of half a dozen.

The 1948 'Interchange of Locomotives' brought a distinguished visitor to our shed. This was the LNER World Speed Record Holder – Sir Nigel Gresley's No.22 MALLARD. I just happened to be on 'shed turning' at the time and, as she came through the coal stage, had to move her to the New Shed ready for the next turn of duty. I clambered up on to the footplate, took a moment to familiarise myself with the controls and, opening the regulator, dropped down to the front of the Old Shed, where the driver on the turning duty worked the points for me to reverse on to the 'back road' towards the New Shed.

He left me to turn the points at the eastern end of the shed myself, while he set the points for stabling in the correct road in the New Shed. I was quite enjoying myself on this locomotive and, as I passed the back of the coal stage, spotted the point which had to be turned, to reverse back and into the sidings for New Shed. So I applied the brake. Now, on Great Western engines, this would have permitted me to swing down from the footplate, landing exactly as the engine stopped with the wheels clear of the point. This time, I swung down and turned the point, only to see MALLARD sail gaily on. I had not allowed for the fact that the braking was different from ours, and had a 'delay' effect. Worse still, this special locomotive, in the spotlight of publicity, was now heading for the catch point which protected the running lines outside the shed. She was in immediate danger of derailing and, worse, terminate my career at the same time. Running after her I climbed up on the footplate, wound the reversing lever into forward gear and opened the regulator wide. With much protesting the engine stopped within inches of the catch point, and started to move in the right direction. I had escaped ignominy (and worse) by the skin of my teeth.

Like anyone, I am aware of the problems encountered on the present day railway when late running is caused in autumn by leaves on the track. As I understand the problem, the lost adhesion when the wheels run on to the leaves cause the wheels to 'slip' and increase in revolutions. The power unit then automatically engages a higher gear ratio, which only adds to the difficulty, and the train grinds to a halt. The problem with leaves is not a modern one, however, and certainly existed in my days on the footplate. It caused us a headache or two, and some very hard work, especially on the early morning goods to Tavistock. All would be going well, Claude and myself probably feeling quite relaxed and satisfied with the progress we were making on a heavy train up the branch towards the top of the incline at Yelverton. With no warning, there would be an almighty roar of the exhaust out of the chimney as the wheels spun at full revolutions. The fire in the firebox would start to disappear out of the chimney with the vastly increased draught placed upon it. A shouted command would come from Claude (hardly needed, it must be said) for me to get sand on the rail, while he would frantically shut the regulator to take power from the wheels, hoping to give them a chance of regaining adhesion. The problem with this course of action was that it was the last thing either of us wanted, for it meant that a slow train became very much slower and if we weren't careful, we'd grind to a halt. That in itself created additional difficulties. The action of shutting the regulator, applying sand, opening regulator, wheels slip, shutting regulator and applying sand would go on repeatedly until, with a feeling of huge relief, the wheels would pick up and, to the delight of all, the train would carry on normally. Except, of course, it was now travelling at a much reduced speed, making more demands on steam and water, and thus making the task that much harder.

A further seasonal hazard of course, was frost and snow. On the main lines signalmen would find points blocked, the lens on the signal arms obscured; at the least it might be a struggle to trudge to a (possibly) remote box. The teams of lengthmen would battle manfully to keep the track in use, and might be reduced to huddling up in various retreats – huts, signalboxes and so on. In the Plymouth district the most vulnerable line was the Princetown branch and I've already mentioned the elderly pannier with snow plough at Laira, kept in steam at vulnerable periods. With the withdrawal of these veterans ordinary panniers served for the last winters on the branch – it closed in 1956.

The 'Regulations for the Operation of Trains' at those times were contained in an 'Appendix of the Timetable' and included the following under the heading 'Snow Storms': *When there is a drift of snow in prospect, the engine working on the Princetown Branch, provided there is an opportunity to do so, must be run to and fro over the threatened spot. The Station Masters at Princetown and Yelverton must direct this to be done according to the end*

Old Plymouth 14. The Gents Bathing Pool, Plymouth Hoe, in July 1922. For those who wished it, the facilities allowed for a degree of privacy.

Old Plymouth 15. July 1922 and the Ladies Bathing Pool. As the Gents, so the Ladies had the privacy of their own pool. It appears that they also had water slide, which seems a bit unfair.

of the Branch at which the engine is at that time. If the use of the snow plough becomes necessary, a telegram to that effect must be sent to the District Traffic Manager and to the Locomotive Foreman at Laira.

I was booked on a spare turn at Laira in January 1952, a cold and wintry day, and I was hoping for something better than shed duties. Prepping engines or similar did not exactly appeal to me. After booking on, however, my driver, Frank, informed me that we were to take the snow plough-fitted pannier tank to Laira yard, collect some brake vans and take them to Yelverton. Although we'd had no snow in Plymouth, there had been a considerable fall on Dartmoor. Ensuring that the bunker was heaped with coal and 'topping up' the water tanks, we took off to Laira yard, collected the vans and a guard, and made our way to Marsh Mills. Arriving there, we found a number of permanent way staff waiting to board, together with a ganger; he would ride on the footplate with us to Yelverton, and on the way could explain to Frank what was to happen. There was so much out of the ordinary happening that I have to confess, as a youngster I was getting a little excited. I recall Frank suggesting that I 'settle down' adding ominously: 'It could be a long hard shift'. As it turned out he was only too right.

As we went down to Yelverton the weather became ever more wintry with flurries of snow and when we arrived there we could see the Moor towards Princetown, carpeted in white. We picked up more P.W. men at Yelverton and after turning the engine and plough, to get it the right way round for the branch, running around the vans and filling both boiler and tanks with water, we set off towards Dousland. Relatively little snow had accumulated on the first stretch of line and we cleared it quite easily; it proved easy too, on to Burrator Halt. It was here that we could see deeper snow ahead, and the ganger warned that usually the worst area was near Peek Hill at Edgeworthy, where drifting could occur, blocking the cutting. A 'V' blade snow plough is good enough as long as the shifted snow can clear the sides of the blade. Come to a cutting where the sides of the banks restrict that clearance and the snow just gets pushed forward and compacts. At Edgeworthy this was exactly what happened. The cutting was full with drifting snow, piled high. With all of the men now out of the vans, we approached the drift with some fair force; regulator half open, lever well forward. Into the drift we plunged until the wheels started to slip under the pressure. Then it was: close regulator, reverse, and have another go. The problem with the white stuff if that the more you (literally) 'plough' into it, the more it can tend merely to compact further. This I was finding out, in a very practical way. Back once more and Frank opens the regulator wide and in we went full blast. It sounded good, but it was like hitting a solid wall. All that happened was that we were *derailed*. I have to confess I welcomed the reassurance that this was quite normal, though someone might have mentioned it, I thought (that footplate humour again...). The presence of the re-railing jacks and skids on the top of the pannier tanks was now explained. The ganger rallied some of his men to place the skids in position, and to clear some of the snow around the drift, and after a couple of attempts, we were back on the rails. I was very aware of conserving water, for if we were stuck for very long our loco could be in serious trouble.

This was the slogging, battering ram manner in which we worked our way forward. Over and over we rammed, derailed, re-railed and tried again, the same procedure until at last we pushed our way through each serious drift. On and on up towards Princetown we laboured and yes, the novelty certainly did wear off, until eventually the gladsome sight of Princetown station came into view and we were able to enter the place with a flourish of speed and flying snow. What a welcome we received, reminiscent of the relief of Mafeking, I suppose! All that was missing was a brass band. The locals plied us with all sorts of wonderful fare to satisfy our hunger, and I enjoyed a drop of liquid which looked like cold tea, but certainly did not taste like it. Eventually we were able to get free to turn the locomotive, take on much needed water, and work our way back to Yelverton, this time with little bother. We were relieved at Yelverton by a Laira crew sent up to meet us, and we rode home as passengers. It was an experience hard to match, but my most vivid memory is of how tired I was. Absolutely shattered!

One problem I encountered by moving back to live in Saltash in 1952 was collecting my pay on a Thursday, if on night duty. It meant breaking my sleep, whereas when we lived at Lipson Vale, I could slip to the shed and back in half an hour or so. It now took the best part of a couple of hours. Not a 'hazard' in itself I would accept, but could in all innocence cause one!

I was very proud, as all fathers are, when my daughter Susan was born. She has always complained though, that when she was very young my shift work meant that I was either asleep or at work when she wanted me to spend some time with her. This was not wholly true; there was one Thursday when she was two or three years old when I, *unselfishly,* offered look after her for an entire afternoon to give my wife, Joyce, a break, as of course, all loving husbands and fathers did!

It was Thursday, I had to collect my pay and, having learnt to drive, borrowed the father-in-law's car to go to Laira. I would be taking Sue, for obviously an essential part of any little girl's upbringing should be a visit to an engine shed; the earlier the better, I'm sure we'll all agree. Joyce, recovering from her shock, duly got our daughter ready and pretty as a picture she was, in a spotless white dress with embroidery upon it I recall, a bonnet (as all young ladies of that age wore in those days) white socks and shoes. What proud father could resist the chance to show her off?

And this I did. I made her secure in the front seat, though no one dreamed of seat belts in those days, and drove with great care all the way to Laira. I am sure that Sue was as excited as I was for she chattered away all of the time. At Laira I parked the car, and walked with Sue holding my hand to the timekeeper's office window, there to pick up the little envelope of money. On the way I pointed out engines on the coal stage having their fires cleaned and the tenders replenished, and I could see that she was enjoying it already. Introducing Sue to everyone we met, including the foreman, I could tell, being a father, that she wanted to see more so, lifting her up in my arms, carried her round the whole of Laira shed. Roundhouse, cleaners cabin, the stores, New Shed, the boilersmiths shops, and finally, as icing in the cake, as it were, up and on to the footplate of a King.

What better way to finish the visit, and without doubt she was impressed. She kept reaching out to touch the regulator and all the controls, and sat on the fireman's seat. I even helped her to lift the shovel. Her finest moment came when she sat on the drivers seat and I at least could see the thrill and the excitement that welled through her. Tears came into her eyes, though it turned out to be due to a bit of coal dust. We drove back to Saltash and our daughter was back in the arms of her mother, her doting father anticipating the gratitude and the gushing story of how she had spent her first exciting foray in the world out there. Instead I was taken back by wifely admonishment, all because a little coal dust and oil had got on to the dress, bonnet, socks and, yes, the shoes. Nothing had escaped but, Good God, we had been to an engine shed! What did she expect? Even though Joyce did of her best, the dirt would not come completely out and those clothes could never be worn in public again. Yet had this not been a small price for my daughter's exciting experience, and for my wife's free afternoon in the process? Was I not a fine father and a dutiful husband? Unfortunately some did not think so.

4410 standing in the Princetown branch platform at Yelverton, on 5 July 1955. To the left is the signal box at the Plymouth end of the down platform. The little turntable sits neatly between the up and branch platforms. It came into its own when the snowplough was out on the branch, having, of course, to work 'blade first'. *R.C. Riley/Transport Treasury.*

Old Plymouth 16. A lovely picture of the Old School House at Cremyll, on the Cornish side of the entrance to the Hamoaze and River Tamar. It appears that the pupils are enjoying the open air of a summer's day and are acting out some sort of a play. The premises to the right of the Tower, with a flagpole, is now a very popular 'watering hole', The Cremyll Arms.

Four car auto train at Royal Albert Bridge, 'the gateway to Cornwall', on 13 April 1952. Having collected the 'staff', the fireman on the 64XX class pannier tank has opened the regulator for the short passage of the bridge. Although on the footplate on his own, it was still his responsibility, the rules clearly stating that the staff, or 'token', should be carried on the footplate. The driver sat in the vestibule at the front end of the leading coach. Although the driver had a 'regulator' lever attached by rodding to that on the engine, and a vacuum brake in the vestibule, the regulator was cumbersome to use and he usually left this to the fireman to operate. The bridge really 'belonged' to the autos, for after all they plied some 35 to 40 journeys across her daily in each direction. In the days before the road bridge, the autos were very popular and extensively used. Four coaches denotes a busy time of the day, late afternoon probably, when the Devonport Dockyard stopped work for the day; the 78 seater coaches would be full, with passengers standing. *R.E. Vincent/Transport Treasury*.

CHAPTER 13
Small Coal

Great Western fireboxes were well suited to the best soft steam coal from South Wales but, for all its qualities there were times when some small coal, 'fines', were needed, to help to 'hold' the fire together; it filled up the holes and give the fire some body, as it were. In preparing this story, I realised that I had some small incidents and thoughts which did not fit easily under the chapter headings so far but, nevertheless, were a part of the whole, like the small coal on the fire, hence the title of this Chapter.

Senior fireman, after passing their examinations, became known as 'passed firemen'; that is, fireman *passed* for driving and when and where a vacancy occurred they could apply for a position as a driver – the official title for the grade. This method of progression was open to all firemen, so long as the exam was passed. There was discussion (heated at times) in the cabin at Laira to the effect that being a driver did not necessarily make you an *engineman*. The point was that anyone, given the training and experience, could drive a steam locomotive but a certain higher expertise, in the manner in which that driving was carried out and so on, distinguished a 'driver' from an 'engineman'. It was a fine distinction, though there was no intention to denigrate the expertise of

either, driver or engineman. One who regarded himself as an *engineman* might not be happy to be called a *driver* by his peers while one accustomed to *driver* might find *engineman* something of an honour, coming from a man who was a junior. If that makes sense!

From debate in the enginemens cabin (as it was officially called – did that mean all of us who used the cabin were enginemen? no...) it seemed that some drivers, in a fashion difficult to define, were more particular in their method of driving than others. A touch on the regulator up or down to make a fine adjustment, continual alteration of the reversing lever to suit the work of the locomotive, perhaps only a percentage point at a time, nevertheless made all the difference. And that difference affected the demands on the fireman. So, therefore, came the final explanation: only the fireman rightly knew if his mate was a driver or an engineman!

Naturally enough, we came into daily contact with signalmen, the 'bobbies' (so-called from their 'policing' of traffic one supposes) especially on local services – the branch lines, the Saltash auto service and so on. Against the rules we regularly topped up their coal with some choice selection of 'nubby' and in return could scrounge a can of hot water from their

ever-boiling kettle, to make the tea. As a fireman I came into direct contact most of all when in the Goods Link. On a freight, we'd be stopped at a signal for an undue time or directed into a loop for a more important train to pass and under the aforementioned 'Rule 55' I'd 'proceed' (as the Rule Book had it) to the box to remind the bobby that we were there, signing the box register as proof. I've described this already and it usually went without any problems; in fact it was sometimes quite pleasant to enter a warm, cosy box, after the cold and draught of the footplate. A few pleasantries would be exchanged and, as often as not, by the time these were done with, the road was clear for our train to proceed. The one place that did not quite work like that was Wearde signal box immediately to the west of Saltash.

Wearde box was in an idyllic setting, sat on the bank above the River Lynher with views to the east of Plymouth and the Hamoaze reaches of the Tamar. On the opposite bank were the grounds of Anthony House, and Jupiter Point, the river base for the training ships of HMS Raleigh and HMS Fisguard, the Naval Training Bases. The box was at the west end of Wearde loop which ran alongside the Lynher from Coombe-by-Saltash viaduct, and immediately to the west was

The east end of the bridge with the up 8.50am Penzance-Plymouth stopping train, leaving the eastern portal behind a Hall on 13 April 1952. Both signals at the end of the bridge are 'off', so the train has a clear road ahead to at least Keyham. *R.E. Vincent/ Transport Treasury.*

the line of the original route of the former Cornwall Railway towards St Germans. The beginning of that line now forms a coaching siding. When placed in the loop, it was the fireman's job to trudge to the box to carry out Rule 55. The problem at Wearde was that the floor was covered in a very highly polished red linoleum. The signalmen (one I remember was called Ivor Richards) even wore slippers on their feet, and under no circumstances was a fireman with coal dust on his overalls and dirty boots going to walk on that hallowed floor covering. Even when raining, the register and pen (with nib; no biros then) together with a bottle of Great Western

ink, was brought to the doorway, and the signing duly done. The same would apply if hot water was needed for a can of tea. Always pleased to be of service but, the kettle would be brought to the doorway.

Observing the rule was painful on one occasion. In 1955 Claude and I were working a mixed goods back from Newton Abbot, something like 2.35am away from Hackney Yard, and the night was wintry. Although up to that time we had only had flurries of snow in the wind, with a shower or two of hail, there was nothing to worry us unduly. However, while we were in the loop at Aller Junction waiting for a banker and a clear road, it started

to snow in earnest. Claude reflected gloomily that if this kept up, it would be a long night before we reached Plymouth. If we were delayed too much we would fall foul of the early morning traffic; the postal, newspaper, London passengers, and the parcel train, all due between 4 and 6am. Eventually we were 'let out' and sent on our way. There were no problems with the management of the train, although the poor old guard looked a bit cold when he came up to put down brakes after Dainton tunnel. We travelled on to Totnes without delay and up the next bank to Rattery and Marley tunnel. All the time it had been snowing steadily and

5919 WORSLEY HALL piloting 6800 ARLINGTON GRANGE on an up passenger train, passing Wearde signal box (the infamous 'hallowed ground') on 13 July 1957. Prominent is the water tank on up side, feeding the water column which is just out of sight to the left of the box. The line of the original Cornwall Railway can be seen to the left, 'circling' around the signal box to leave the existing line, again leftwards. The signal box, like many others, was always kept in immaculate condition (the lino was so highly polished you could almost comb your hair looking in it!) but the 'bobbies' took it a bit far, barring entry to enginemen and their perceived dirty boots. *R.E. Vincent/Transport Treasury*.

it was noticeable that it was settling and building up ever quicker, in the way snow does, as it 'gets a hold'. The banker left us by Rattery box and through the tunnel we hurried, feeling a little confident that we just might be allowed to keep running through to Tavistock Junction yard.

But no, our hopes were dashed as we approached the distant signal for Brent to find it at caution; the ATC siren sounded its warning and we were signalled into the goods loop at the eastern end of Brent station. After waiting a little while and seeing the postal go by, Claude remarked that more than likely we would be here until all of the early trains had gone through. It was now about 3.30am and that meant another 2-3 hours at least. Under the prevailing conditions, nothing would be running to time, and no signalman would take any chances putting out a goods in front of a more important train and thereby risk delaying it. It was decided that I should go to the signal box and inform the signalman that we were where we were (in all probability, I thought, he will know. He put us in there!) sign the register and fill the can with water to make a cup of tea when I got back.

I put on my Mackintosh and pulled my cap down about my ears, and grabbed the hand rail to swing out over the side of the cab, at the same time dropping down to reach for the middle step with my left foot. This I managed but did not notice in the dark that the snow had piled up on to the step, and had turned icy. My foot slipped off, I lost my grip and fell heavily to the ground, my back catching the bottom step on the way. I landed with a terrible thud on to the ground, my bottom hitting the end of the sleeper. A bit dazed I shouted out and Claude came to help. Well, after a time, I felt able to carry on, though it was very sore indeed around the base of my spine. I went to the box and arrived looking like Nannook of the North after a close encounter with a polar bear, carried out my duties, signed the register and got the news that we would be held until possibly 5.30-6am. There was nothing to do but fill the tea can and return to Claude. Telling him the news and making the tea, I could not sit down for soreness, but assumed I was suffering merely from bruising. After an age we were let out and proceeded to the yard and off to Laira shed without further difficulty. Claude made certain that I reported my fall and had it registered in the accident book. The next morning I was worse and decided on a visit to the doctor. He prodded and poked and I winced and groaned and the diagnosis was that I had broken the very lowest bone of my spine, the coccyx. To me, a young man this seemed a bit serious, and I admit to a little panic. But I was assured that this bit of the spine was of no use to humans, only monkeys who swung from trees with it! A course of painkillers and I was sent on my way. The occasional twinges from that coccyx still remind me of Rule 55 of the Great Western 'Bible'.

Later on when I lived in Saltash on the Cornish side of the Tamar, I needed to cycle across the Royal Albert Bridge at night in order to get to Laira for duty. In those days there was no road bridge and the ever-faithful ferry did not run after midnight, except in a case of a dire emergency – ambulance, fire engine or suchlike. I must pay tribute to the signalmen on both sides who turned a blind eye to the rules and regulations and kept a watch to see that I had crossed with safety. On the south side there was plenty of room once I had cleared the rodding for the points and could ride at a reasonable speed. The problem arose when a train crossed at the same time. It demanded dismounting and tucking the bicycle and myself under the 'coping' of the span. I was always surprised how much clearance there was, but then the mighty thing was built to the broad gauge. What was also mysterious was the number of occasions that my crossing and taking shelter coincided with the fireman on that train washing down the footplate! I can assure you that to be deluged with a shower of dirty black water interspersed with a liberal amount of small coal in the early hours of the morning is not the best start to a shift. I'd arrive at Laira looking like I'd already done eight hours at the coal stage.

Of all the adjectives used to describe life on the footplate, 'tedious' is probably the last that would spring to mind. Yet I have a candidate to submit – a stopping passenger train that would well fit the description. This was the 1.55pm Penzance-Newton Abbot, which we worked forward from Plymouth North Road. At times departure could be delayed unduly; the stock used was from the 7.30am stopper from Newton Abbot and because of the congested traffic at that time of the day it could (I quote from a train controllers log) 'be late arriving at Penzance (due 11.50am) which gave the marshalling shunters and carriage cleaners little time for the turnaround'. Remember too, that the carriages had to be removed and stabled to release the locomotive (usually a Hall) to go to Long Rock shed for turning, watering and coaling before returning to Penzance station to work the same carriages back to Newton Abbot.

The loading was about right; five or six 'on' to give something like 170-200 tons, but it was scheduled to stop at almost every station, platform or halt between Penzance and Newton Abbot. If I recall rightly there were only two exceptions, Probus & Ladock (still in use at this time, not closing until 1957) and Dockyard Halt. The train could be held up between Truro and St Austell by the Truro-St Blazey pick-up goods. This was scheduled to go into the sidings at Burngullow, just west of St Austell, to permit the 1.55pm passenger to go through. Laira crews relieved the Penzance men at North Road station for the journey through Devon. We too were booked to stop everywhere: Plympton, Cornwood, Ivybridge, Bittaford, Wrangaton, South Brent, Totnes and Newton Abbot. Due away from North Road at 5.20pm, we were not due to arrive at Newton Abbot until 6.52, more than an hour and a half to travel some 25 miles

or so and not exactly exhilarating. The problem for the fireman was when and how much to fire.

Leaving North Road there was a chance to put the fire in a semblance of good order on the short pull up to Mutley tunnel. Normally thoughts would turn to getting a full head of steam and a boiler of water for the bank at Hemerdon. But this time we were to stop at Plympton, just under four miles ahead and at the bottom of the bank, so I did not want the engine blowing off excess steam at the station stop. Hemerdon was always challenging and though five or six coaches were within the limits for a single engine, there was still plenty to do. Over the top of the bank and it was a short run to the next stop at Cornwood; again boiler management was crucial. Maintaining steam was not difficult, for the regulator would be shut for each of the stops. Once away again, there was not a lot to be done to the fire despite the slightly rising gradient for the next two or three miles to Ivybridge. Then it was a short haul of some two miles to Bittaford, followed by the same to Wrangaton. As soon as the regulator was opened and speed got up, it was time to shut down again. A bit of work was needed going towards South Brent to prepare for the long run, seven miles or so of falling gradient to Totnes and with the Dainton bank to tackle afterwards. I recall that we had more passengers getting off and on at Brent than all of the other stops put together, with the possible exception of Ivybridge. My driver reminded me upon leaving Brent that we were to take the engine on to shed at Newton Abbot, a timely reminder to work the fire down low as possible for the eventual attention of the fire-droppers. By now the stop/start was getting – yes – tedious, but that did not mean we could afford to relax, with still some seven miles from Brent to Totnes and a further seven or eight to Newton Abbot after that.

Eventually, after a stirring climb up to Dainton and the tunnel, which levelled down my fire for me, and the run down past Aller, we came into the station right on time. This did not alter the fact that it had taken almost five hours to come from Penzance and that we had been an hour and a half from Plymouth. It wasn't exactly a matter of breaking records. Our return working was with a semi-fast goods from Hackney (Newton Abbot) goods yard to Tavistock Junction, and the journey back home did not take much longer than the passenger working. But there it was, part of our job; a service to the paying public and, after all, we *were* paid to do it.

I gave much thought as to whether to detail a darker episode of life at Laira but after a talk with a very senior former Laira engineman, I accepted his opinion that it involved very important matters of principle to us at that time. Enginemen's memories were long – too long maybe – and, as I understand it, the beginnings of a strike in the 1950s lay in the Second World War, and related to the working of ammunition trains. The crux of the problem arose from the fact that a munitions expert from an Ordnance

Depot would accompany the train and ride in the brake van. It came to the notice of the train crews that they received an enhancement of pay known as 'danger money' for the risks involved. Train crews felt somewhat aggrieved at this, for they remained on the same rate of pay no matter what. An approach was made by the unions, the Associated Society of Locomotive Engineers and Firemen (the footplate crews) and the National Union of Railwaymen (the guards) for a similar 'danger' payment. The consultation, as always, became quite protracted and heated, to the extent that eventually the representatives of the unions *hinted* that if the matter was not soon brought to an acceptable conclusion (after all, these trains were still to be worked while all the negotiations were going on) it might, very reluctantly result in 'industrial action'.

At this stage, it seems, the dispute came to the notice of the Prime Minister, Winston Churchill who called upon the railwaymen to understand that there was a war going on and that the enemy was indeed the Germans not the British railways. It is said that he urged all sides to be aware of their first responsibility, to the country and the war effort. There was it seems an understanding, which to the unions looked more like an assurance, that after the war had been brought to a successful conclusion, the loyalty of the railwaymen would be acknowledged. This, to the unions and their members, was virtually a promise that there would be wage increase to compensate. Satisfied, this was how the matter remained until hostilities were over.

Whatever the arrangement, it was never honoured (as the unions saw it) and it remained a thread of discontent running through subsequent pay negotiations, by now with the nationalised British Railways. It was a factor in the 1949/50 round when the unions informed the BR Board that they

would be calling for strike action. This was where I became involved. A very young man, I was instructed by my union to go on strike. I confess to mixed feelings. Loyalty firstly – should it be to my employer, or to the union? Well, I was most impressionable as with most young men, and decided upon the latter – to strike. This in itself created a major problem for, although there was strike pay, this would be nowhere near enough for my board and lodgings in Percy Terrace, Lipson Vale. I discussed this with Frank Hawkey, the union representative, and he agreed to me going home to stay with my parents at Saltash, but that I was to make a contact with him each morning. My landlady, 'Ma' Beedle told me not to worry, she would keep my room for when the strike eventually ended.

Arriving back home, I got a warm son's welcome from mum, of course, though she warned that dad was 'not all that pleased'. When he came in for lunch he demanded to know why I was on strike; I was not directly affected by what happened during the war, so what did I think I was I up to? And what did I hope to gain personally from this misguided action? From his point of view, of course, being one of 'the old school' (which we are all destined to attend eventually) after family first loyalty belonged to your employer, who after all gave you the means to keep family clothed and fed. Added to that he had served in the Army during the Great War and had 'done his bit' probably for a lot less pay than some who were safe at home in a 'reserved occupation' like the railway! Being a dad, though, he soon relented and made me feel welcome.

The strike lasted for two weeks, I believe, and eventually we were instructed to return to work. It was then I found that there was serious ill-feeling towards some men who had not come out on strike and had continued to work. They

were given the inevitable titles; 'blackleg', 'scab' and worse. 'Strike breaking', crossing picket lines and so on brooked no forgiveness. I arrived one day to book on with one of these men as my driver, to be met at the timekeepers window by Frank Hawkey, who took me to one side and gave a very stern lecture on how I was to conduct myself whilst firing to this driver. It was how things were and how they remained until the 1960s and 1970s, before rapidly declining as the older industries waned. Firstly, I was to carry out my duties in a correct and proper manner. Secondly, I was to inform my driver of all the usual information that was required for the undertaking of those duties. But that was it; I was to make no general conversation – no welcome, such as good morning, the weather etc., *and in no way to either make or share a can of tea.* Lastly, I had to remember that whilst the members who struck endured a hardship, those who continued working received their full wages and even made additional money with overtime. I was left confused and, frankly, disturbed. The driver in question, it turns out, was wholly accepting of the situation and made no attempt to start a conversation, make a cup of tea or anything else. He accepted the 'sanctions' and almost, it seems, approved the 'verdict'. It was not an easy way to work though, and I was glad to return to my regular driver once more.

Two coach auto train making its way over the bridge towards Saltash on 18 April 1949. To the right can be seen the remains of supports for the landing stage where US soldiers from the St Budeaux camp embarked for the D-Day Landings. On the left can be seen one of the entrances to the underground ammunition and explosive stores, served by rail. *R.E. Vincent/Transport Treasury.*

Looking west, 13 April 1952, a view that shows the essential simplicity of the design, a lasting tribute to the genius of Isambard Kingdom Brunel. *R.E. Vincent/Transport Treasury*.

6855 SAIGHTON GRANGE (see also page 95) at Royal Albert Bridge signal box on 13 April 1952, with the 8.50am ex-Penzance; the fireman can be seen preparing to hang the 'staff' on the 'bull's horn' which can be seen on the post at the near end of the signal box. The post to which the staff is attached for pick up can be seen opposite, on the down side, connected by a little boarded crossing. *R.E. Vincent/Transport Treasury*.

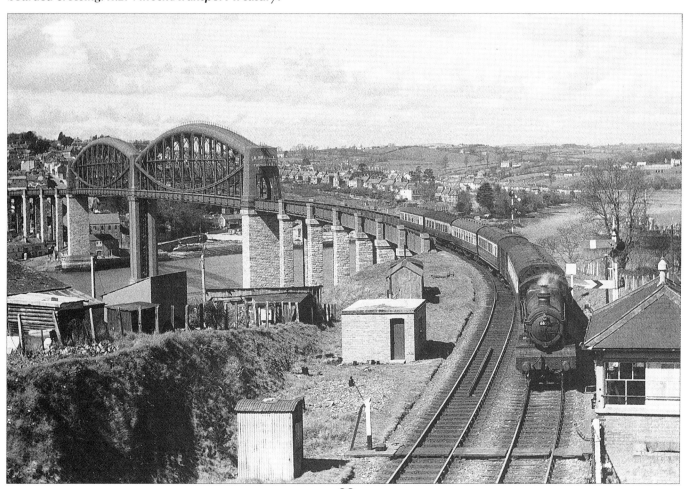

Old Plymouth 17. The Fish Market, Plymouth Barbican in the 1920s. Most perishable trains in the West Country included a fish van in the loading, and for a certainty some of the fish landed at the Barbican would have been destined for markets further afield. The picture shows a fine assortment of fish dealers, buyers and dockside workers proudly displaying some of the day's catch. Of interest is the poor fellow extreme right who appears to be suffering from toothache.

By September 1960 steam is being phased out, and 4950 PATSHULL HALL is piloting D602 BULLDOG on an up express. The location is the former Lipson Halt between Mutley tunnel and Laira shed, and in the background the chimney of Beechwoods Food Factory dominates the skyline. 4950 is without a shed plate on the smokebox door, and I wonder if she is destined to change sheds for the short time left to her. It was just below this location, on the left side of the picture, that I once had lodgings. *R.C. Riley/Transport Treasury.*

CHAPTER 14
Gradients

St Blazey men jealously claimed the Newquay branch as their own, and did not take kindly to re-arrangements in the mid-1950s, when it was decided that certain 'through' trains destined for Newquay should be rostered to Laira instead. Later, the Cornish sheds took over the working of the first part of the down 'Limited' on summer Saturdays Newton Abbot-Truro and this was either a 'sop' to the Cornish or a logical improvement to working practice, depending on your view. Whatever the reason, honour appeared to be satisfied. One such train was the Saturday-only 9.30am ex-Paddington; being on a spare turn I found myself paired with a No.2 Passenger Link driver called Albert Stansbury. It was something like 1.00pm on duty to prepare 6949 HABERFIELD HALL, to work to Newquay and return. I had very little knowledge of the line, but my brother had told me of Luxulyan bank, 1:37 to 1:40 at the severest part. At North Road station we coupled up to our train on Platform 2, and the guard came up to inform Albert that our load was twelve, just over 400 tons or so, which meant that we had our work cut out, though we would have assistance for the bank from Par by an engine or engines from St Blazey shed. We were booked away at 14.25pm and scheduled to stop at Saltash and

Liskeard before Par. From the start the heavy load meant I had to get stuck in to get the fire right. HABERFIELD HALL responded and up the pull to Devonport and again to the Royal Albert Bridge, she steamed very freely; all boded well for the rest of the journey.

At Par station we were directed into the branch platform and found that St Blazey had sent out a 53XX 2-6-0 to assist us in front with a small 45XX prairie to 'bank' us at the rear as far as Luxulyan. First we had to uncouple and place the 53XX behind us. Great Western rules decreed that where there were both up and down gradients, a locomotive that did not have a leading bogie could not be coupled in front of one that had. This, however, also meant that Albert remained in control of the train; moreover I did not have to worry about catching the staff at the single line sections, which was a relief in this unfamiliar territory. It also determined that, in order to get so many coaches within the confines of the platform at Newquay, we would uncouple before reaching the station at Penrice Junction and leave the 53XX to take the rest of the train the last short distance on her own.

Departure from Par was something like 3.30pm and with a short blow on the whistle exchanged between the three

locomotives we eased the train out of the platform and on the line towards St Blazey. It was a bit 'curvy' past the shed and yard and across the main road level crossing, when a proper start towards Ponts Mill could be made, gradually increasing speed for the bottom of the bank. With all the 'hanging about' at Par, my fire had become a little ragged, so after leaving the station I had put an iron in to liven things up and allow it to brighten again before adding fresh coal. At Ponts Mill she was perfect, with a full head of stem, just slightly blowing off at the safety valve, and the fire was red hot. I started now to build it up again and with each shovelful was pleased to note that short puff of smoke from the chimney to indicate that the coal had been placed exactly right. Up the bank now, both locomotives on the front working flat out, and a glance back the train showed the little 45XX at the rear also playing her part. This incline certainly was all that it was reputed to be; it looked steep, it felt steep. The sound of three engines was very impressive, and in a way I was enjoying it, never having been in that situation before.

Working steadily away with the shovel, I was conscious of the chimney of the 53XX against our tender, and could see the puffs of smoke as the St Blazey fireman

Prairie tank 5519, the Luxulyan banker, assisting the 9.30am Paddington-Newquay on 9 July 1955. This train loaded to twelve coaches and needed the banker at the rear as well as two engines in front. *R.C. Riley/Transport Treasury.*

carried out his work. He, of course, had an advantage, this being home ground for him. I confess to having heard stories from other Laira fireman that, because of the so-called grudge that the Cornish shed nursed when this work was allocated to Laira, they did not give of their best when assisting the Laira crews over the branch. This most assuredly was not the case on this occasion and I regard it as just another of those 'dark mutterings'. The 2-6-0 behind us was 'flat out', without doubt. The bark from her chimney, and the steam blowing free from her safety valves told the true story. I caught the eye of the other fireman part way up as I had a breather looking out over the side of the cab, taking in some gulps of welcome clean air. He gave a wave and did a thumbs-up; like me, he seemed happy with how things were going. He also pointed back to the third engine and, sure enough, that fireman was looking out, so all three of us were suddenly waving to one another. If anyone noticed, they must have thought it was some sort of highly technical means of communication between engines. After nearly half an hour we gained the station at Luxulyan and without the train stopping and with a pop of his whistle the 45XX dropped away from the train, his work done. As Albert commented, he'd 'done a good job,'

The steepness grew easier from hereon until near enough St Dennis Junction and the Tregoss Moor. But before that came the stations of Bugle (famous for the Cornish brass band festivals) and Roche (known locally as Victoria, and famous for the Roche Rock with the ruins of St Michael's Chapel). We rounded the corner at St Dennis Junction where the china clay mineral lines came in from Melador

Mill and Burngullow, the latter linking again ultimately with the Plymouth-Truro main line which we had left at Par, some forty minutes or so earlier. The line was now double track across the expanse of the Goss Moor, and we watched the traffic on the main road running alongside. We had one stop to make, at St Columb Road, delaying the holiday makers travelling by road and earning their curses as we blocked the level crossing with our long train. Now for the last leg of the journey; with luck another ten minutes will take us through Quintrell Downs and on to Tolcarne Junction, where the Newquay-Chacewater line joins ours, and then Trenance where we will uncouple. Right on time we arrive, some 20 miles or so from Par, and for the passengers exactly seven hours after leaving Paddington. Our task done, we have to turn our engine, take on water and get some coal forward for our return booked work, which turns out to be the 6.00pm passenger train to Plymouth. No help needed with this one, just five coaches on with stops at Par, Lostwithiel, Bodmin Road, Liskeard and Saltash; no trouble at all for a Hall.

I have to admit it was a pleasure to sit down while descending the Luxulyan bank this time, as we dropped down beneath Treffry's ten arch, 98 feet high aqueduct/viaduct. The homeward journey was without incident, and after the novelty and exhilaration of the earlier trip, a bit of an anti-climax. Our Hall steamed her head off both ways in the best of Western locomotive fashion. We arrived back at Plymouth at 8.15pm and left the coaches for the station pilot to deal with while we ran to Laira to put the engine on the coal/ash road and to book off duty. A memorable and enjoyable day's work.

For a fireman the lines in Devon presented two distinct challenges, in both directions. Working east from Plymouth, first there was Hemerdon bank, and then the west side of Dainton after Totnes. Working westwards from Newton Abbot towards Plymouth, first came the east side of Dainton summit (from Aller Junction) and then Rattery from Totnes to Marley tunnel. It was a fact that if all was in good order the banks, despite a sometimes fearsome reputation, did not present any great difficulty if an engine was in good order, though they demanded respect and needed the all out effort of both locomotive and crew. The banks had an individuality, each its own; no two were alike, and could not be treated as such.

Starting from Plymouth the first to be overcome was Hemerdon, 2½ miles of continual climb with the ruling gradient of 1:41 for most of its length, but other than the long curve in the track as the woods were reached, the track is reasonably straight. An experienced crew would be aware that a full boiler of water at Plympton would take you to the distant signal for Hemerdon box. However, once over the immediate 'hiccup' of a summit, the track makes a short fall, and it was imperative to have at least a third of a boiler showing in order to protect the fusible plugs at the rear of the firebox. If they became uncovered the plugs, being made of lead, would melt and the water left in the boiler would flood into the firebox and extinguish it. There was little hope if this happened, once the foreman got you in front of him. For the banking engines this was a good practice, for with the long run back down to Tavistock Junction after reaching the top and leaving the main train, it allowed plenty of time to replenish the boiler and top up with water. For a through train, however, the criteria was quite the opposite. Although we always considered Hemerdon signal box to mark the top of the bank, the gradient continued to climb, although not as severely, to Wrangaton. Therefore it was important with any 'prestige' train to go over the top in as good a condition as possible. From Wrangaton the track starts to fall but the regulator would stay open until Marley tunnel, where the true fall to Totnes occurs. At Totnes there was chance for some recovery if required before the next gradient to Dainton.

Dainton at times seemed to go on for ever, although it is 'only' some 3½ miles long. The worst problem lies in the curvature of the track together with the final part steepening to 1:32/1:33. The combination of curves and grade imparts a considerable drag on the wheel flanges, and will make a long heavy train even more so. Once through the tunnel of course it is downhill all the way to Newton Abbot.

East of Newton Abbot the track is virtually level all the way to Exeter, and especially so for the eight miles to Dawlish. Still, a bit of 'collar' work was required on the part of the fireman, for the regulator would stay open for the whole distance. A beautiful stretch of line when the weather is fine, but at times it can be very different. The line meanders a bit through Teignmouth, and looking ahead thoughts would turn to topping up the boiler in order to take on plenty of water from the troughs at Exminster. The sea wall at Dawlish and Dawlish Warren must be one of the most photographed railway locations there are. It is renowned for a pleasant and relaxing climate for most of the year, yet when it is stormy the sea front becomes one of the most

troublesome areas on the whole system, and the line can be closed. The giant waves whipped up by gale force winds, combined with high tidal levels, regularly and spectacularly (to this day) wash out the sea wall and undermine the track. The water troughs at Exminster were now only four miles ahead; time to top up the boiler to ensure that, all being well, as much water as possible is taken on. Thoughts too, of the coming stop at Exeter, and then the long climb to Whiteball and the tunnel. The gradient gradually starts to rise a couple of miles before St David's station, but not enough to raise a sweat on the brow.

Twenty miles or so of steady pull faces the crew once the right away has been received at St David's station. After clearing the platforms, on the way to Cowley Bridge Junction, there is a chance to put the fire iron in and give the fire a rake over. A fireman does not like to use these tools too often, for that in itself can let cold air up through the firebars and hasten the formation of clinker. The driver's thoughts and attention are all about keeping the train 'swinging along', keeping a good speed up to lessen the effects, if possible, of the final pull to the tunnel at Whiteball. The regulator is gradually eased across until on the second port, and the reversing lever is controlled a 'snick' at a time as it is dropped to alter the stroke of the pistons to suit the terrain and the speed of the engine. He will be listening to the beat of the exhaust as well as keeping a watch on the steam gauge and gauge glass on the fireman's side, to judge how the engine is responding to the added demands. Through Tiverton, and the final effort begins. There are just over five miles to the top at Whiteball, and the beat becomes heavier and louder from the

chimney. Sampford Peverell and the train begins to 'hang'; the shovel becomes almost a blur and Burlescombe and the top can almost be seen. The expression 'to hang' referred to train *seeming* to become heavier – the loss in speed combined with the curving rail flanges to increase the drag. Despite this, it all works in text book fashion and, as we pass the signal box the front end dips to go down hill. No problem now, it will stay like this till Taunton. The fireman has a chance to tidy up. Get some coal forward; have a sweep up and damp down, and only then, when all is completed and the needs of the locomotive are seen to, he is able to have a sit down, all the way to Taunton.

Top left. Laira's 5972 OLTON HALL on the former St Blazey hallowed ground of Luxulyan bank, 9 September 1955. The train is the 9.30am Paddington-Newquay. The severity of the incline, 1 in 37/41, together with the loading of twelve coaches, required an additional locomotive in front all the way to Newquay (in this instance a St Blazey mogul) and a further St Blazey 55XX 2-6-2T at the rear as far as Luxulyan. *R.C. Riley/Transport Treasury.*

Below. 5969 HONNINGTON HALL, a Penzance engine, at St Dennis Junction on the Newquay Branch, 11 July 1955. The engine has overcome the climb up the Luxulyan Bank and now has a level track to the station. In the background are the tank engines which have been at work on the Retrew and St Dennis clay mineral lines. *R.C. Riley/Transport Treasury.*

When Kenneth Leech rode on the footplate, he invariably took a photograph of the crew and then presented them with a copy. This is 6012 KING EDWARD VI and men at Laira when Kenneth travelled to London with them. From left to right: Fireman Bill Rundle, Footplate Inspector Bill Andress and Driver Edgar Stephens.

CHAPTER 15

Men of Laira

Running an engine shed needed a great number of men, and they nearly all were men, then, in administration, trades and of course on the footplate. What they often had in common was a profound knowledge of locomotives and how they worked and operated – in their own particular area of expertise at least – as well as, very often, something of a devotion to the job. I always felt that at Laira we excelled with the number of 'other' trades with just those qualities. At the top was Chief Foreman Harold Luscombe. Although, as you might have noticed, as a cleaner boy I was pretty much below his notice, the fact is that we could not have had better at the top. He ruled and managed in a very quiet but authoritative way, as the best did back then. All going well, you hardly knew that he was there. Step over the line, and then look out. He was however, as I found out, a forgiving man.

Looking after the day-to-day operations were the shift foremen and first among them was Harold Cook, liked and respected by everyone. He always appeared unruffled whatever the crisis, which in essence meant he was just exceptionally competent. He was also of a pleasant disposition. Next was Vince Joiner who, for whatever reason, scared

the daylights out of me, especially in my early days. It was worth anything to avoid him, but I know now I was wrong. If one did one's job then there was little to fear from him. When I came out of the chief foreman's office after the uncovering of the Western Drive house number plot, Vince was waiting. I quaked, expecting a blast but got none, just a tap on the shoulder from him and a quiet but firm message of 'Good one – don't do it again though'. The third shift foreman was Fred Manley. Fred liked a smoke and usually found time to light up a cigarette no matter where or when or how. He also knew his crews. He knew those who would oblige no matter what the task might be, who were prepared to work long hours, and Fred was very often able to oblige.

In addition to these gentlemen there were two assistant foremen, Mark Peplar and Jack Chaston. I always got on well with Mark, although in hindsight, I knew very little about his background. Jack Chaston had been a driver at the remote Moorswater shed, an outstation of St Blazey. The work there covered the Looe branch, and it was because of this that I worked with him on one occasion. In the late 1950s the station master at Looe requested a special train to move stock from the local cattle market. As the

drivers at Laira were not familiar with the Looe line, it was decided that Jack would take a 45XX 2-6-2T and a fireman, collect a train of cattle empties from Laira yard, run to Looe and return with the cattle. The theory worked perfectly for most of the day. The cattle were duly loaded at Looe, and we prepared for the journey back to Laira yard. Unbeknownst to us, while we had been at Looe a small section of the bank alongside the line between Coombe Junction and Liskeard had slipped, blocking the track and effectively locking us within the confines of the branch. We were held with the train at Coombe Junction where I spent most of the time helping the guard fetch water from the nearby stream, for the cattle. Jack, fortunately, lived close by and was able to nip home and came back loaded down with food and drink. Eventually the line was cleared and we were released, to take the train to Laira and book off, some 18 hours after we had booked on – the longest shift of my career. The line suffered another slippage many years after I had left the railway, but it brought the memories back clearly.

'The Office' was overseen by Chief Clerk Cecil Elson, with the assistance of three booking-on clerks who worked a rotation of shifts to cover the 24 hours.

Laira shed; the view westwards from the coal stage on 17 July 1960. From the left is the 'New Shed' (now housing diesels), the 'Middle Sidings' with the Stores (windows open) and the sand road, with a solitary engine standing on it. Alongside is the sand house (sloping roof) and, this side of it, the enginemens cabin. The main building is the 'Round Shed' which housed the turntable and was home to the fitters, boilersmiths (at the back) and the cleaners cabin. To the right were the main offices. *R.C. Riley/ Transport Treasury*.

Laira shed yard on 17 July 1960, with engines lined up to take coal at the stage; the pannier tank is engaged in bringing new, full, wagons of coal from the adjacent siding. To the left are the outgoing roads from the shed; to the right in front of the road bridge can be seen Laira Junction signal box, and the lines of the goods yard. *R.C. Riley/Transport Treasury.*

Of them I recall Terry Nicholls, who became a celebrated railway photographer and I am grateful for kind consent to use some of his material in this book. There was also Miss (Lil) Dowell, a very efficient pay clerk, and Frank Adams, the roster clerk. Frank had to be very conscious of the seniority of footplatemen. Seniority, relative to each other, was jealously guarded, especially when it came to spare turns. The roster board would be minutely examined and Frank would soon need to explain himself if it was found that a more prestigious job had been allocated to a junior man. A whole days roster (*hand* written and rewritten) has been re-scheduled on occasion to appease a particular driver or fireman! The trade union for footplatemen at Laira was the Associated Society of Locomotive Engineers and Firemen, ASLEF. Our branch secretary was Frank Hawkey, a driver, while the sectional council representative was Frank Thomas. Frank was also a driver but union duties occupied most of his working time, seeing him 'away from home' for meetings and the like. He would periodically return to undertake driving duties in the No.2 Goods Link, in order to maintain his status, and his road knowledge. One of the most popular men was Albert Stuckey; he was the 'appointed person' who distributed the tea and sugar rations for manual workers. This practice of course continued for some years after the war had ended.

Locomotives coming on shed at the end of a period out at work required attention, in turn, from various grades. The fire droppers descended on a loco first. There

were no rocking grates (movable fire bars) or self-emptying ashpans on the Western in my day. The only way for the hot coals and ash to be removed was by the same way that it arrived, back through the firehole. A long handled metal shovel, an iron bar with a flattened end, known as a 'slice' (named somewhat ironically, one imagines, after a 'cake slice') and a long handled scraper were the tools. Repeatedly introduced into the firebox, as you might imagine, the handles became very hot. They had no company-issue gloves, only bits of cloth or sacking to hold on with; a fire dropper's hands became very hardened with the heat and consequently cracked and sore. It was a thankless task, and only the ever-present heaps of smouldering embers on the north side of the coal road bore mute testimony to their efforts.

Next attention for our locomotive was at the coal stage where the tender would be refilled by coalmen on the coal stage. Using only shovels, they would empty the wagons of coal into four wheeled tubs holding ten hundredweights each. The tubs would then be pushed on to ramps overlooking the tender. With a flick of the hand to release the catch on the front face of the tub and a strong heave to lift the back end, the coal would be dumped in the tender. They were one of the trades on shed to work at 'piecework' rates and were thus inclined to get frustrated if the empty wagons were not replaced by full ones quickly enough. The fire-droppers were paid in similar fashion and they too looked for an unending queue of locomotives to be moved to the 'fire pits' and their piles of ashes so that they could keep working. The area around the coal

stage was always very busy; noisy, dusty and dangerous at times. While the tender was being filled the 'ash men' would open up the smokebox door and clear the spent char which had collected. Left unattended this char would block the tubes. The tubes would be 'uncorked' if needed, using a pointed poker, and the tubes then blown through with a steam lance, connected up to a nozzle on the smokebox front, thus tapping the steam of the locomotive itself.

After stabling the locomotive would have a small fire lit in the back end of the firebox, ready for the fireman whose task was to prepare the fire and engine for its next turn of duty. These 'fire lighters' were easily recognisable from their 'flare' lamp carried on the coal pick and their unique 'framework of sticks' used to light the fire. These were produced in millions by apprentices all over the system, 'recycled' (though we didn't use the term then) from old planks – typically at the district wagon works. They consisted of lengths of old wagon planking (about 9in.) nailed together in an open box-like structure, which meant they caught fire very quickly and efficiently

The ashes and dross from the firebox and char from the smokebox would be regularly loaded on to empty metal loco coal wagons and taken away for ground fill and other railway purposes. An old Ruston Bucryus grab crane was kept for this work on a special road, laid alongside the ash road. There were many more, highly skilled grades too, principally the boilersmiths and coppersmiths who carried a whole host of jobs from boiler washouts, re-tubing the boilers and repairing leaking steam pipes on the footplate to creating, for a small consideration (a packet of Woodbines, say) a copper capped tea can! Add to the list the electricians, carpenters, storemen, the shed handyman/cleaner and not least the locomotive fitters and you have some idea of the kaleidoscope of trades and specialisms to be found at a big engine shed.

The locomotive fitters would repair any defect reported by a driver at the end of his shift. Many drivers had a favoured fitter, and I recall that Claude would send me chasing around the place to find Len Olver, later to become the shed foreman and, ultimately, the 'Shedmaster' in charge of the Diesel Depot. His fitters mate, a refugee from Europe during the war, was called Strudinsky, and known as Fitter Strud. I have never since come across a man with such strength; he would lift cast brake blocks and hold them in position for Len to hammer the securing pin in as though they were made of paper. I tried to lift one once and could just raise it from the ground; I can hear the laughter and comments of 'Strud' even now. Locomotive fitters were seldom able to carry out their work in comfort, and would have to do the job wherever the engine was stabled, often outside in rain or frost. I cannot recall ever hearing one complain though. Well not that much.

I've deliberately left till last the group of Laira men I know best – these of course are the men of the footplate. It is only possible to mention a relative few – there were hundreds of them after all. Early

from my cleaning days, I became aware of a driver at Laira by the name of Tom Cock. Tom was in the Top Link, and of course to me he was *Mister* Cock! A renowned engineman, he was 'great' in all senses of the word. My final driver at Laira was Jack Holway, who fired to Tom in the top link. It was from Jack that I learnt that, as a driver 'there was none better'. As a mate, Jack declared that 'he was all that I could have wished for when I needed help'. As a character, there was 'none to compare'. That, to me, would seem a perfect summing-up of a man great in build, great in nature, great in expertise. They appeared to us as giants, with names from a lost age; Walter Cooper, Len Amery, Edgar Stephens, Arthur Trethewey, Fred Newcombe, George Hammett, Joe Harris, Lou Underhill, Joe Endean, Bill Harris and countless more, all from the Top Link – 'the London men'. Robert (Bob) Wheatley, was one and I include a picture of him at Paddington station during the war, with his locomotive cab windows covered by a metal plate for the blackout. Bob's fireman at that time was a passed driver, Horace Carlyle.

Horace started his railway career at St Blazey shed as a cleaner boy. When his promotion came he was 'made' fireman for Laira and eventually, having passed his examinations for driver, was fortunately able to stay at Laira. While a driver there, Horace got a fireman called Bill Rundle. Bill, as we've heard, started cleaning at St Blazey, was 'made'

fireman for Laira, and eventually became a driver there too. I recall firing to Horace on one occasion and soon realised that he had a 'thing' about cleanliness. He was spotless himself, his overalls with nary a stain on them. He liked the footplate to be kept the same and used a page of a newspaper to line the cabside where he rested against it. His enginemanship almost caught me out. My brother Bill had often recounted how 'light' Horace was on the regulator and I did not fully realise his meaning until I was with him. I found myself on more than one occasion being seriously near to 'blacking' the fire out. As I explained in Chapter 7, coal should only be placed in the firebox on the top of fire; that is, coal that has burnt through. If a fireman 'overfired', coal would land on top of unburnt coal, creating a dead spot so far as heat was concerned. This was known as 'blacking' the fire out and led to falling steam pressure.

Horace's handling of regulator and the reversing lever was superb and he would always put a clean piece of white card (well, a cigarette packet) behind the sight glasses of the mechanical lubricator. He regularly checked and adjusted the oil flow to the cylinders depending on the speed and power. In the days that Bob and Horace were in the Top Link, there was no hostel at Oak Common for the lodging (termed 'double home' on the GW) crews and men were put up in homes round about, often those of railway widows. In their case it was 'Hilda's'. I have tried to find out more, but know only

The RCTS 'Plymouth District Tour', run in connection with the 'Brunel Centenarian' (Paddington-Saltash) on 2 May 1959, on the main line to the SR station at Friary. Four auto coaches sandwiched between 64XX pannier 6420. Much of the 'New Shed' and the coal stage, with its various wartime extensions and additions, is in full view. One of the first and unlamented D600 Warship Type 4s is in the yard and another is on the curving 'Speedway'. This formed a part of a triangle of lines whereby locomotives could be turned without the need of a turntable. It was used mainly by the engines stabling in the New Shed. The 'Mullet Pond' to the right. *Peter W. Gray.*

Laira shed in June 1960, a tank engine under the hoist. A Grange has been brought from the siding by the coal stage and is to be turned or transferred to the set of rails on the left to go off shed. A driver is in deep conversation with a shift foreman. The Hall and 53XX appear to have been 'prepared' and are in steam. Note the 'fire devil' beneath the gantry of the water column, ready to be lit up at the approach of winter frosts. *W. Potter.*

that the house was off Old Oak Common Road, fairly adjacent to the ramp leading down to the shed. Upon entering Hilda's a notice read 'remove your boots', and a notice board on the wall had instructions as to your room. Not by name but by turn of work. Thus it would state *Laira Men on 3.45pm. ex-Plymouth, use Room 6, after vacated by ? Men for the ?pm train to ?.* The ? of course would be actual shed names and train times. Imagine a fireman having sweated and slogged all of the way from Plymouth, via Bristol, perhaps, and having *to wait* to get into bed, *only just-vacated and the sheets not changed.*

I have mentioned my brother Bill at various times throughout this book. His reputation as a fireman was well deserved, though at times perhaps I could have done without being reminded of that fact. He served the railway until he retired, a driver in his own right who made the transition from steam to diesel. He does admit however, that there were occasions when he felt that he might have been better off making a change. If asked to come up with the 'highlight' of his career, I believe a particular firing turn might figure prominently. It was at the end of April 1964 that Bill received an instruction from the foreman that he keep the 9th of May 1964 clear for a very important roster. It seemed that *Railway World* magazine had come up with an idea to commemorate the exploits of Great Western 4-4-0 CITY OF TRURO sixty years earlier when the mail special had achieved a record speed down Wellington Bank. It was proposed to run three specials, hauled by selected Castles. The

first, behind 4079 PENDENNIS CASTLE would run from Paddington to Plymouth and the second, from Plymouth to Bristol, would be headed by 7029 CLUN CASTLE. 5054 EARL OF DUCIE would take the third, Bristol to Paddington. Reserve Castles would to be on 'stand-by' at selected places in case of emergency. Each crew was to consist of a driver and *two* firemen so you can see nothing was being left to chance. The Laira trio selected for 'our' special was made up of Driver Harry Roach (my brother's regular driver), Firemen W.L. Rundle and W. Watts. (I had done my cleaning with Bill Watts.)

The great day for the CITY OF TRURO Sixtieth Anniversary was to be Saturday 9th May 1964. Bill arrived for work that day to find that CLUN CASTLE had already been prepared for the trip, by none other than Inspector Harold Cook, a well known and highly respected officer. It seems that Inspector Cook had been at Laira for the best part of a week and had undertaken the whole of the preparation personally; examination, oiling (even new wicks in all the oil wells), fire building, trimming the tender and cleaning up the footplate. Some said that he had even slept on the locomotive, he was so concerned for the success of the great day. Joining Harold, he and the three-man crew made their way to the engine and met up with Inspector Cook, together with Jack James, the Chief Inspector, Mechanical and Electrical Engineering Dept. Paddington, and Norman Tovey, Mechanical Inspector, Paddington. I understand that the usual pleasantries were exchanged.

Upon climbing on to the footplate, Harry Roach was greeted by Inspector Cook with the information that 'all was in good order and that, *he had cleared out the tender of coal, and had had it replaced by specially selected Ogilvie coal, cracked up to the size of a man's fist and just right for shovelling.* This was unreal but not good enough for Driver Roach. He asked him to repeat the statement, only to inform Inspector Cook that he should *clear the Ogilvie out again* and mix it up with some dust: 'I won't take the engine off shed', he said. Presumably dumbfounded, the inspector looked at him, and asked something like: 'You don't mean that?'

Harry assured him that he did, adding, 'get it off and mix it, or we'll drop the firebars' and with that, the instruction was given. This turned out to be an inspired decision by Driver Roach, for it turned out that on the trip from Paddington, PENDENNIS CASTLE had failed at Edington, and the train had to change locomotives at Westbury. The cause? Dropped firebars, believe it or not, could melt and fail if a fire was 'too' hot. The selected coal proved 'too hot'. Fireman Godden, who was on PENDENNIS that day, blamed the state of the coal in their tender. CLUN CASTLE's run to Bristol on the other hand, was straightforward enough, given the special circumstances and at no time was the fireman extended beyond what might have expected from such a train. A tribute perhaps to the enginemanship of their Driver.

The *Railway World* account of the whole day came in the July 1964 edition, of which I am proud to have an original copy, with 7029 CLUN CASTLE featured on the cover at the head of the special, Z48 with its special bell code 4-1-4 ('Must Run Strictly to Time'). The report, by Cecil J. Allen, gave great credit to the achievement of the Laira crew. He reported that their work was 'brilliant', especially on the climb from Sampford Peverell to Whiteball. The entire run of 127.4 miles from Plymouth to Bristol took 128 minutes net, a clear gain of 15 minutes on the booked time and 'a triumph for both engine and crew'.

The often asked question is *did they do a ton?* Harry Roach was given all the usual notices of speed restrictions etc. when booking on, which would have included Whiteball to Taunton, and speeds of 100mph had been forbidden. Chief Inspector Andress was on the footplate and he had had overall control over the locomotive arrangements from the start. He had inspected some twelve locomotives (the remaining Castles were getting run-down by this time) before making the final selection. Standing as usual behind the driver for the early part of the journey, at Whiteball he altered position; CLUN CASTLE started downhill and, leaving the tunnel for the long run down to Wellington, Norton Fitzwarren and Taunton, Driver Roach closed the regulator and opened it up a little on to the 'drift' position to allow a little steam into the cylinders to act as a cushion for the pistons, and to keep the flow of lubricant moving. With that Inspector Andress moved to his side and, catching his eye, made a little 'upward' movement with his hand two or three times, a footplateman's signal for 'open

her up', before moving to the fireman's side of the footplate and looking out over the side. Harry looked at Bill, and with a characteristic forward thrust of his chin (a favourite action of his) nodded, and lifted the regulator upwards a fraction or two wider, and wound back the reversing lever. Best estimate of those on the footplate that day is that speeds of 96, 97 and then 98 were reached, until the need to apply the brakes around Norton, and the restriction of 80mph for Taunton, brought the adventure to a close

The mystery of the coal lingered in the minds of those involved; Old Oak Common men, Driver A. Perfect, Firemen D. Godden and D. Green and the crew from Bristol Bath Road, Driver F. Higby and Firemen R. Gitsham and C. Richards, got the *same* picked coal and instructions as the Laira men and it would not have been coincidence. The only logical explanation is that the Inspectors received the instruction to clear the tender and refill it from some person 'higher up', and whatever they might privately have thought, had to act upon it!

Laira, of course, was host to footplatemen from many other sheds, of which the furthest-flung was Old Oak Common, in London. Some of the Old Oak drivers, lodging on 'double homes' were very familiar, a few of whom I recalled from my days at Slough: Walter Harris, Charlie Brown, Percy Steer, Tommy Worth, Bill Bateman and, by no means least, Bert Potter, a regular driver of the Royal Train. Closer to home, there were any number of men every day from as far west as Penzance and from most points east; Bristol, Exeter and such places.

The aptly named Driver Leonard Rail,

of Penzance, was always ready to give me a lift from Saltash to Laira or return, if he was in the vicinity with a goods, especially when I had to be on an awkward night shift, or it was teeming with rain and I did not fancy a five mile bicycle ride, including the hazardous passage of the bridge.

Keeping a watchful eye on us at times were the footplate inspectors. Renowned in the London Division were Inspectors Andress and Price, who would turn up on 'special occasions'. At Laira we came under the Newton Abbot Division and Inspectors Bill Buttens and Varcoe, both very 'fair' men and railwaymen to the core, but one was always *concerned* if they had occasion to visit your footplate. Often though the true reason was nothing to do with the crew at the time, but the locomotive. A previous crew might have experienced difficulty when working her, and perhaps could not keep to the time schedule. Inspectors would then take a test run, and depending on their findings, the engine might well be 'shopped' for certain improvements to be carried out.

My last driver was Jack Holway, a 'character', in every sense of the word. Way ahead of his time, Jack was a 'mod' before the term had even been thought of. Every day was different working with him, and very often his mood determined his style of dress. At one time he had a passion for the American railroads, and regularly wore striped overalls with the US type of head gear. Certainly working with him was never dull but, above all, for a young driver, his enginemanship was without fault; I cannot recall a single bad trip with him. I was not really aware of it at the time, but firing to Jack gave one a sort of

Auto fitted pannier tank 6400 under the hoist with her trailing pair of wheels and connecting rods removed, 30 April 1961. *R.C. Riley/Transport Treasury.*

a reputation! In these later years when I visit various railway social clubs, I am often introduced with the comment 'He fired to Jack Holway'. That seems to have quite an effect, imparting near-celebrity status, and I get all sorts of queries as to what it was like with Jack, and then listen to their recollections of him. He was a very heavy pipe smoker and had a 'Sherlock Holmes' as he liked to call it, with some affection. The first time that I truly was aware of him was at Newton Abbot, on a return working waiting to assist a down express to Plymouth. When it ran in to the station, both Claude and myself were surprised (and a little shocked) to see that the engine was painted *blue*. The first blue King! On coupling up to the front end, the fireman, who was Jack Holway, asked if I liked the colour, and straight-facedly informed me that he personally had requested the paint job, *and if it caught on Swindon would re-paint the whole class!* A character, as I said, and I believe that they broke the mould after he was born.

I am well aware that these notes can make mention of only so many of the men at Laira, as well as a few of the visitors. This part of my story could be twice as long and still only touch the fringes; I have been fortunate, however, to have had access to some of the surviving roster and crew details of the Laira links. I've been able to include some details as appendices, and trust that most of the former Laira men who may read this book might find their names there. Those who are not, please forgive me.

The shed at Laira never slept. It was a 24 hour, 7 days a week, 365 days a year operation. Bank Holidays and festive celebrations made no difference, the trains still ran, and they needed locomotives to haul them. The quietest time of the whole day was probably the very early hours of the morning. The engines for the sleepers (the 'midnight' and so on) to London had disappeared and the loco which had brought it from Penzance was already on the coal road. The Millbay shunter was back on shed after dealing with 00.45 Penzance goods. An engine from Tavistock Junction, off a goods train, might amble in and come to halt at the coal road.

As the early hours unwound, the shed grew busy in various ways. Activity around the coal stage grew and night shift fitters were busy sorting out defects reported by drivers booking off the night before. The boiler washers were in action and the night shift cleaners would be busy making the early morning passenger locomotives gleam (probably singing while doing so). The fire lighters would be at work for the first engines of the day, as would the crews rostered on 'prepping'. The odd crew booked on to relieve another crew or to take an engine off shed for the 1.30 Bristol, 1.40 Penzance goods, 2.45 Newton Abbot or similar. From about 2am the pace would be quickening and crews would be turning up to book on for

the early Paddington service and the Penzance trains; the postal, papers, and parcels. The two crews for the Saltash autos would arrive, then the crew for the first passenger train up the branch to Tavistock and the goods which followed it and those for the pilots shunting Tavistock Junction (three) and Laira yards. Crews would appear for bankers and the transfer locomotives, and the early morning freights heading off both east and west.

Come the grey dawn the place would be absolutely 'buzzing', drivers hurrying to stores for oil, firemen searching high and low for shovels or fire irons, or simply fetching sand from the furnace to top up the sand boxes. This was a job in its own right, given the weight of sand and the distance to some engines. Flare lamps guttering and 'smeaching', pools of light from the anaemic yard lamps, blowers forcing fires bright; every type of activity came together to make sure that the trains ran. But of course the old shed had seen it all before. The early morning rush over, the tempo would slow down to a steady rate of comings and goings; crews booking on and off, locomotives arriving and departing.

The engine on the ash road crane would start with a cough and a blast of smoke and then settle to a steady chug-chug as the operator cleared the piles of ash and clinker into empty coal wagons. And as always the coal stage men would be complaining that they were waiting on

Saddle tank 1363 on the coal road, 30 April 1961, having finished her shift at the Millbay Docks. Her fire is being cleaned – note the fire dropper's shovel resting against the cab. On Great Western Locomotives all ash and clinker had to be cleared from the firebox the same way as it went in – through the firehole door. *R.C. Riley/Transport Treasury*.

full wagons, and their precious piece rate pay was suffering as a result. The shift foreman would be busy organising the 'spare' sets; perhaps a job on shed, or relieve a crew who were on long hours, or a last minute substitute for someone calling in sick. No chance of being bored here.

The Laira Links
No.1.Passenger Link. The senior link and home of the 'elite'. The enginemen were, of course, the most senior and the most experienced on the shed and were accordingly highly respected and 'looked up to'. The firemen were in many cases men who had 'passed' their examinations to become drivers themselves, and were just waiting for a suitable vacancy to arrive in a lower link. From there they would work there way up through the links all over again. At Laira the six most senior amongst them (I mentioned this quite a way earlier on in the book) would be temporarily promoted in the summer season to drivers in order to accommodate the additional burden of work. They would be placed in the junior link, the Pilot Link, and this would then allow for a move up of the senior six in every other of the links, both drivers and fireman. Of course at the end of the summer everyone reverted back again.

No.1 Passenger Link covered the 'double home' prestige work to London. This necessitated taking 'rest' (a minimum of eight hours) at Old Oak Common and then working the 225 miles back to Plymouth the following day. A modern hostel was eventually provided at Old Oak, replacing the private 'digs' round about, of the sort mentioned. The offerings of 'Hilda' and her ilk fell out of favour somewhat. Not everyone was enamoured of this type of work, with its constant separation from the family, but compensation came in the shape of enhanced payment. A days work was measured against the number of miles worked by the engine crew, and the excess was paid at a bonus rate (a type of 'piece' work really). As I recall, 150 miles constituted a 'day's pay', and a London trip paid something like 10 hours pay. Not bad one might think, but for both men it required much continuous concentration and effort. For the fireman came the additional problem that the further they went, the further he had to reach into the tender to get the coal. On the way home to Plymouth this meant that when tiredness started to tell and the coal was furthest away, he had his hardest work to do, on the South Devon banks. So yes, I always felt that the extra money was well earned. Of course not every day was 'double home', for to afford a bit of relief the London jobs were interspersed with workings to either Penzance and return, or to Exeter and Taunton.

No.2 Passenger Link. The Drivers 'learnt the road' from Plymouth to Taunton and Penzance. The workings of the link covered passenger, parcels and perishable trains including fast perishable freight to Bristol and (on double home lodging jobs) Westbury. Additional rosters included the branch passenger trains to Launceston and to Exmouth Junction over Southern metals. This latter was an interchange between the footplatemen of the Great Western at Laira and Exeter, and of the Southern Railway at Plymouth Friary and Exmouth Junction whereby each familiarised themselves with the 'opposition' line between Exeter and Plymouth. The reason was the regular breaching of the sea wall and consequent flooding of the Western track at Dawlish during extreme stormy weather. In that event, the Southern route, far inland, could be used instead. Quite high around Dartmoor, it in turn could be clocked by snow or storm, and accordingly the SR trains would use the GW route.

No.1 Goods Link. This was a bit of a misnomer for it covered passenger work as well as freight. The area of operations was Plymouth to Taunton and Truro, and to Launceston on the branch. The rosters also included spare turns to cover for specials, holidays, sickness and so on.

No.2 Goods Link. I have covered this in the general text; workings were similar to the No.1 Goods Link except that the drivers in No.2 learnt the road only between Plymouth and Newton Abbot and to Truro on the main line and to Tavistock on the branch.

Car Link. Worked the Saltash suburban railcar service ('the motors') with 54XX and 64XX pannier tanks. The service extended partly to Plympton in the east and to Liskeard and Doublebois to the west. The enginemen in this Link were 'regular' (they had elected to stay in it) but for the firemen it was a 'progressive link' and they were on their the way through to the upper links.

Transfer Link. As the name suggests, the work covered mainly the transfer of wagons around the various goods yards in the Plymouth area. Additional work included shunting at Millbay Docks, the Yealmpton and Sutton Harbour goods trains and relicving crews on rest days, shunting at either Millbay or North Road station.

Pilot Link. Covered the shunting turns in the three yards at Tavistock Junction and two yards at Laira; one turn at North Road. Additional work involved the Hemerdon banking (later transferred to No.2 Goods) and shed duties at Laira – turning, preparation, coal stage pilot.

In addition to the above regular links, there were crews stationed at Plymouth Millbay who covered the shunting duties at North Road station and Millbay. Two further sets of men were permanently based at Princetown. It is probably true to say that the measure of the prestige of an engine shed was the type and number of the locomotives stationed there. In this respect Laira counted among the premier sheds along with Old Oak Common, Bristol Bath Road; Cardiff Canton, Tyseley and Wolverhampton Stafford Road. The shed code LA carried on the framing behind the buffer beam in GWR days denoted the Laira engines; it was replaced after nationalisation by a small oval shaped plate mounted on the lower section of the smokebox door bearing the BR code 83D, changed to 84A in September 1963 when Stafford Road, 'owner' of that code, was closed. Laira closed in 1989; a glorious lifespan of some 88 years. In 1950 the allocation was:

King 4-6-0 (10)
6010 KING CHARLES,
6012 KING EDWARD V1,
6016 KING EDWARD V,
6022 KING EDWARD III,
6023 KING EDWARD II,
6024 KING EDWARD I,
6025 KING HENRY III,
6026 KING JOHN,
6027 KING RICHARD I,
6029 KING EDWARD VIII.

Castle 4-6-0 (18)
111 VISCOUNT CHURCHILL,
4032 QUEEN ALEXANDRA,
4087 CARDIGAN CASTLE,
4088 DARTMOUTH CASTLE,
4089 DONNINGTON CASTLE,
4097 KENILWORTH CASTLE,
5012 BERRY POMEROY CASTLE,
5021 WHITTINGTON CASTLE,
5023 BRECON CASTLE,
5026 CRICCIETH CASTLE,
5057 EARL WALDEGRAVE,
5058 EARL OF CLANCARTY,
5060 EARL OF BERKELEY,
5090 NEATH ABBEY,
5095 BARBURY CASTLE,
5098 CLIFFORD CASTLE,
7027 THORNBURY CASTLE,
7031 CROMWELL'S CASTLE

Star 4-6-0 (1)
4054 PRINCESS CHARLOTTE

County 4-6-0 (3)
1006 COUNTY OF CORNWALL,
1022 COUNTY OF NORTHAMPTON,
1023 COUNTY OF OXFORD.

Hall 4-6-0 (11)
4966 SHAKENHURST HALL,
4968 SHOTTON HALL,
4972 SAINT BRIDES HALL,
4992 CROSBY HALL,
5964 WOLSELEY HALL,
5998 TREVOR HALL,
6907 DAVENHAM HALL,
6913 LEVENS HALL,
6949 HABERFIELD HALL,
7905 FOWEY HALL,
7909 HEVENINGHAM HALL.

Grange 4-6-0 (3)
6949 WALTON GRANGE,
6855 SAIGHTON GRANGE,
6873 CARADOC GRANGE.

Manor 4-6-0 (4)
7801 ANTHONY MANOR,
7804 BAYDON MANOR,
7809 CHILDREY MANOR,
7814 FRINGFORD MANOR.

Fast Freight. 2-8-0 (1)
4703.

Heavy Freight 2-8-0 (3)
2875, 3832, 3864.

Freight/Passenger 2-6-0 (3)
5318, 5376, 6319.

WD 2-8-0 (2)
90148.

Large Prairie 2-6-2T (4)
5148, 3178, 3186, 3187.

0-4-2T (2)
1421, 1434.

Small Prairie 2-6-2T (12)
4407, 4409, 4517, 4518, 4524, 4528, 4542, 4583, 4591, 5540, 5567, 5569.

Auto-fitted Pannier Tank (8)
5412, 6406, 6407, 6414, 6417, 6419, 6420, 6421.

Pannier Tank (24)
1973, 1990, 2148, 3629, 3639, 3675, 3686, 3705, 3787, 3790, 4653, 4656, 4658, 4679, 4693, 7762, 8709, 8719, 9671, 9673, 9711, 9716, 8765, 9770.

Saddle Tank (Docks) (4)
1361, 1363, 1364, 1365.
2251 0-6-0 (1)
2258.

The GWR engine shed at Laira was in fact the third to be constructed in the city. The first had been at Millbay, built around 1850 by the former South Devon Railway. It stood on the up side of the line above Millbay station, just south of Cornwall Junction. It seems to have been known as Harwell Street, which was on the down side of the railway; a substantial carriage shed was also put up here. The Great Western added a second, timber building with four roads in the mid-1880s and at the same time updated and improved the whole shed. At some time later the name appears to have changed to 'Belmont' which was much more appropriate as the sheds and sidings were adjacent to that street, rather than Harwell Street. This shed was to remain in operation until 1931, when all the locomotives were transferred to the new depot at Laira.

There was another shed, a little single road stone built affair, within Millbay Docks, adjacent to the southern end of the Inner Basin and to the approach lines entering the docks from Millbay. I regret that I have been unable to ascertain the date of construction, but it was certainly there when I worked the 'dockie' with Tren, though it did not seem to be in use, at least for locomotives.

Driver Harry Roach preparing an engine for a special banker job at Tavistock Junction (see page 22 for instance).

April 1962 and 5024 CAREW CASTLE (Newton Abbot), 5065 NEWPORT CASTLE (Old Oak Common) and 1004 COUNTY OF SOMERSET (Wolverhampton). *Terry Nicholls.*

My big brother Bill, holding up an unidentified Castle on the coal stage road at Laira. The Castle has had its firebox cleaned, it's coaled up and the smokebox was being cleared of char, in readiness for placing on shed for its next job.

Small prairie 4552 shunting Moorswater sidings on the Looe branch in July 1960. The box wagons mark the spot where we were held with the cattle wagons from the final Looe Cattle Market. *R.C. Riley/Transport Treasury*.

The bucolic view (from above Saltash Passage) across the River Tamar from the Plymouth side, to Coombe by Saltash viaduct on 13 April 1952. Of interest is that area of land showing whitish in the top left-hand corner, a section of market garden where my father was the head gardener. The whole of those fields, including the garden, has been developed and no green land now exists. *R.E. Vincent/Transport Treasury*.

The Royal Albert Bridge viewed from above Coombe Creek, 14 April 1952. An up passenger train has crossed to the Devon side, the boundary between Cornwall and Devon lying the middle of the channel. The high ground immediately behind the train hides a warren of tunnels and chambers which housed ordnance for the Royal Navy's warships. It was said that if the area exploded it would take out not only half of Plymouth but Saltash as well! *R.E. Vincent/Transport Treasury*.

CHAPTER 16
Saltash

Once I moved back to Saltash with my family to live, travelling to Laira to work, I found myself daily involved with the staff at the station and the workings of the place. Even before that, in our courting days, we were befriended by a lovely lady called Mrs Moore who managed the Wymans bookstall on the station. Going to Plymouth for shopping, or St Budeaux for the latest film at the *State Cinema*, we would always have a chat with her and exchange the very precious coupons from our ration books, for sweets and a morsel of chocolate. I am sure that at times we were given something extra to our allowance. We also remember her gift to us of a very lovely wedding present.

My first experience of the station as a railwayman had come back in the spring of 1945 when, as a lad porter at Devonport, I'd been 'loaned out' by the station master there to Saltash for 'temporary duty'. This turned out to be a week in the goods yard; I had to report to Ted Lewis, and was to assist with the additional work brought about by the seasonal flower traffic. During the early spring, the market gardeners in the Tamar Valley would send untold boxes of freshly cut flowers, by rail, to various destinations in London and the Midlands. They were either delivered direct to Saltash by the producers or collected by GW lorry; the traffic was immense and brought in a considerable revenue. At the height of the season a parcels van would be coupled up to the auto train at North Road station and brought to Saltash, to be placed in the goods yard and brought out on to the up platform whenever a clear opportunity permitted. There duly ensued a frenzy of loading until the signalman shouted of the need to clear the track for an approaching train. Whenever possible the auto train, with its two coaches, would be utilised to propel the van back into the sidings until another clear period arose; this was quite routine, for it shunted a couple of milk trains in the same way on a daily basis. When it was not available porters used 'pinch bars' to manoeuvre wagons. This was hard work and if a GW delivery lorry turned up, that would be pressed into service, using a tow rope. Thankfully the suburban service was so frequent that there was never an undue period when an auto was *not* at Saltash, so resorting to these measures was rare.

While all this went on there was no rest, for all the boxes had to be recorded, weighed, stamped and ticketed with destination label and then loaded onto platform trolleys to await loading. They were very busy and tiring days, only relieved by the chance to go out on the lorry with Driver Bill Hingston and to assist him with the loading and unloading. During this time, my station master at Devonport, Charles Devonshire, became responsible for Saltash as well and when he retired he was succeeded by Geoff Axford. I recall Jack Staddon, Bill Stanton and Roy Morris as porters on the station. In the ticket office were booking clerks Jim Lewis, Clifford Stephens and Ken Nodder; Reg Roberts was the ticket collector. I have no doubt that there were others, and to them I offer my apologies for the omission.

We lived at that time in a flat on Fore Street Hill and live in that road still, and though it has since been renamed 'Lower Fore Street', we have the magnificent sight of the Royal Albert Bridge whenever we look out of our window. Every time I'm reminded of edging my way across that bridge to get to work during the night time, and the regular drenchings (see Chapter 13). As mentioned then, there was of course no road bridge in those days and our ferry across the Tamar stopped at eleven or so. If I was on duty in the small hours of the morning, I would cycle to the station, see the signalman on duty, and let him know I was crossing over. This was downright illegal but in all cases Allan Wingett, Tom Bunker or Alf Freeman were happy to conspire with me. They'd let me know if there was a suitable goods to hand and I'd drop the bike by the box and 'hitch a ride' to Laira. Otherwise

7823 HOOK NORTON MANOR runs through the now closed and increasingly derelict Defiance Platform in July 1957, with a up passenger train. The trees on the skyline surround the 'House on the Hill' where my father was gardener, and my parents lived in a bungalow behind the trees to the left. *R.E. Vincent/Transport Treasury.*

it was a matter of cycling across and running the gauntlet of cab-washing firemen! Cycling across, I'd give a shout so that the bobby at Royal Albert Bridge box, having got the nod from Saltash, knew I was safely across, though what they'd have done if I didn't appear I can't think. One of the signalman there was a Saltash lad, Martin Dennis, whose father was also a railwayman.

Joyce and I married in 1951, and for a time rented a room in the house in Lipson Vale where I had lodged as a single man. Almost a year after, I requested special permission from the authorities to live at Saltash. At that time it was generally a requirement of the Locomotive Department that footplate crews should live within a mile radius of the shed. Permission was granted and we duly set up home in the lower part of Fore Street, close to Brunel's famous bridge. A little way below us, immediately adjacent to the bridge, lived a lady called Mrs Penfound, who was very ill with tuberculosis. She had to spend all her time in bed, and this she had moved in front of the window, so she could see, amongst other things the trains travelling up and down. Laira men and others from St Blazey, Truro and Penzance came to know this and most times when working a train across the bridge would blow the whistle by day or shine the gauge glass lamp at night to let her know that they were thinking of her. Each whistle or shining lamp was always acknowledged by a wave or the flashing of her torch. At each shed a collection took place before Christmas and a bouquet of flowers and perhaps a small gift taken to her. There was some considerable sense of loss felt by the crews when she finally died. We had lost a friend.

At the top of the hill, now called Lower Fore Street, in Saltash is an old-fashioned grocery shop now turned into a museum piece. In its working heyday it was run by twin brothers by the name of Elliott, and it stocked every imaginable sort of comestible, displayed and served almost as it was in Victorian times. Frank Elliot undertook most of the running of the shop, while brother Harry, who was a qualified pharmacist, travelled daily to Plympton on the eastern outskirts of Plymouth to work. His train was the 7.50am, one of the local suburban services which extended at peak travel times to Plympton instead of terminating at Plymouth North Road. Harry would always delay leaving the shop to catch the train until the last possible moment, and then could regularly be observed running at full pelt past the Guildhall and Saint Nicholas & Faith Parish Church, haring around the corner by the old Police Station – almost hopping on one foot – to arrive at the station. Here, without pause, he would dash straight into the carriage and sit down as though nothing at all untoward had occurred. It is said that he did not even seem out of breath. The station staff would smile; the fireman always had the brake 'blown off' and the reversing lever wound ready for the off. The staff to let

the train across the bridge was ready in the signalman's hand and being passed to the fireman on the engine, and the driver in the vestibule of the leading railcar would revert to his seat. Right away could be safely given and the whole scene reverted to normal. It is said that he *never* missed the train.

Saltash station was bounded by two bridges. To the east of course is Brunel's Royal Albert Bridge, magnificent and regal in design; spanning the River Tamar between Devon and Cornwall, the bridge gives the impression that it was ever there – as old as the land itself. Much has been written with regard to the history and construction and a multitude of photographers have recorded it from all angles. As a fireman my greatest concern (so great was it, I've expressed it several times in this book – an indication of how it haunted me) so far as the bridge was concerned was to ensure that I caught and collected that darn single line token, 'the staff'. To miss it was mortifying; to suffer the humiliation of stopping the train and trudging back to collect it, pink at the neck with embarrassment, unthinkable.

The second bridge at Saltash stands immediately at the western end of the platform, and carries Culver Road over the railway. Both bridges have had replacement work at times during their long lives and in each case the work could be undertaken in a spectacular manner.

The Culver Road bridge to the west was originally of stone construction, and, because Culver Road was there before the station was built, it restricted the length of the up platform. With locomotives of ever greater power and trains ever longer, together with the increasing number of trains using the station, it was decided in 1906 that the platform should be extended to the west. This meant demolishing the stone arched road bridge and replacing it by one of steel girder construction, with a greater span. This would then permit the up platform to be lengthened westwards. I have been unable to ascertain the actual dates on which the work was carried out, nor the total costs involved. I do know the contractors were a local firm, Relph & Son, and that the foreman in charge of the work was Emmanuel Davy, a forebear of Andrew Barrett, the present chairman of Saltash Heritage, to whom I am indebted for the information. For the demolition of the original bridge, some 50 tons of timber was laid upon the line to protect it from falling masonry; a formidable charge of nitro-glycerine brought down an estimated 150 tons of stone, much of which was salvaged to make the abutments for the new steel girders to rest upon.

One of the regular inspections of the Royal Albert Bridge revealed in 1927/28 that the land span girders had deteriorated and needed replacement. Engineers devised a special piece of apparatus (shades of the manner in which the cantilevers were placed on to the outside of the present Tamar road bridge) which transported a section of new girder to the site, lifted the old girders and

moved them sideways two feet, and then placed the new sections in place, all in one operation. The replacement of the seven approach spans on the Devon side was undertaken by some fifty men working on Sundays April-July 1928. The eight Cornish spans were dealt with September 1928-January 1929. My driver in the No.2 Goods Link, Claude Bolt, once told me that when he was a fireman, one of his drivers recalled working a couple of the Sundays on the locomotive used to propel the spans to and from the bridge.

There was a third bridge, Coombe-by-Saltash viaduct, situated immediately to the west of the station. It spanned Coombe Creek which was the natural boundary between the Parishes of Saltash and St Stephens. The original viaduct was constructed in 1859, part of the final section of the line between Truro and Saltash. Completion between St Germans and Saltash had been held up for almost a year, through some of the viaducts awaiting completion. The first viaduct at Coombe had spans at 64ft. 6ins. centres. It was rebuilt in masonry in 1893, with the new structure erected alongside the existing one. At some stage in its life the viaduct acquired a 'footbridge' attached to the up side. Made of iron support work, secured into the viaduct itself, it carried a sleeper laid walkway approximately six feet in width with a high railing safety barrier on the outer edge. At each end access was through a 'kissing-gate'. Although constructed and maintained by the railway, it became recognised as a 'public' path to connect at the western end with the path to the quay and houses at Wearde on the River Lynher, the two houses at Coombe Green and the 'House on the Hill' which, until latter years, had extensive market gardens stretching down to Coombe. Thereby was a connection between myself and the viaduct.

In 1945 my father was appointed the gardener for the House on the Hill, and we moved as a family from our previous home on the western outskirts of St Austell to live in a small wooden bungalow adjacent to the 'big house' as we came to know it. I have some fond memories of the viaduct. Firstly, of our courting days when, wishing my future wife Joyce 'goodnight' on the far side of the town (she lived right by the Royal Albert Bridge, and just a little way up the hill from our present home) we would, without fail, prolong the moment of parting and make myself late for getting home (parents were strict in those days). I used to run all the way and across that bridge. It never occurred to me that the sleepers made quite an echo with the 'thumping' of my feet pounding across them. It could be heard a mile away, and most certainly by my parents in the bungalow at the top of the adjacent fields. At the top of the garden I would pause for a moment to catch my breath and then walk in as though nothing was amiss, and wonder why they were smiling!

After our daughter Sue was born we purchased a very 'up-market' 'Swan' pram. It was massive and poor Sue often looked lost in it. The problem arose with negotiating the kissing-gates. They were not designed to accommodate prams, and we had to lift it over the top, and at the same time attempt to move the swing portion so the Joyce could get through. Joyce is not very tall, and she found it difficult to lift the pram, with its 12 inch wheels, over the gate, and at times feelings could get a bit high. We had to repeat the process once more at the far end, and again twice on the way home.

The market garden had its attractions... The area was set out in plots which ran lengthways up and down the garden and they were divided, in the main, by soft fruit; raspberry canes, gooseberry bushes and apple trees. The latter were of especially good quality and flavour. It was most noticeable at weekends and especially on a Sunday afternoon, that after the Plymouth railcar arrived (we could see the station from our bungalow) young people would appear, crossing the viaduct with the sole intention of pinching the produce. This was serious scrumping. Mr Gerry, the owner of the gardens, was outraged and quietly suggested that dad should do something about it. In his spare time my father was a 'special constable' with the Cornwall Police Force and, after discussing the scrumping problem with the station sergeant a solution was arrived at. As soon as the miscreants were seen upon the footbridge, dad would call the Police station and a constable would be despatched to the end of the viaduct. Simultaneously, dad, and if I was home, I

would accompany him, would walk down towards the garden and confront the fruit thieves. They would take flight back across the walkway to where the constable was waiting; trapped. By this time we were on our end of the walkway, and they had nowhere to go. They would be made to empty out their pockets and in some cases bags, given a stern, if not faintly terrifying lecture by the constable who also took their names and addresses. Then they were sent back on their way. It was a sign of those days that mostly the admonishment had the desired effect, and after a time the raids ceased altogether.

Finally, it is only too noticeable that the other two bridges, the Royal Albert and the road bridge, are looking a little neglected at this present time. In 2009 we shall be celebrating another anniversary of the Royal Albert Bridge. 150 years! Perhaps those responsible will give their own Birthday Present – A Coat of Paint.

****

At the beginning of this chapter I mentioned being sent, as a lad porter, to Saltash to assist with the seasonal flower traffic. It was not until I arrived there that I realised that the station dealt with a considerable trade in fruit too. I recollect being instructed one Thursday afternoon to board the motor train which arrived at 1.30pm. The train was being extended to Wearde, approximately one mile to the west, there to load up a consignment of strawberries from the

local market gardens. It was impressed upon me that the task was to be carried out at all speed as the train was due to depart from Saltash once more at just before 2pm. I was astonished at the number of 'ponnets' of strawberries which were to be loaded, but we achieved the task in time and the train was not delayed. The 'station' at Wearde was known at that time as Defiance Platform, and had originally been Defiance Halt. It was named after H.M.S Defiance, the Royal Navy Training Establishment moored below Wearde in the River Lynher. The Establishment carried a complement of about 800 officers and ratings, who were trained in torpedo and wireless operation. It was felt that they would benefit from a railway connection close by, and an approach was made to the Great Western. The first halt was on the line of the former Cornwall Railway, running along the hillside above the River Lynher and Wearde Quay. It has been said that the halt was built by the sailors of HMS Defiance to a design provided by the Great Western, but I have not been able to confirm that. Even the opening date is not recorded, but was given the name Defiance 'Platform' instead of 'Halt'. It was used by the local residents as well as the Navy and was mostly served by the local auto trains. At one time there were eleven trains stopping every day and the unusual preponderance of 'pagoda' style shelters was to segregate the officers from the 'lower ranks' and the general public from both!

The Royal train brought Her Majesty, Queen Elizabeth II and the Duke of Edinburgh to Saltash station on 25 July 1962, at the start of a tour of the Duchy of Cornwall estates. Her first visit was to be to a local tenant farmer, Mr Roberts, just a couple of miles outside Saltash, at Landulph. This photograph shows the frontage of the station bedecked for the occasion, with the local dignitaries arriving, to be presented to Her Majesty.

The up platform at Saltash with a flurry of activity as the Royal Train approaches. In the entrance, wearing his Chain of Office, is the Mayor of Saltash, Councillor (now Sir) Vernon Seccombe J.P. along with Mrs (Lady) Margaret Seccombe, and the Town Sergeant.

The Royal Party arrive, and Her Majesty is shaking hands with Sir Douglas Marshall, the Member of Parliament for East Cornwall. Also in the picture, right to left: Mr J.B. Stainer, Duchy of Cornwall Land Steward, His Royal Highness Prince Philip, Mrs Margaret Seccombe, Councillor Maurice Huggins, the Mayor (hidden by Her Majesty), Mr Gordon Bellingham, Town Clerk of Saltash, Mrs Muriel Bellingham and, extreme right, Mrs Suzanne Marshall.

Saltash station from Culver Road, on 14 September 1952. The two onlookers are clearly interested in the passenger train crossing the Royal Albert Bridge towards Plymouth. From the left is the road to the station forecourt, station buildings on the up platform, the footbridge, Royal Albert Bridge, the terrace of houses adjacent to the down platform and the top of the water tank on the down platform. *R.E. Vincent/Transport Treasury.*

Pannier 6414 propels a two coach auto into the down platform at Saltash from Plymouth on 13 July 1956. The fireman has just 'hung up' the staff which can be seen still swinging on the 'bull horn'. When the timetable called for an immediate turn around, the train would leave from the same platform, hence the need for the additional 'starter signal' at the end of the platform. *R.C. Riley/Transport Treasury.*

Royal Albert Bridge Repairs 1. December 1927, and a view looking west through the centre spans. The simplicity, yet magnificence, of the structure can readily be appreciated. Note the additional cross bracing fitted in 1905, as well as the pipe on the left of the decking, bringing drinking water across from Plymouth to Saltash. Of note, too, are the rounded tops on the spans; these are originals which exist still at this present day. They have never been renewed, unlike the land spans.

Royal Albert Bridge Repairs 2. An unusual view of a section of one of the tubes, showing the fixing of a main truss and the cross bracing struts. The chains and rope hawsers were essential for safe working when hoisting materials and so on.

Royal Albert Bridge Repairs 3. Replacement of land spans at the eastern end, 1928. A special wagon was constructed, with cross beams on which the replacement sections were taken to their intended position. The old sections were unpinned and slung outwards on the cross beams to permit the new sections to be dropped in place. This photograph shows a new section in place, with the originals slung to the outside.

Royal Albert Bridge Repairs 4. Replacement of land spans, July 1928, and the special wagon with its cross girders. The old girders have been slung to the outside and the new ones are being placed in position. Once that is done, the wagon will be prepared for the journey back off the bridge, carrying the old sections.

Royal Albert Bridge Repairs 5. A 45XX small prairie tank coupled to the special wagon, with the old section (note the rounded top plate – the replacement has flat top plate) being carefully removed under the watchful eye of one of the workmen.

Royal Albert Bridge Repairs 6. A view from the eastern pier in June 1928. A section of old girder has been slung out on each side and the new girders are being prepared to replace them. The difference in the shape of the tops can readily be seen in the lower part of the picture.

Royal Albert Bridge Repairs 7. It is 28 November 1928 and the engineers pose for a 'Job Well Done!'

A scene well known to my wife Joyce and myself, for this is where we walked when we were courting! This is Babis Lane, Saltash, in September 1949, with Coombe by Saltash viaduct framing the River Tamar, a ferry nicely positioned in the left-hand arch. The Devon span of the Royal Albert Bridge just shows above the viaduct. *R.E. Vincent/Transport Treasury*.

A lone seagull swoops over the Saltash Ferry, crossing towards the Devon shore in April 1952. The engineroom man has stoked the fire up to produce a dense smoke from the chimney – something that was unlikely to be appreciated by those passengers riding outside on the upper deck! *R.E. Vincent/Transport Treasury. R.E. Vincent/Transport Treasury.*

Royal Albert Bridge and Saltash station – conversion from broad gauge 7ft 0¼ in. to standard gauge 4ft 8½ in. during 17-20 May 1892. *Saltash Heritage Museum.*

6911 HOLKER HALL approaching Wearde box with the up 8.05am Newquay-Paddington on 13 July 1957. HOLKER HALL will come off the train at Plymouth North Road and a King or Castle will take over for the run to London. The train has just crossed Forder viaduct, overlooked by Trematon Castle and House above. *R.E. Vincent/Transport Treasury*.

7925 WESTOLL HALL with a Liverpool-Penzance train has now cleared the speed restrictions for Saltash and the Royal Albert Bridge and is picking up speed for the run to the first stop at Liskeard, 13 July 1957. The location is the eastern end of the former Defiance Platform with Wearde loop (the old Cornwall Railway line) alongside. *R.E. Vincent/Transport Treasury*.

6803 BUCKLEBURY GRANGE at milepost 252 near Wearde signal box, 19 April 1949; the carriages are very much 'of their time'. The fireman has the right-hand injector on to place water into the boiler, but it seems to be in need of a little attention as it is not 'picking up' properly. The footpath to the left ran from Forder to Wearde, and was a private railway-owned path at that time. *R.E. Vincent/Transport Treasury.*

1006 COUNTY OF CORNWALL between Wearde and Shillingham tunnel, 18 April 1949. On home ground and in full flow, 1006 heads a down express on the final stretch before the tunnel. She is still in her original form with single chimney. Their draughting and steaming was improved with the introduction of a double blast pipe and chimney. *R.E. Vincent/Transport Treasury.*

The Saltash Corporation steam ferry, en route from Saltash Passage on the Devon side to Saltash on the Cornish shore, April 1952. Last vehicle on the ferry is a milk lorry with its traditional churns, destined for Daws Creameries on the opposite side of the road from the large white roofed building under the western span of the bridge. That building was formerly Bennets & Palmers Store but was converted to a vehicle repairers - SALTASH GARAGES L^{TD} on the roof could be read for miles. *R.E. Vincent/Transport Treasury.*

Coombe by Saltash viaduct on 25 June 1955, with a 42XX 2-8-0T (almost certainly from St Blazey shed) crossing with what appears to be a train of clay empties. These could be from Ponts Mill at Fowey, destined for Lee Moor Works at the east end of Plymouth. Of interest is the spare Saltash ferry berthed on the 'groynes' on the Plymouth shore, probably for maintenance and repair. *R.E. Vincent/Transport Treasury.*

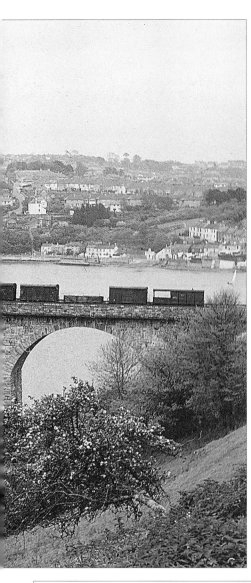

Left. Coombe by Saltash viaduct on 15 May 1954, with a Hall on an up goods, approaching Saltash station. The home signal is 'off' and indicates that in all probability the train has a clear run across the Royal Albert Bridge. The fireman will be thinking about collecting the single line token (the staff) from the signalman or, more to the point, not missing it. The footbridge clinging to the side of the viaduct was installed and maintained by the railway and over the years had become an informally 'private' access and shortcut for the residents of Coombe Green, Wearde and the 'House on the Hill', avoiding a longish detour. *R.E. Vincent/Transport Treasury.*

Bottom left. Through one of the arches of Coombe by Saltash viaduct on 14 April 1952, framing its illustrious big brother. Note that the Royal Albert Bridge has been painted a dark grey. I believe that this only happened on one occasion and that subsequent repaints returned to the lighter shade. I am reliably informed by my wife, Joyce, that at one time it was possible to cross Coombe Creek on foot at low water. Alas not now, the creek is sadly silting up with thick mud. *R.E. Vincent/Transport Treasury.*

Below. Coombe by Saltash viaduct on 15 May 1954, with what looks like a Grange on a down goods. A person in a light-coloured coat can just be seen approaching the kissing gate on the left end, at the beginning of the slope up to the walkway. It just *could* be my mother, returning from shopping... *R.E. Vincent/Transport Treasury.*

6863 DOLHYWEL GRANGE and 7022 HEREFORD CASTLE at home outside New Shed. The Grange is in BR black which, though not liked at the start, seemed to suit the class fairly well. The paintwork of both locomotives have that distinctive appearance which comes from cleaning with an oily wad of cotton waste. *Terry Nicholls.*

6008 KING JAMES II and 6013 KING HENRY VIII with the second part of the down Cornish Riviera Express, at Stoneycombe sidings on 19 July 1958. The leading King would have brought the first part from Paddington to Newton Abbot where it would have handed over to a pair of Cornish locomotives for the remainder of the journey. It would then have waited for the second part, and coupled up to assist over the Devon banks. Although not all that popular with the crews, it gave a chance for a sight and sound of two Kings working in unison, something that is unlikely to be repeated. *R.C. Riley/Transport Treasury.*

CHAPTER 17
Conclusions

The question is sometimes asked: 'who was actually of most importance on the railway? Well, the guard often gave the impression that he was. After all he was 'in' the train and could be aware of all that was going on; he waved flags to start trains. Yet he could wave his green flag for all he was worth, that did not mean that the train would move. The driver then? but again he could not move the train until a signal that cleared the road ahead was pulled off. So was it the signalman, the 'bobby'? He was in the same position as the guard; he could pull signals as much as he liked but that would not move a train. So the driver it is! But wait, he could not move a train unless there was a track for the train to run on. So it was the ganger and his happy band of men. They had nothing to do with moving a train but were none the less vital to the operation of a railway. The truth was that, on the great Western, as on all the other companies, we were all as important as one another. It needed all of us working together in unison. A team, each one of us doing our own thing and to the best of our ability; equal in responsibility and skill at our job – running a railway!

The section of line between Plymouth and Saltash was at one time as busy as any part of the Great Western. The Saltash suburban service, as it was advertised, ran over thirty rail motor cars ('autos' as we called them) between North Road and Saltash, with occasional extensions to Plympton in the east and to St Germans and Liskeard westwards. On a Saturday night the last 'auto', the 11.18pm. from North Road, extended to Doublebois arriving at ten minutes after midnight. The return journey was as empty stock (there are tales of late night revellers hitching a lift) terminating at Laira sidings just before 1am.

In addition at night there were the postal, milk, newspapers, parcels and through and stopping passenger services, making up more than thirty trains in their own right in and out of Cornwall together with perhaps 10-12 freight trains. It can be appreciated that the timing of trains over the single line of the Royal Albert Bridge was critical and, at times, could give the district controller quite a few problems – hence my dread of dropping the staff. And then, in the season, came the Cornish new potatoes and broccoli, the flowers, fruit and so on to add to the congestion. Somehow it all worked. How, no one really could say. Possibly with a great deal of good fortune, but I like to think it was because all of us, signalmen, controllers, station masters, inspectors, porters, footplate crews and all the rest, had a *Pride in the Job*. We were Railwaymen. And so it was over the entire GW system and I am sure, although it could never be admitted, it was true of the 'other' railways too!

Life on the footplate could never be called 'humdrum', for no two days were ever the same. Locomotives differed in their condition, the coal in the tender, the state of the fire. Some were free steaming while others could be 'difficult'. The job to be done differed. At Laira it ranged from the 'lowly' shunting turns, to adventures over the banks to Newton Abbot, Exeter, Taunton, Bristol or London. There was so much variety; the branches to Yealmpton, Tavistock and Launceston, and to Princetown, local work in Millbay and the docks, Sutton Harbour and transfers/banking on Hemerdon. We worked the auto passenger trains from *everywhere* to destinations on the main line, and in the summer connected with services to Looe, Newquay and Falmouth.

Emergencies would occur, and when 'spare' on shed, helping to 'prep' an engine in a hurry, assisting the turners, or just sitting in the enginemens cabin, waiting, praying even, for a job to relieve the

6019 KING HENRY V with the down Cornish Riviera Express passing Lipson Junction on 4 July 1957. Laira roundhouse and coal stage down the embankment on the right; goods loops in between. Over 220 miles after leaving Paddington, the crew of 6019 have just to run up to Mutley tunnel and then drop down into Plymouth North Road Station. *R.C. Riley/Transport Treasury.*

boredom, you could suddenly be told to grab your things, hop on a footplate and sent who knows where. The short experiment in oil-burning came and went and I had one experience of firing an engine so equipped. At first it seemed straightforward – just twiddle a wheel or shift a lever but somehow, at the end of the day it did not feel right for me. To sit on a padded seat was relative luxury but I was not used to that, and not having to wield a shovel felt unnatural. Impressed as I was in some respects, I recall saying to my driver at the end of our shift *that it wasn't for me*. We were glad when the oil project floundered.

To arrive on shed on a summer day was usually a delight, with gleaming engines; dry underfoot even if, sometimes, it was too sunny. Sweat would be running off your back, and the dust blowing in your eyes as you prepared your engine. Then you would hope for a shower of rain to cool and damp things down a little. But, to arrive on a cold and wet winter day, with everything dull and dreary, was to find the ground beneath your feet almost a quagmire of sodden ash and coal dust. Everything you touched would be filthy, and rain water dripped down your neck when trimming the tender. Then you yearned for a that warm summer's day again. It was no good, the circumstances were never right! And yet; and yet, afterwards it did not seem to matter. It was a part of The Job.

To start the day on one of those locomotives was to forget all the bad times; the trick was to concentrate on the trip ahead. Which, of course, was going to

be the finest train work ever. Once that signal came off for the passage off shed, you were committed to the task in hand, to be done to the best of your ability.

Locomotives on the Great Western owed everything to their lineage. The early designs of Gooch and Dean were afterwards developed into the modern era by Churchward and Collett. From the Saints and Stars came the familiar Halls and the magnificent Castles and Kings. John Keeble, a well known writer of hymns, had in a way immortalised the 'Saint' class in his *Word Supreme Beyond Creation*. In its first verse comes the following phrase: *Well Thy Saints Have Kept Their Station*. Can this mean that there are great Western locomotives, even in Heaven? and if so, might I have the privilege to meet again my former colleagues, and to make steam with them once more on the *Heavenly Railway?*

****

Circumstances, or fate, determined that my career on the footplate was to be shorter than most. The need to live in Saltash had itself created difficulties; long hours meant that less and less time could be spent with my wife and young daughter. At the same time we were sadly witnessing the demise of the steam age; our locomotives, in which we took so much pride, were becoming run down and scruffy. So it was that in 1962 I decided to leave the railway and try my hand at something different. It was a very hard decision to make at the time, with many sleepless nights and much heart

searching, but it was the right choice, and once done I had no regrets. And yet, and yet... although I did very well for myself after obtaining qualifications in highway engineering and maintenance with the Cornwall County Highways Department and afterwards as a Technical Officer with the local Caradon District Council, I will never forget those days.

Above. 6873 CARADOC GRANGE on an up passenger train and 5003 LULWORTH CASTLE with a down 'special', about to pass each other on St Pinnock viaduct, 6 July 1955. The former Cornwall Railway had an interesting rule concerning 'trains meeting' – see text. R.C. Riley/Transport Treasury.

Right. **Laira shed, east end, 17 April 1958 and 6419 might be ready to go off shed to the up sidings to collect her auto carriages, though normally these engines left with bunkers piled as high with coal as safety would permit. A 46XX pannier is on coal stage duty. Six wagons were normally up at one shunt; the position of the engine suggests that three have already been unloaded and the next three are getting emptied out. The coal stage men were paid at a 'piece-work' rate so that soon they will be shouting for the replacements. W. Potter.**

Laira on 27 August 1961, 'dockie' 1363 on the coal stage. The little saddle tanks needed a good run from the back of the shunting spur to push a full half dozen wagons up the incline. When I was on the duty with one of them, my driver generally kept to three at a time. A Laira engine, 6873 CARADOC GRANGE stands in the sidings. Smoke is coming from the chimney, but by the look of the tender which is still piled high, I'd say the firelighter has just 'lit her up'. *R.C. Riley/Transport Treasury*.

The east end at Laira, 15 July 1958. 1434 is full of steam as she waits in the siding for the crew, to go off shed. Auto fitted, her next turn of duty is probably to work the Tavistock branch passenger from North Road Station. A 94XX 0-6-0PT is on coal stage duty. *R.C. Riley/Transport Treasury*.

Laira's oil-burning Hall 3955 (formerly 6949) HABERFIELD HALL in the 'intermediate' sidings in June 1947. Converted to oil in May 1947, she was restored to coal in April 1949. The short-lived oil-burning fiasco commenced in 1946 and was over after a couple of years. I only worked on such an engine one time, and although it was cleaner and the fireman had a padded seat, it just did not 'feel right' to me! *R.C. Riley/Transport Treasury*.

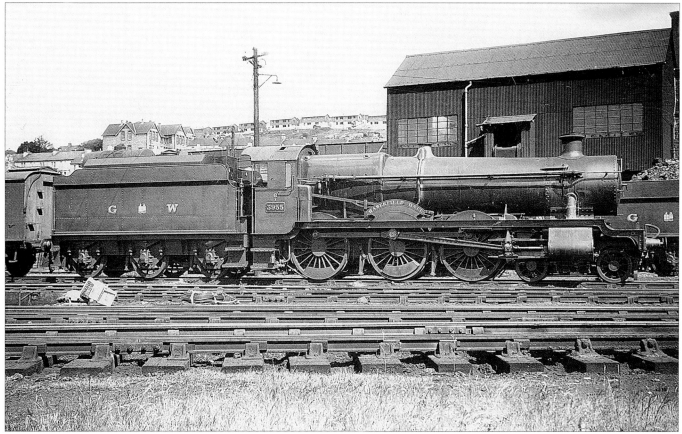

Old Plymouth 18. A final view of Plymouth Hoe, in July 1922, from the waters of Plymouth Sound. Although earlier photographs in the book give the impression of it being somewhat compact, this view shows that the Hoe was quite extensive, with a considerable distance between the buildings at the back of the Esplanade and Bandstand, and Bandstand and Smeaton's Tower.

By April 1963 the steam era is rapidly moving to a close, and prairie 4591 and pannier 6438 look very lonely in the shed at Laira. *Peter Groom.*

The New Shed at Laira, 10 September 1957, with 4088 DARTMOUTH CASTLE and an unidentified Hall standing outside, on the middle two roads. The Castle has been stripped of her connecting rods on the driver's side, and there they are on the ground. Perhaps a sign of decline, for at one time they would have been placed on a flat top cart to keep them clean. The shed has already been partitioned to accept the diesels, although a steam locomotive is standing inside on the left-hand road.

The horse-worked Laira Junction & Lee Moor Tramway; I could not resist this as an endpiece. Out of view in the background but nevertheless close by, is all the hustle and bustle of a big, busy engine shed; the panniers, prairies, Granges, Halls, Castles and Kings. An age away from all this, the Lee Moor 'locomotives' quietly haul their load, 'double-headed' no less! Just give them a feed of oats and a bucket of water once in a while and they'd go all day. The Lee Moor Tramway was used to take china clay from the Lee Moor Clay Works, above Plympton on the eastern outskirts of Plymouth, to the Quay at Sutton Harbour. Constructed about 1830 as part of the Plymouth and Dartmoor tramway, it was built to a 4ft 6in gauge. The trucks had a capacity of 4 tons and were drawn by horses; normally two were necessary for 4-5 trucks. The tramway crossed the Tavistock/Launceston branch approximately two miles north of Marsh Mills station and ran to the north of the main line until Laira, where it then crossed the Main Plymouth-Exeter line, to run alongside Laira Yard and on to Sutton Harbour. The tramway closed in 1947, but the crossing remained in place for many years after.

Laira Rosters – Explanatory Notes

It was not until I decided to include the working rosters of the footplate crews at Laira that I realised how mammoth a task this would be, and therefore I have, of necessity, been able to only show a section of the rosters for certain of the links. The Goods Links comprised some 35-40 turns, with the Pilot Link only a few less. However, I believe that I have still been able to show a balanced and fair representation of the duties of these links.

The inclusion of names also created problems inasmuch as the rosters which I examined were full of additions and deletions to take account not only of promotions, but also seasonal temporary promotions to cater for the increased demands of the summer period. This meant that at times names were duplicated in more than one link. I have attempted, to the best of my ability and from the information at my disposal, to ensure that no member of that select band of 'Laira men' has been omitted. I feel sure, however, that this could be a possibility, and therefore I offer my sincerest apology to anyone whose name either does not appear, or is shown with the wrong driver or in the wrong link.

Where possible I have included explanatory notes with each of the rosters to clarify abbreviations etc. In all cases the original rosters were hand written but in only a few have I had to make an 'educated guess' in deciphering the content. I am sure former Laira men will note that, for the sake of brevity, I have taken a 'liberty' with No.1 Transfer Link!

No. 1 Goods Link (part) Summer 1955

Turn No	1	2	3	4	5	6	7	8	9	10	11	12	13	14	15	16	17	18
Sunday	1/15 Asst.	off	6.20 Truro	off	9/45 Asst.	off	10th Spare	off	3/42 Truro	off	4th Spare	off	8th Spare	off	7/30 Stock	off	2nd Spare	off
Monday	9/10 Taunton	5.10 NA	3/30 Spare	6.40 Truro	9/0 Spare	2.45 NA	11.0 Spare	4.20 Exeter	5/30 Spare	1.50 Truro	8.0 Spare	4/8 St A.	10.30 Spare	3.45 Exeter	12/0 NA	3.5 Truro	2/0 Spare	3.0 NA
Tuesday	9/10 Taunton	5.10 NA	3/30 Spare	6.40 Truro	9/0 Spare	R	11.0 Spare	4.0 Spare	5/30 Spare	12.5 NA	8.0 Spare	2/0 Spare	10.30 Spare	2.30 Spare	12/0 NA	3.10 Truro	1/15 Truro	6.0 Spare
Wednesday	9/10 Taunton	R	3/30 Spare	6.40 Truro	9/0 Spare	5.0 Spare	11.0 Spare	4.0 Spare	5/30 Spare	12.5 NA	8.0 Spare	2/0 Spare	10.30 Spare	2.30 Spare	12/0 NA	3.10 Truro	11.0 Par	5.10 NA
Thursday	8/0 Spare	5.10 NA	3/30 Spare	R	9/0 Spare	5.0 Spare	11.0 Spare	4.0 Spare	5/30 Spare	12.5 NA	8.0 Spare	2/0 Spare	10.30 Spare	R	10/0 Taunton	3.10 Truro	11.55 Truro	2.30 Spare
Friday	8/0 Spare	5.10 NA	4/8 St. A.	6.40 Truro	9/0 Spare	5.0 Spare	11.0 Spare	R	5/30 Spare	R	8.0 Spare	R	10.30 Spare	2.30 Spare	10/0 Taunton	R	12/8 Lans	3.10 Truro
Saturday	8/0 Spare	5.10 NA	3/30 Spare	6.40 Truro	9/0 Spare	6.0 Lans	9.30 Car	4.0 Spare	5/30 Spare	off Turn	8.0 Spare	2/0 Spare	10.30 Spare	2.30 Spare	12.15 (Sun) NA	3.10 Truro	11.40 Car	R

Notes: Time; 10.30 denotes am - 10/30 denotes pm.
Abbreviations; NA – Newton Abbot; Lans – Launceston; St A. – St Austell; R – Rest day Car: Auto working

Driver.	Fireman.	Driver.	Fireman.	Driver.	Fireman.	Driver.	Fireman.
Curtis W.	Burrows A	Thomas F.	Collings R.	Porter W.	Carrivick E.	Norman W.	Wilson G.
Finch P	Williams K.	March T.	Symons C.	Ackrell W.	Walker J	Down H.	Hatton R.
Davies T.	Dick	Aldgate P.	Parsons R.	Newman H.	Kelly R.	Carter W.	Chapman J.T.
Guscott C	Stevens H.	Metherell H.	Pinhey F.	Bunce J	Stonehouse R	Bolt C.J.	Burt J.
Kiver F.	Platt R	Watson W.	Pattemore E.				

The following Drivers and Firemen were in this Link, but because of promotion etc., I am unable to 'pair' them up.
DRIVERS:- Nosworthy R.; Joslin S.; Smith L.; Hurd A.; Cousins E. ; Lineham A.;
FIREMEN:- Rowe T.; Hobbs A.; Blindy S.; Hawkey A.;Himsworth G.; Gill R.; Foster T.G.;Chapman C. .

No.1 Passenger Link Summer 1955

Turn No.	1	2	3	4	5	6	7	8	9	10	11	12	13	14	15	16	17	18
Sunday	10.30 x Pdn	off	off	7.40 Truro	off	off	9/50 x Pdn	off	12/20 Pdn	off	10.30 X Pdn	off	off	2/0 x Pdn	off	off	5/0 x Pdn	3/30 x Pdn
Monday	9.11 Pz	off	8.30 Pdn	3/55 Pdn	9.36 Truro	11.15 Pdn	8/15 Spare	10.13 Exeter	9.30 xPdn	12/30 Pdn	5/6 Truro	off	4/20 xPdn	10.30 xPdn	3/45 Pdn	6.50 Pz	4/10 Truro	2/38 Pz
Tuesday	8.30 Pdn	3/55 Exeter	AO Pdn	4/10 Pdn	5.30 xPdn	off	7/50 Truro	12/30 Pdn	4/20 Exeter	9.30 xPdn	5/6 Truro	11.15 Truro	3/45 Pdn	6.50 Pz	5/30 xPdn	4.50 Pz	1/30 xPdn	2/38 PZ
Wednesday	AO Pdn	3/45 Pdn	12/30 Truro	9.30 xPdn	11.15 Truro	4.50 Pz	5/6 Truro	5/30 xPdn	3/55 Pdn	off	4/10 Pdn	6.50 Pz	3/30 xPdn	5.14 Pz	2/38 Pdn	12/5 Pdn	4/20 Exeter	off
Thursday	9.11 Pdn	4/15 Pz	9.30 xPdn	off	11.15 Truro	12/30 Pdn	7/50 Truro	6.50 Pz	5/6 Truro	12/5 Pdn	1/30 xPdn	5.14 Pz	3/55 Exeter	off	2/38 Pz	5.30 xPdn	4/20 Exeter	4/10 Pdn
Friday	12/30 Pdn	AO Pdn	6.50 Pz	11/45 Assist	11.15 Truro	5.30 xPdn	11/45 Pdn	5.14 Pz	3/45 Pdn	9.30 xPdn	2/0 Pdn	12/5 Pdn	4/10 Pdn	AO Pdn	2/38 Pz	off	4/20 Exeter	9.30 xPdn
Saturday	10.30 xPdn	10.35 xPdn	5.14 Pz	11/45 Assist	10.45 Truro	11/30 xPdn	5/30 Pdn	off	11.5 xPdn	10.51 Pdn	9.25 xPdn	9.30 xPdn	11.0 xPdn	6.55 xPdn	4/20 Exeter	11/45 Pdn	2/50 Pdn	12/30 Pdn

Notes: Time; 10.30 denotes am - 10/30 denotes pm.
Abbreviations; Pdn –Paddington; xPdn – Ex Paddington; Pz – Penzance; off: Rest Days. AO Pdn – As Ordered (no booked return working from Paddington so usually, as a means of getting the engine back to Laira, it would be on a double headed passenger train Paddington-Plymouth.

Driver.	Fireman.	Driver.	Fireman.	Driver.	Fireman.	Driver.	Fireman.
Hammett G.	Luscombe	R.Amery L.	Harris W.	Bolt F.C.	Knapman J.	Bright W.	Hext W.
Harris J.	Green R.	Solomon J.	Lewis A.R.	Underhill L.	Henwood P.	Simons N.	Hill L.
Newcombe F.	Hawker J.	Friend J.	Courtnary. ?	Hawkey F.	Roberts S.	Endean F.	Gahan R.
Kent C.	Giles J.	Giles. R.	Giles R.	Jarvis E.	Barrett E	Bunce F.	Yendall R.
Down F.C.	Lewis G.	Trethewey A .	Stonehouse R.				

No. 2 Goods Link (part) Summer 1955

Turn No	1	2	3	4	5	6	7	8	9	10	11	12	13	14	15	16	17	18
Sunday	off	9th Spare	off	5th Spare	off	15th Spare	off	9.20 Lisk	off	5.0 Orders	off	off	2/0 Orders	off	9/30 Bkr	off	3.0 Orders	off
Monday	10/35 Bkr	10.0 Spare	5.0 Spare	4/25 NA	2.0 Spare	5/0 Spare	6.0 Spare	4/15 Bkr	12.0 Spare	6.10 Spare	9/0 Spare	11.0 Spare	3/0 Spare	R	6/0 Spare	5.35 Tavi	1.25 N.Rd	1.0 Spare
Tuesday	6/35 Bkr	10.0 Spare	5.0 Spare	R	2.0 Spare	5/0 Spare	6.0 Spare	4/15 Bkr	12.0 Spare	5.35 Tavi	9/0 Spare	11.0 Spare	3/0 Spare	6.10 Lisk	6/25 NA	R	4.30 Mbay	1.0 Spare
Wednesday	6/35 Bkr	10.0 Spare	5.0 Spare	4/25 NA	2.0 Spare	5/0 Spare	6.0 Spare	R	12.0 Spare	5.20 Tavi	9/0 Spare	11.0 Spare	3/0 Spare	6.10 Lisk	10/15 Bkr	5.35 Tavi	11.30 Spare	R
Thursday	6/35 Bkr	R	5.0 Spare	4/25 NA	2.0 Spare	5/0 Spare	6.0 Spare	4/15 Bkr	12.0 Spare	6.0 Trans	12/0 Asst	11.0 Spare	3/0 Spare	6.10 Lisk	9/0 Spare	5.35 Tavi	1/15 Truro	1.0 Spare
Friday	6/35 Bkr	10.0 Spare	5.0 Spare	4/25 NA	2.0 Spare	R	6.0 Spare	4/15 Bkr	12.0 Spare	3.20 Truro	10/35 NA	R	3/0 Spare	6.10 Lisk	5/0 Spare	5.35 Tavi	2/0 Spare	1.0 Spare
Saturday	off Turn	10.0 Spar	5.0 Spare	4/25 NA	2.0 Spare	5/0 Spare	6.0 Spare	4/15 Bkr	9.25 Truro	R	10/35 NA	11.0 Spare	3/0 Spare	6.10 Lisk	6/52 Truro	5,35 Tavi	12.0 NA	1.0 Spare

Notes: Time; 10.30 denotes am - 10/30 denotes pm.
Abbreviations; NA – Newton Abbot; Tavi - Tavistock; Lisk – Liskeard; Mby – Millbay; N.Rd - North Road Station; Bkr – Banker; Trans – Transfer Gds. R – Rest day;

Driver.	Fireman.	Driver.	Fireman.	Driver.	Fireman.	Driver.	Fireman.	Driver	Fireman.
Carnell V.	Ravensdale G	Cooke B.	Watts W.D.	Tipton T	Saville S.R	Goff H.	Lavers D	Odell T.	Hansford A.
Jenkins D.	Leatham R.	Williams C.	Easterbrook V.	Carlyle H.	Coombe D.	Gulley A	Churchward C.	Hard A.	Harper J.
Crook C.	Rowe T.	Knight R	Hancock F.	Roach H.	Cremen W	Treverrow G	Morris C.	Boase J	Snell T.
Johnson L	Stephens K	Beal R.	Johnson F	Willcocks S.	Fulton R	Brown E.	Nicholson L.	Bryant E.	Porter R.
Stephens E.	Blyth.	Plummer L.	West S	Martin E.	Fraser J.	Eddy D.	Parry A.	Chaston J.	Cremen M.
Brayan L.	Lock D	Avery B.	Furneaux P.	Petite C.	Clarke W.	Bice C.	nk	Slee I.	Waterfield C.
Dunstan W	Coulling J.	Holway J	Rundle P.E.	Sanders J.	Viant P.	Everitt J.	nk	Leach E	Hawkey P.

No. 2 Passenger Link (part) Summer 1955

Turn No	1	2	3	4	5	6	7	8	9	10	11	112	13	14	15	16	17	18
Sunday	5/5 NA	off	9.35 Nqy	off	5.33 Pz	off	Lifton Milk	off	11/45 NA	off	4/10 Taunton	off	4.50 Pz	off	9.20 NA	off	9/45 Taunton	off
Monday	3/15 Asst	R	2/35 SR	2.0 Spare	8/5 Taunton	5.14 Pz	1/0 Exeter	5.0 Spare	off turn	7.10 Lans	7/15 Spare	6.25 Wby	2/8 Nqy	4.50 Pz	5/40 Exeter	6.15 Sp	10/5 Taunton	R
Tuesday	3/15 Asst	6.25 Wby	2/35 SR	R	8/5 Taunton	R	1/0 Exeter	5.0 Spare	1.30 Bsl	7.10 Lans	7/15 Spare	xWby	2/8 Nqy	9.11 Pz	5/40 Exeter	6.15 Spare	10/5 Taunton	5.14 Pz
Wednesday	3/15 Asst	xWby	2/35 SR	2.0 Spare	8/5 Taunton	9.11 Pz	1/0 Exeter	5.0 Spare	1.0 Exeter	7.10 Lans	7/15 Spare	6.25 Wby	3/10 Lans	8.0 Spare	5.40 Exeter	R	10/5 Taunton	6.15 Spare
Thursday	3/15 Asst	6.25 Wby	3/0 Lans	2.0 Spare	8/5 Taunton	7.10 Lans	1/0 Exeter	R	off turn	R	7/15 Spare	xWby	2/35 Exeter	4.50 Pz	5/40 Exeter	6.15 Spare	10/5 Taunton	5.0 Spare
Friday	3/15 Asst	xWby	3/0 Lans	2.0 Spare	6/30 Taunton	9.11 Pz	2/8 Nqy	5.0 Spare	1.30 Bsl	7.10 Lans	7/15 Spare	R	2/35 Exeter	4.50 Pz	7/50 Exeter	6.15 Spare	10/5 Taunton	2.30 Pz
Saturday	3/19 Pz	5.43 Pz	3/0 Lans	2.0 Spare	8/55 Taunton	9.11 Pz	2/26 Nqy	4.19 Pz	12.1 Exeter	6.50 Pz	7/15 Spare	6.29 Nqy	2/35 Exeter	R	4/28 Pz	6.15 Spare	10/5 Taunton	4.50 Pz

Notes: Time; 10.30 denotes am - 10/30 denotes pm.
Abbreviations; Pz – Penzance; Nqy – Newquay; SR – Southern Railway; NA – Newton Abbot; Bsl – Bristol; Wby – Westbury; Lans – Launceston; R – Rest day

Driver.	Fireman.	Driver.	Fireman.	Driver.	Fireman.	Driver.	Fireman.
Littlejohn F	Hughes J	March	Rundle W.L.	Nanskivell A.	nk	Vicary	Symons S.
Ball R.	Bennett H.	Clarke A.	Willson	Davies	Sargeant R.	Newham	Liddicoat W.
Sprague A.	Dodderidge L	Vokes	Monk A	Eade	Mills A	Langman S.	Boyes B.
Stansbury A.	Hockeday A.	Foster A.	Platt R.	Bunce F.	Watson	Cornelius F.	Warne J.
Saunders W.	Yabsley W.	Tregenza R	English	Cooke	Stonehouse	Paul	Hindworth?
McCarthy J.	Williams	Watson	Hodgekins?	Acknell	Joyner?	Nk	Cole R.

Pilot Link (part) Summer 1955

Turn No.	1	2	3	4	5	6	7	8	9	10	11	12	13	14	15	16	17	18
Sunday	10/8 Prep	off	10/0 Ee	off	6.0 Turn	off	2/0 Turn	off	9/40 New Yd.	off	6.0 Ee	off	9/5 Up Side	off	2/0 Prep	off	1/30 New Yd	off
Monday	10/0 Ee	4.5 Bkr	11/55 Up Side	11.15 New Yd	10/0 Prep	R	2/0 Turn	2.30 Prep	11/55 New Yd	6.0 Prep	2/0 Prep	4.55 New Yd	11/55 Dn Yd	6.0 Turn	3/55 Tavi	R	5/35 Up Side	6.30 Loco Spare
Tuesday	10/0 Ee	4.5 Bkr	11/55 Up Side	11.15 New Yd	10/0 Prep	1.25 N.Rd.	2/0 Turn	4.55 New Yd	11/55 New Yd	6.0 Prep	2/0 Prep	R	11/55 Dn Yd	6.0 Turn	3/55 Tavi	2.30 Prep	5/35 Up Side	6.30 Loco Spare
Wednesday	10/0 Ee	R	11/55 Up Side	11.15 New Yd	10/0 Prep	1.25 N.Rd	3/55 Tavi	4.55 New Yd	11/55 New Yd	6.0 Prep	2/0 Prep	4.55 New Yd	11/55 Dn Yd	6.0 Turn	2/0 Turn	2.30 Prep	5/35 Up Side	R
Thursday	10/0 Ee	4.5 Bkr	11/55 Up Side	11.15 New Yd	10/0 Prep	1.25 N Rd	3/55 Tavi	R	11/55 New Yd	6.0 Prep	2/0 Prep	4.55 New Yd	11/55 Dn Yd	6.0 Turn	2/0 Turn	2.30 Prep	5/35 Up Side	R
Friday	10/0 Ee	4.5 Bkr	11/55 Up Side	11.15 New Yd	10/0 Prep	1.25 N Rd	2/0 Turn	6.0 Turn	11/55 New Yd	6.0 Prep	3/55 Tavi	4.55 New Yd	11/55 Dn Yard	R	2/0 Prep	2.30 Prep	5/35 Up Side	6.30 Loco Spare
Saturday	10/0 Ee	1.15 Mbay	11/55 UpSide	R	10/0 Prep	1.25 N Rd	2/0 Turn	6.0 Turn	11/35 New Yd	R	1/25 Tavi	4.55 New Yd	9/45 Old Yd	6.0 Turn	2/0 Prep	2.30 Prep	5/35 Up Side	6.30 Loco Spare

Notes: Time; 10.30 denotes am - 10/30 denotes pm.
Abbreviations; Prep – Preparing Engines; Turn – loco Turning Duties on Shed; Tavi - Tavistock; Mby – Millbay; N.Rd - North Road Station; Bkr – Banker; Tavi – Tavistock; R – Rest day; Ee- East end of Coal Stage; Up Side, Dn Side, New Yd are the three marshalling Yards at Tavistock Jct (Marsh Mills)

Driver.	Fireman.	Driver.	Fireman.	Driver.	Fireman.	Driver.	Fireman	Driver	Fireman
Howard G.	Russell T.	Ryder K	Squires B	Hancock T.	Haddock S.	Finch R.	Short C.	Wilson C	Reynolds T.
Richards N.	Easton D.	Rogers R.	Launder D	Barwick G.	Mathews J.	Nance W	Townsend S.	Hoskings S.	O'Leary A.
Birkenhead L	Harris D.	Gould F.	nk	Hoskings E.	Beable L.	Ough H.	Wheeler R	Downing E.	Edgecombe C.
Williamson W.	Cole F	Bryant R	Griffiths D.	Coker S.	Lock K.	Lang P.	Congdon D.	Williams N.S	Thomas V.
Sharman F	Battishill D.	Hood W	Guy E.	Vicary F	Atkinson G.	Full M.	North E.		

A not wholly accurate artist's impression of the eastern end of Saltash station and the approach to the Royal Albert Bridge.

Rail Car Link (Saltash Suburban Service)
Summer 1955

Turn No	1	2	3	4	5	6
Sunday	off	4.25	3/25	off	9.56	off
Monday	3.0	11.0	3/0	R	6/32	11.45
Tuesday	3.30	11.0	3/0	4.47	6/32	11.45
Wednesday	3.30	R	3/0	4.47	6/32	11.45
Thursday	3.30	11.0	3/0	4.47	6/32	11.45
Saturday	3.30	12/37	3/0	4.47	6/32	R

Notes: Time; 10.30 denotes am - 10/30 denotes pm.
Abbreviations; R – Rest days.
We always knew it as the 'Car Link' though the original rosters titled it the 'Railcar Link'

Driver	Fireman.	Driver.	Fireman.	Driver.	Fireman.
Hocking J	Lee D.	Mathews C.	Couch K	Warne A	Conday G.
Mitchell E.	Wickett C.	May W.	Cole R.	Hill W.	Speare F

Transfer Link 1 Summer 1955

Turn No	1	2	3	4	5
Sunday	off	off	off	off	off
Monday	9.0 Trans	6.45 S.H.	2/5 S.H.	4.55 Up Side	2/5 Up Side
Tuesday	9.0 Trans	6.45 S.H	R	4.55 Up Side	2/5 Up Side
Wednesday	R	6.45 S.H	2/5 S.H	4.55 Up side	2/5 Up Side
Thursday	9.0 Trans	6.45 S.H.	2/5 S.H.	4.55 Up Side	2/5 Up Side
Friday	9.0 Trans	6.45 S.H	2/5 S.H.	4.55 Up Side	R
Saturday	7.0 Trans	6.45 S.H	1/30 Spare	4.55 Up Side	2/5 Up Side

Notes: Time; 10.30 denotes am - 10/30 denotes pm.
Abbreviations; Trans – Transfer Gds; S.H. – Sutton Harbour; Up Side , Tavistock Jct. Yard; R – Rest days.
The link split after my time into these, 1 and 2, about 1954.

Driver.	Fireman.	Driver.	Fireman.	Driver.	Fireman.
Giles F.	Davison W.	Cuthbert C.	Lemin R.	Goddard A.?	Hyatt K.
Hawker W.	Kirby D	Triscott P.	Curtis T.	Webber C.	Jones R.

Transfer Link 2 Summer 1955

Turn No	1	2	3	4	5	6
Sunday	off	6.0 Spare	off	1.25 N.Rd.	off	off
Monday	8.5 Lisk	6/15 Trans	3.5 D/Bois	11/25 St.G	6.0 Trans	12.15 Trans
Tuesday	8.5 Lisk	6/15 Trans	R	11/25 St. G.	6.0 Trans	12.15 Trans
Wednesday	8.5 Lisk	6/15 Trans	3.30 D/Bois	11/25 St.G.	6.0 Trans	12.15 Trans
Thursday	8.5 Lisk	6/15 Trans	3.30 D/Bois	11/25 St.G.	R	12.15 Trans
Friday	8.5 Lisk	6/15 Trans	3.30 D/Bois	11/25 St.G.	6.0 Trans	12.15 Trans
Saturday	R	6/15 Trans	3.30 D/Bois	9/16 St.G	6.0 Trans	off turn

Notes: Time; 10.30 denotes am - 10/30 denotes pm.
Abbreviations; Trans – Transfer Gds; St.G – St, Germans Pick-Up Gds.; D/Bois – Tip Gds to St. Austell(Change Over Crews at Doublebois); N.Rd – North Road Station; R – Rest days.

Driver.	Fireman.	Driver.	Fireman.	Driver.	Fireman.	Driver	Fireman
Warren J	Teague R.	Mack F.	MacKeen R	Yendall T.	Preece S	Lowden C.	Curran A.
Tall F.	Peart E.	Sampson W.	Prescott J.	Gale B .	Hocking K.	Flashman W	Rosser W.
Goodman H.	Chapman R.	Phasey S	Whale N	Smith H.	McCarty M.	Crook F	Duckett E.

In the autumn of 1854 the great cylinder is in position in the centre of the river, with the compressed air machinery and pumping engines supplying the work which is going on below the water level. The Cornwall land spans are being placed on to the masonry piers, and the western truss is nearing completion on the eastern shore.

BIBLIOGRAPHY

Auto Trains by Colin Veale and Rev. J. Goodman (G.W. Society Didcot); *Branch Lines to Longmoor* by Vic Mitchell & Keith Smith (Middleton)*; B.R. Steam Motive Power Depots* by Paul Bolger (Ian Allan); *Castles and Kings at Work* by Michael Rutherford (Ian Allan); *Churchward Locomotives* by Brian Haresnape & Alec Swain (Ian Allan); *Early Years of West Country Steam* by P.M. Alexander/Michael Whitehouse (Wild Swan); *Encyclopaedia of the Great Western Railway* – LRGP; *Great Western Album 1 & 2* By R.C. Riley (Ian Allan); *Great Western in the 1960s* by Brian Stephenson (Ian Allan); *Great Western 4-6-0s* by Brian Stephenson (Ian Allan); *Great Western at its Zenith* by Brian Stephenson (Ian Allan); *Great Preserved Locomotives. No.7* by Brian Dodd (Ian Allan); *Great Western Steam in South Devon* by Keith Beck & John Copsey (Wild Swan); *Halls, Granges and Manors at Work* by Michael Rutherford (Ian Allan); *Illustrated History of Plymouth's Railways* by Martin Smith (Irwell Press); *Model Railway Journal* - Article on Laira Locomotive Shed by John Dornom (Wild Swan); *Peto's Register of Great Western Railway Locomotives Vol.1* (Irwell Press); *Newton Abbot to Plymouth* by Vic Mitchell and Keith Smith (Middleton Press); *Plymouth to St. Austell* by Vic Mitchell & Keith Smith (Middleton Press); *St. Austell to Penzance* by Vic Mitchell & Keith Smith (Middleton Press); GW Sheds in Camera by Roger Griffiths (OPC); *Steam Around Plymouth* by Bernard Mills (Tempus Pub); *The Cornish Riviera* by Stephen Austin (Ian Allan); *The Great Western Railway in East Cornwall* by Alan Bennett (Run Past); *The Great Western Railway in Mid-Cornwall* by Alan Bennett (Kingfisher**);** *The Great Western Railway in West Cornwall* by Alan Bennett (Kingfisher); *The Last Days of Steam in Plymouth and Cornwall* Maurice J. Dart (Alan Sutton); *Tribute to the Great Western* by Richard J. Blenkinsop (OPC); *Shadows of the Great Western* by Richard J. Blenkinsop (OPC); *West Country Engine Sheds* by Maurice Dart (Ian Allan); *Western Main Lines* by J.H. Moss & R.S. Carpenter (Middleton Press); *Yelverton to Princetown Railway* (Oakwood Press) *Appendices courtesy W.L. Rundle, and the Late Frank Thomas.*